An Assessment of the Strategic Importance of the Hardwood Resource in British Columbia

by

M.R.C. Massie
Nawitka Renewable Resource Consultants Ltd.
Victoria, B.C.

E. B. Peterson and N.M. Peterson
Western Ecological Services Ltd.
Victoria, B.C.

K.A. Enns
Larkspur Biological Consultants Ltd.
Victoria, B.C.

July 1994

CANADA-BRITISH COLUMBIA PARTNERSHIP AGREEMENT ON FOREST RESOURCE DEVELOPMENT: FRDA II

Canada

BC

Funding for this publication was provided by the Canada–British Columbia Partnership Agreement on Forest Resource Development: FRDA II — a four year (1991–95) $200 million program cost-shared equally by the federal and provincial governments.

Canadian Cataloguing in Publication Data

Main entry under title:
An Assessment of the strategic importance of the hardwood resource in British Columbia

(FRDA report, ISSN 0835-0752 ; 221)

"Canada–British Columbia Partnership Agreement on Forest Resource Development: FRDA II."
Co-published by B.C. Ministry of Forests.
Includes bibliographical references: p.
ISBN 0-7726-2220-5

1. Hardwoods – British Columbia. 2. Forests and forestry – British Columbia. I. Massie, M. R. C. II. Canadian Forest Service. III. Canada–British Columbia Partnership Agreement on Forest Resource Development: FRDA II. IV. British Columbia. Ministry of Forests. V. Series.

SD397.H3A87 1994 333.75'09711 C94-960280-9

This is a joint publication of the Canadian Forest Service and the British Columbia Ministry of Forests.

For additional copies and/or further information about the Canada-British Columbia Partnership Agreement on Forest Resource Development: FRDA II, contact:

Canadian Forest Service
Pacific Forestry Centre
506 West Burnside Road
Victoria, B.C. V8Z 1M5
(604) 363-0600

or

B.C. Ministry of Forests
Research Branch
31 Bastion Square
Victoria, B.C. V8W 3E7
(604) 387-6719

EXECUTIVE SUMMARY

Utilization

British Columbia has six important hardwood species. Red alder, bigleaf maple, and black cottonwood are primarily coastal species, while aspen, paper birch, and balsam poplar (frequently called cottonwood) are more prevalent in the Interior.

On the Coast, species that have sufficient volumes for potential use are alder (32 million m^3), maple (5 million m^3), and black cottonwood (3 million m^3).

In the Interior, there are 20 million m^3 of paper birch, 41 million m^3 of balsam poplar, and 338 million m^3 of aspen. These figures reflect only a portion of the total resource, but where concentrations occur they do indicate development potential.

There is a potential for maple utilization in the Vancouver and Powell River areas. Alder also has potential in these areas, as well as on Vancouver Island. Black cottonwood could be developed around the Vancouver and Powell River areas and on northern Vancouver Island. In the Interior, there is good development potential for birch in the Fort Nelson–Fort St. John area, as well as the Kamloops-Okanagan area. Some potential also exists in the Prince George and Hazelton areas. Cottonwood in the Interior has a high potential in the Dawson Creek–Fort St. John area and farther north in the Fort Nelson Area. Considering both Coastal and Interior cottonwood, potential also exists in the Terrace-Hazelton area. Aspen has widespread development potential in the central, north-central, and particularly the northeast portions of the province.

Hardwood harvesting is in a developmental stage in British Columbia, and only some quotas and allowable annual cuts for various species have been identified. Based on concentrations of hardwoods, estimated by lead species analyses, a conservative interim estimate for the annual harvest potential of coastal areas is 0.6 million m^3, mainly in alder. The Interior is estimated at 6.4 million m^3, mainly in aspen. About 1.4 million m^3 of hardwood was harvested during 1989–90, but the harvest had increased to an estimated 1.9 million m^3 by the end of 1992. The increase can largely be attributed to the new pulp mill near Chetwynd. About 0.6 million m^3 is now harvested on the Coast and some 1.3 million m^3 in the Interior (largely aspen in the northeast).

Based on a hardwood harvest of 1.425 million m^3 in 1990, direct employment was estimated at just under 1200 jobs and total employment at just under 4000 jobs. The same harvest is estimated to have created about $44 million in direct employment income and about $97 million in total employment income. As hardwood harvesting increases, both employment and employment income will rise. Should a harvest of about 7 million m^3 develop over the next several years, it could generate about 19 500 jobs and annual employment income of $475 million.

Market opportunities for British Columbia hardwoods appear to be expanding. Sawn products from coastal alder and maple are in demand both domestically and in the United States, and some further opportunities may be available in Europe. Chips from alder are well accepted in Japan, but shipments have slowed because of the recent downturn in the Japanese economy. The market for alder chips in adjacent Washington is strong and is expected to increase. Black cottonwood chips are being used domestically and sold to export markets. Veneer production from black cottonwood is increasing domestically.

The use of birch for veneer and specialty products is also increasing domestically. Waferboard/Oriented Strand Board (OSB) made with aspen has been increasingly accepted for domestic use and further export potential to the United States is expected as economic conditions improve. Greater use of balsam poplar for this product may be expected if markets continue to expand. Aspen pulp competes in world markets. Increased production will depend heavily on future economic conditions and social attitudes concerning recycling as well as wood supply opportunities, production costs, and the relative value of the Canadian dollar.

Greater use of the provincial hardwood resource has development, management, and research implications. New policies will be required that reflect both large volume uses and small specialty product uses. A greater diversity of products will be produced than is the case with conifers, and sawmilling will not have as important a role. Regulating timber supply will be more difficult because increasing age can mean loss of quality. Uses for low-quality stands (or imbalances in mature and overmature age classes) will be of great initial concern. New (hardwood) manufacturing equipment will be needed and harvesting equipment and procedures will differ significantly from those used for softwoods. New inventory and reporting systems will be required as will increased forest management expertise for both pure and mixed stands. Similarly, tenure and allocation policies will require revision and rationalization.

Ecology

The ecological importance of provincial hardwood species is identified and roles, characteristics, and processes are described in relation to increased resource use and multiple-use demands.

Hardwoods serve several important ecological roles. They are commonly viewed as a nurse crop for other commercially important tree species. Their nutrient cycling characteristics differ from those of conifers. Although not well documented, hardwoods are thought to exert different microclimatic and hydrologic influences than do conifers. Hardwoods are prominent early colonizers of disturbed sites, and in this context they provide rapid carbon fixation during the period of fast juvenile growth. At the other end of their life-cycle, hardwoods have a relatively early release of carbon because most stands break up at younger ages than do coniferous stands. Hardwoods are relatively resistant to airborne pollutants because they carry a receptive surface area of foliage for only part of each year. Several of British Columbia's hardwood species are important for stabilization of soil erosion and protection of aquatic habitats in alluvial and riparian ecosystems. Hardwood-dominated ecosystems are also important contributors to the overall genetic and biological diversity of provincial forests.

The discussion of silvicultural aspects of hardwood management focuses on:

- maturity ages and rotation lengths,
- acceptance as advance regeneration,
- re-establishment of hardwoods after old-growth or young natural stands have been harvested,
- fire relations,
- methods of control on sites where hardwoods are not wanted,
- opportunity for intensive management of short rotations on very productive sites, and
- challenges of managing hardwoods in mixed rather than pure stands.

Management implications and research needs are suggested and are summarized by subject area (in descending order of priority), as follows:

Forest Health

- Better definition of the ecological basis for the nurse crop concept for each of the main hardwood species.
- Increased attention to disease and insect influences in young stands of the key hardwood species.

- Continued documentation of the circumstances and ecosystems in which hardwoods may play a moderating role on diseases or insects of importance in coniferous or mixedwood stands.

- More precise definition of site associations where a silvicultural choice between hardwood and softwood species would aid forest health through long-term management of nitrogen supply, a major determinant of forest productivity.

- Hydrologic comparisons of hardwood, softwood, and mixedwood stands in relation to snow and rainfall interception, snowmelt rates, subsurface and overland flow of water, and water quality.

Hardwood Silviculture

- A continued search for innovative ways to encourage and manage conifers and deciduous species in mixedwood stands.

- Better definition of the circumstances where deciduous–conifer mixtures, including silvicultural underplanting of conifer seedlings, might enhance the wood supply of both hardwood and softwood components.

- Improved background information on desirable stocking levels for hardwoods, particularly in relation to incremental silviculture.

- Increased attention to silvicultural methods for maximizing the beneficial role of hardwoods in riparian zone management.

- More precise information (except for black cottonwood where there is already a good information base) on the definitions of hardwood maturity in managed and unmanaged stands, and in relation to presence or absence of conifers.

Ecology

- Better quantification of the hardwood-dominated land areas involved and the hardwood biomass production rates in the most productive ecosystems of the province's biogeoclimatic zones and subzones.

- Long-term studies of managed stand growth in hardwood and mixedwood stands, and the effects of management practices on stand dynamics, including the nutrient capital lost from whole-tree logging.

- Continued definition of competition thresholds in various conifer-deciduous mixtures that occur naturally in the province.

- Increased attention to soil and humus factors that influence vegetative reproduction of the main hardwood species.

- Increased attention to hardwood features that influence whole-tree utilization, including tree dimensions, production structure, and physiological characteristics.

Multiple-Resource Use

The importance of provincial hardwood resources to multiple-resource uses (e.g., wildlife, fisheries, recreation, native cultural importance, and aesthetics) is described and discussed. The database for hardwood forests is re-examined and some uncertainties are identified. The main hardwood-using species (primarily birds, ungulates, large and small mammals, and some amphibians) are identified.

The biogeoclimatic classification (BEC) is used as a tentative link between wildlife in TSAs and their hardwood habitat needs. Fish distributions in main rivers and lakes are identified and some elements of hardwood importance to riparian fish habitat are described. Salmonids and trout are the economically important species. They require streamside and lakeshore contributions to organic material, channel stability, temperature control and coarse woody debris, which originate to a great extent from hardwood species in the riparian zone. There are many unknowns surrounding the diversity, abundance, and species distribution of fish, especially in first- and second-order streams. This adds to the uncertainty about the importance of hardwoods to their habitats.

Native use of hardwoods was, and still is, extensive for medicines, food, and building materials. Many hardwoods have religious significance and there are important cultural sites associated with riparian hardwoods, especially in the northeast.

Recreational use of hardwood-dominated land areas is difficult to quantify because the information available is not specific to this forest inventory type group. However, the main recreational uses of hardwood stands include birdwatching, photography, hunting, fishing, and fall colour viewing. Many of the most popular recreation areas in the province have some element of riparian vegetation. Many of the hardwood stands have semi-primitive nonmotorized status, particularly in the far northeastern part of British Columbia. Aesthetics of hardwoods are discussed, mainly in relation to American literature on the subject. Hardwood green-up following harvesting is rapid and the visual softening effect of hardwoods and related species in cutblocks is considered valuable to some forest recreation planners.

Sources of uncertainty and management concerns are discussed. These relate primarily to the lack of information about multiple resource uses, but many topics of concern and potential research projects are identified. Some suggestions are made about the new forest inventory, including the need for a multi-disciplinary approach.

ACKNOWLEDGEMENTS

We thank the many people who assisted with this assessment, especially Marilyn Blache, Phil Comeau, and Kathy Hopkins for providing us with several hardwood-related reports that were not otherwise available and for assisting in many other ways.

Robert Hyslop, R.J. Hyslop and Associates, Vancouver, contributed substantially to the section on products and markets.

The people listed below contributed comments and access to materials and literature:

Ralf Aldrich	Native Affairs Branch, Ministry of Forests, Victoria
Anthony Britneff	Inventory Branch, Ministry of Forests, Victoria
Mike Brownlee	Integrated Resources Branch, Ministry of Forests, Victoria
David Campbell	Range Branch, Ministry of Forests, Victoria
Bill Chalk	Inventory Branch, Ministry of Forests, Victoria
Steve Chatwin	Research Branch, Ministry of Forests, Victoria
Dave Clark	Wildlife Branch, Ministry of Environment, Lands and Parks, Victoria
Ray Coupé	Research Section, Ministry of Forests, Williams Lake
Garry Darychuck	Research Section, Ministry of Forests, Nelson
Stu Hawthorn	Fisheries Branch, Ministry of Environment, Lands and Parks, Victoria
Peter Rennie	Ministry of Forests, Kamloops
Charles Scrivner	Department of Fisheries and Oceans, Environment Canada, Nanaimo
Geoff Tomlins	Binary Image Corp., White Rock
Peter Tschaplinski	Research Branch, Ministry of Forests, Victoria

We also appreciate the technical and editorial suggestions made by members of the reviewing committee during review of an earlier draft.

" Though the birches seemed dream-like on account of that frosting,
with 10 miles behind me
and ten thousand more to go. "

James Taylor

TABLE OF CONTENTS

APPENDICES

FIGURES

TABLES

1 INTRODUCTION

The broadleaved, or hardwood forest resources of British Columbia have historically been underestimated or ignored in both economic and ecological dimensions. Until recently, conifers have dominated the forest resource picture.

The economics of wood use has also favoured conifers for both structural and paper products. Therefore, it is not surprising that forest management techniques and forestry and products research have concentrated on softwoods.

However, three broad sets of circumstances have converged in the past decade to change the status of the hardwood resource in this province, and elsewhere:

- Global changes in production technology for, and market acceptance of, fibre and solid-wood products that can be made from hardwood species (together with increasing scarcity of economic wood resources of traditional types in North America and the world).
- Growing scientific and public concern about the environmental impacts of forest harvesting and management practices, the sustainability of basic resources (soil, air, water), and the long-run conservation of biodiversity.
- Growing knowledge of the silviculture and ecological importance of hardwood forest types.

The primary purpose of this study is to document the strategic importance of the hardwood resource in British Columbia, within a framework that will be useful for management, research, and development plans.

The sections on Resource Identification and Inventory, and Utilization and Economic Benefits (Sections 2 and 5), were prepared by Michael R. C. Massie of Nawitka Resource Consultants. E.B. and N.M. Peterson of Western Ecological Services prepared the Hardwood Ecology section (Section 3). The Multiple-Use Potential of Hardwoods in British Columbia section (Section 4) was prepared by K.A. Enns of Larkspur Biological Consultants.

2 RESOURCE IDENTIFICATION AND INVENTORY

To determine the potential for hardwood use in various geographic regions of the province, basic information was summarized from the statistics compiled for each Timber Supply Area (TSA) using the Provincial Summary Reporting System.

In addition, estimates were included for most of the Tree Farm Licenses (TFLs) within TSA boundaries. No data were available for five coastal TFLs and five TFLs in the Interior. Therefore, the statistics for coastal areas could be understated by about 10% and the Interior statistics by 5%. Until better inventory estimates are available, however, current data should be adequate for broad planning purposes.

Certain information is necessary to find out if there is enough hardwood in a geographic area to merit further investigation of its use and management. The summary that follows identifies TSAs and groups of TSAs that have a significant level of hardwood on both an areal and on a volumetric basis. Volume is further classified as "near-mature," "mature," and "overmature" (footnote [b], Table 1). This helps to determine both quality and the potential for use over the development period.

The analysis that follows needs further refinement before any utilization scheme is contemplated. However, it does provide a good indication of where the best potential for hardwood resource development exists. The areas and volumes shown are based on lead species (i.e., the most prevalent species in a stand[1]) for a hardwood type and are not estimates for a specific hardwood species. The "purity" factor (percent hardwood volume of the total volume of the inventory type group) can range from about 60 to 90% depending on the specific type, although in general purity in leading hardwood types tends to be fairly high.

Only the major tenures on which timber can be harvested have been considered. These include private lands, forest management Crown land, miscellaneous provincial reserves, TFLs, and woodlot licences. Reference maps are shown in Appendix 1. They indicate forest districts and major towns, forest regions and TSAs, the delineation between coast and interior TSAs, and for each region, the TSAs with major parks and TFLs

2.1 Lead Species Analysis

Data were compiled on a lead species basis to determine hardwood supply potential. This procedure allows the identification of forest areas with a preponderance of hardwoods and where development interest will likely focus. The magnitude of utilization will depend not only on the "purity" factor for the stands but also on the hardwood component where the lead species is coniferous. The reader is cautioned, with reference to the volumes shown, that not all of the volume is hardwood.

[1] Inventory type group refers to a specified species mix that can be identified by numbers or letters.

On a forest utilization basis, however, hardwood from coniferous stands would be off-setting. The results of the analysis, presented and discussed by species, are shown in Table 1. The site classes in the table indicate a general ranking of forest productivity.

Paper birch

The largest concentration of paper birch (*Betula papyrifera*) is found in the northeast of the province, particularly in the Fort Nelson TSA. Much lower concentrations are found in the central and south-central areas. In the northeast most sites are poor, while in the central and south-central areas of the province most of the sites are medium. About two-thirds of the volumes reported are mature or overmature.

Cottonwood (Interior)

The largest concentrations of interior cottonwood (balsam poplar, *Populus balsamifera* ssp. *balsamifera*, and black cottonwood, *P. balsamifera* ssp. *trichocarpa*) are found in the northeast of the province on medium and poor sites, and most of the volume is mature or overmature. A much lower, but still significant, concentration can be found in the northwest of the province in the Bulkley, Kalum, and Kispiox TSAs on medium and good sites. This timber is largely overmature.

Alder (Coast)

There are significant concentrations of red alder (*Alnus rubra*) along the coast from the Mid-Coast TSA south to the Fraser TSA. The majority of these concentrations are on good and medium sites. Most of the volumes reported are in the 41–80 year age class (near mature). Given the combination of medium site and relatively large volumes of just-maturing timber, the potential for utilization and management based on strategic planning appears to be excellent. Initial attention might be focused on the Sunshine Coast area, which has both the largest mature and immature volumes.

TABLE 1. Lead species analysis

Region or general provincial area and Timber Supply Area	Area (hectares) by site class that allows harvesting[a]				Volumes (000 m^3) on areas that allow harvesting by maturity[b] class			
	Good	Medium	Poor		Near-mature	Mature	Overmature	
			Paper birch					
Fraser Valley								
Fraser	1 000	3 600	2 000		462	25	0	
Soo	0	425	1 000		24	15	1	
Total	1 000	4 025	3 000	(8 025)[c]	486	40	1	(527)[d]
Northeast								
Fort Nelson	400	24 000	78 600		1 724	5 595	550	
Fort St. John	100	3 600	30 300		1 466	583	111	
Total	500	27 600	108 900	(137 000)[c]	3 190	6 178	661	(10 029)[d]
North-central								
Mackenzie	600	3 900	2 200		133	303	105	
Prince George	100	10 585	5 000		304	609	196	
Total	700	14 485	7 200	(22 385)[c]	437	912	301	(1 650)[d]
Central								
Quesnel	0	4 050	0		135	491	1	
Williams Lake	0	4 500	4 200		167	486	0	
100 Mile House	0	1 900	500		21	233	0	
Robson Valley	0	2 800	2 300		199	186	16	
Kamloops	100	10 735	3 400		589	1 005	87	
Total	100	23 985	10 400	(34 485)[c]	1 111	2 401	104	(3 616)[d]
South-central								
Okanagon	0	15 905	8 000		547	1 629	161	
Revelstoke	200	1 000	500		91	36	1	
Arrow	0	3 290	3 170		210	112	11	
Kootenay Lakes	0	1 800	3 400		123	126	0	
Total	200	21 995	15 070	(37 265)[c]	971	1 903	173	(3 047)[d]
Northwest Interior								
Kalum	315	2 359	472		174	178	0	
Kispiox	0	5 910	3 906		302	383	113	
Total	315	8 269	4 378	(12 962)[c]	476	561	113	(1 150)[d]
Species total	2 815	100 359	148 948	(252 122)[c]	6 671	11 995	1 353	(20 019)[d]

TABLE 1. (continued)

Region or general provincial area and Timber Supply Area	Area (hectares) by site class that allows harvesting[a]				Volumes (000 m³) on areas that allow harvesting by maturity[b] class			
	Good	Medium	Poor		Near-mature	Mature	Overmature	
Cottonwood (Interior)								
Northeast Interior								
Fort Nelson	6 500	40 300	20 400		962	7 193	10 299	
Fort St. John	400	9 000	8 400		661	1 713	1 215	
Dawson Creek	300	28 080	46 880		1 048	7 962	2 244	
Total	7 200	77 380	75 680	(160 060)[c]	2 671	16 868	13 758	(33 297)[d]
North-central								
Prince George	1 300	7 100	1 200		76	279	677	
Mackenzie	100	2 000	1 200		23	91	294	
Robson Valley	0	1 900	800		19	74	215	
Total	1 400	11 000	3 200	(15 600)[c]	118	444	1 186	(1 748)[d]
North West								
Bulkley	200	3 200	400		19	69	412	
Kalum	2 370	5 180	150		45	346	651	
Lakes	0	600	0		0	14	33	
Kispiox	2 746	4 760	200		8	170	1 033	
Morice	600	900	100		13	130	207	
Total	5 916	14 640	850	(21 406)[c]	85	729	2 336	(3 150)[d]
South-central								
Merritt	0	1 100	200		14	132	85	
Kamloops	800	1 700	300		57	163	104	
Okanagan	125	3 775	100		36	366	272	
Total	925	6 575	600	(8 100)[c]	107	661	461	(1 229)[d]
Southeast								
Arrow	790	1 480	110		40	218	40	
Boundary	615	1 340	0		23	255	77	
Kootenay Lakes	400	1 500	100		18	115	110	
Cranbrook	400	2 900	500		150	291	87	
Total	2 205	7 220	710	(10 135)[c]	231	879	314	(1 424)[d]
Species total	17 646	116 815	81 040	(215 501)[c]	3 212	19 581	18 055	(40 848)[d]

TABLE 1. (continued)

Region or general provincial area and Timber Supply Area	Area (hectares) by site class that allows harvesting[a]				Volumes (000 m³) on areas that allow harvesting by maturity[b] class			
	Good	Medium	Poor		Near-mature	Mature	Overmature	
				Alder (Coast)				
Lower Mainland								
Fraser	2 300	24 100	7 200		5 577	646	16	
Soo	794	2 950	1 702		1 113	90	15	
Sunshine Coast	9 560	18 995	9 555		8 478	2 145	92	
Total	12 654	46 045	18 457	(77 156)[c]	15 168	2 881	123	(18 172)[d]
South Coast and Vancouver Island								
Arrowsmith	553	10 781	2 763		3 403	85	0	
Kingcome	1 583	7 915	7 598		2 860	234	3	
Mid Coast	323	5 330	3 231		1 455	233	42	
Strathcona	1 827	14 010	6 395		5 634	232	0	
Total	4 286	38 036	19 987	(62 309)[c]	13 352	784	45	(14 181)d
Species total	16 940	84 081	38 444	(139 465)[c]	28 520	3 665	168	(32 353)[d]
				Maple (Coast)				
Lower Mainland								
Fraser	1 200	9 400	1 000		2 544	1 097	43	
Soo	200	200	100		138	29	0	
Sunshine Coast	790	1 015	226		160	500	24	
Total	2 190	10 615	1 326	(14 131)[c]	2 842	1 626	67	(4 535)[d]
Vancouver Island								
Arrowsmith	0	493	0		140	45	10	
Strathcona	0	360	180		198	20	0	
Total	0	853	180	(1 033)[c]	338	65	10	(413)[d]
Species total	2 190	11 468	1 506	(15 164)[c]	3 180	1 691	77	(4 948)[d]
				Cottonwood (Coast)				
Lower Mainland								
Fraser	3 482	900	200		455	78	20	
Soo	600	2 490	800		115	42	104	
Sunshine Coast	4 592	455	0		732	82	53	
Total	8 674	3 845	1 000	(13 519)[c]	1 302	202	177	(1 681)[d]
Mid and Lower Coast								
Kingcome	2 693	961	0		362	71	262	
Mid Coast	1 789	1 073	0		118	93	235	
Total	4 482	2 034	0	(6 516)[c]	480	164	497	(1 141)[d]
Species total	13 156	5 879	1 000	(20 035)[c]	1 782	366	674	(2 822)[d]

TABLE 1. (continued)

Region or general provincial area and Timber Supply Area	Area (hectares) by site class which allows harvesting[a] Good	Medium	Poor		Volumes (000 m³) on areas that allow harvesting by maturity[b] class Near-mature	Mature	Overmature	
			Aspen					
Northeast Interior								
Fort Nelson	11 000	497 000	542 000		10 972	96 034	40 358	
Fort St. John	2 000	276 000	382 000		8 625	25 901	3 882	
Dawson Creek	0	226 896	246 915		8 680	51 827	2 572	
Total	13 000	999 896	1 170 915	(2 183 811)[c]	28 277	173 762	46 812	(248 851)[d]
North-central								
Mackenzie	1 000	84 000	120 000		2 499	10 893	2 491	
Prince George	2 025	211 562	150 827		8 515	17 491	4 562	
Total	3 025	295 562	270 827	(569 414)[c]	11 014	28 384	7 053	(46 451)[d]
Central and South-central								
Robson Valley	0	16 000	13 000		1 045	1 375	135	
Kamloops	0	25 115	24 000		1 580	2 412	169	
Okanagan	0	10 385	8 000		590	930	40	
100 Mile	0	19 000	26 000		494	2 833	133	
Quesnel	0	42 490	19 690		1 000	6 421	511	
Williams Lake	0	36 000	57 000		1 869	3 039	131	
Total	0	148 990	147 690	(296 680)[c]	6 578	17 010	1 119	(24 707)[d]
Northwest								
Bulkley	0	19 000	11 000		977	1 163	499	
Kispiox	1 058	31 729	17 980		1 246	2 698	956	
Lakes	0	37 000	36 000		1 365	2 551	1 708	
Morice	0	27 000	25 000		1 174	2 668	861	
Kalum	230	3 682	5 370		282	340	3	
Total	1 288	118 411	95 350	(215 049)[c]	5 044	9 420	4 027	(18 491)[d]
Species total	17 313	1 562 859	1 684 782	(3 264 954)[c]	50 913	228 576	59 011	(338 500)[d]

[a] Low site was not considered suitable to establish utilization, although in specific cases, some volumes could come from these areas.

[b] Near-mature is defined as 61–80 years of age for aspen and cottonwood in the Interior, and 41–80 years of age for all other species; mature is defined as 81–120 years of age, and overmature is defined as 121 years or more. Utilization is 17.5 cm close less decay, waste, and breakage to a 10 cm top.

[c] total area (good + medium + poor sites)

[d] total volume (near-mature + mature + overmature)

Sources: B.C. Ministry of Forests, Inventory Branch, Provincial Summary Reporting System, Compilation Reference No. PSR12APJ, March 2, 1992.

B.C. Ministry of Forests, Timber Harvesting Branch, Timber Tenures Section, Tree Farm Licence Area Summary (Including Deciduous), February 11, 1992.

B.C. Ministry of Forests, Timber Harvesting Branch, Management and Working Plans for Selected TFLs, various dates, 1988–1992.

Maple (Coast)

Bigleaf maple (*Acer macrophyllum*) is concentrated in the Fraser TSA and to a lesser extent in the Sunshine Coast TSA. Similar to alder, most of the stands are on good and medium sites. In the Fraser TSA most of the volume is in the near-mature class, while the smaller Sunshine Coast volume is largely mature. Although a much smaller resource than alder, there appears to be a good opportunity for utilization in the Fraser TSA.

Cottonwood (Coast)

Coast cottonwood (*Populus balsamifera* ssp. *trichocarpa*) occurs on the mainland on good and medium sites from the Mid Coast to the Fraser TSA. About two-thirds of the volumes reported are in the near-mature class. The opportunities for management and use appear to be excellent. Volumes can likely be assembled by water transport in most cases, as large areas of concentration do not exist. The floodplains of some major rivers could be dedicated to intensive cottonwood management, but the opportunities appear to be limited in both size and number.

Aspen

Aspen (*Populus tremuloides*) is the major hardwood species and the major concentrations are in the northern Interior. The Fort Nelson, Fort St. John, and Dawson Creek TSAs have the largest areas and volumes where this species dominates. Most of the sites are classified as poor or medium and most of the volume is classified as either mature or overmature. Strategic planning for long-term management and utilization will be difficult because of the age-class imbalance.

Significant areas of concentration also exist in the northwest, the north-central, and the central and south-central areas of the Interior. Again, the sites are almost evenly divided between medium and poor. The age class distribution of these stands, however, is considerably better and about 25% of the reported volumes are in the near-mature or 61–80 year age class.

2.2 Potential Locations for Utilization

The areas and TSAs listed in Table 1 were referred to population centres to link areas of timber supply with communities. The community areas in Table 2 are based on those in the British Columbia Regional Index as used by the Forest Resources Commission (1992). In some cases, where there are many small communities and the potential points of utilization are uncertain, a more general designation is used (i.e., south Vancouver Island, Kamloops–North Thompson, Creston-Nelson-Kaslo). The Vancouver (lower mainland) area, which was omitted from the Commission Study, was included with Powell River as a sub-unit. Some locations or groupings may not be viable as utilization centres not only because of the quantity of the resource, but also because of other demands on the resource, the lack of labour, energy, or transportation, or other factors such as wood quality.

The following estimated annual input volumes (m^3) were considered necessary for a sustainable operation.

Pulp mills	about 450 000 m^3
Oriented strandboard (OSB)	about 400 000 m^3
Pulpchip manufacture (domestic or export)	about 150 000 m^3
Sawmill (medium)	60–80 000 m^3
(small)	25–30 000 m^3
Rotary veneer	30–40 000 m^3
Sliced veneer	10–12 000 m^3

The potential for establishing a facility was considered "high" when the inventory volumes in Table 1 (mature and near-mature) were at least 20 times above the annual usage rates, and the community or area named was central to the inventory area. "Joint potential" was considered on the same basis, but the inventory area was linked to more than one community. "Minor potential" was used to denote communities related to an inventory area, or part of an inventory area, where volumes were lower and facilities of the sizes noted would not be feasible on the basis of current information.

TABLE 2. Estimates of communities favourably located for hardwood use

	Potential for hardwood use[a]				
Species	**High**	**High/joint**	**Joint**	**Minor/joint**	**Minor**
Maple	Vancouver area Powell River				south Vancouver Island Campbell River
Alder	Vancouver area Powell River area		south Vancouver Island Campbell River Port Hardy–Port McNeil		
Cottonwood (Coast)			Vancouver area Powell River Port Hardy–Port McNeil		
Aspen	Fort Nelson Fort St. John Dawson Creek Prince George–Vanderhoof Mackenzie		(1) Hazelton Smithers-Houston Burns Lake (2) Quesnel Williams Lake 100 Mile House Kamloops–North Thompson		McBride-Valemont
Cottonwood (Interior)	Fort Nelson	Fort St. John Dawson Creek	Kitimat-Terrace Hazelton Smithers-Houston	(1) Kamloops–North Thompson Merritt-Princeton Salmon Arm–Vernon-Sicamous Kelowna-Penticton-Oliver (2) Cranbrook Creston-Nelson-Kaslo Castlegar-Slocan-Nakusp Greenwood–Grand Forks	

TABLE 2. (continued)

Species	High	High/joint	Joint	Minor/joint	Minor
			Potential for hardwood use[a]		
Birch	Fort Nelson Fort St. John Kamloops–North Thompson Salmon Arm–Vernon-Sicamous				
			Hazelton (1) Mackenzie Prince George–Vanderhoof (2) Quesnel Williams Lake		
					Vancouver McBride-Valemount 100 Mile House

a The following subjective ratings were assigned on the basis of the volume of the resource present and number of hectares of hardwood located in the general area of the community:

High potential – Sufficient resource available adjacent to the community to support a milling facility.

High/joint potential – Two towns fairly close together in area of concentration of resource.

Joint potential – Resource available in the general area, but the adequacy of the supply and the location of a utilization centre would need further and more specific investigation.

Minor/joint potential – A lower concentration of Interior cottonwood in an area of many small communities.

Minor potential – Relative to other areas, only a limited amount of the resource available. Minor local use may be possible, subject to further investigation.

3 HARDWOOD ECOLOGY

3.1 Study Objectives

There are four main objectives to this review of hardwood ecology:

1. To identify and briefly describe those ecological roles, characteristics, and processes where the presence of hardwoods, either in pure or mixed stands, are thought to create relevant differences from conifer-dominated ecosystems;

2. To summarize the silvical characteristics of the main hardwood species that are considered to be most relevant for forest management decisions, with emphasis on reproductive traits, growth rates, competition, nutrient relations, and responses to silvicultural treatments;

3. To highlight the main management implications of the hardwood-related features outlined in the first two steps; and

4. To suggest research needs related to the identified management implications.

British Columbia's six main species were examined: aspen, black cottonwood, balsam poplar, red alder, paper birch, and bigleaf maple. Alder, aspen, and cottonwood are probably the best known of these species in terms of ecological and growth characteristics.

3.1.1 Study approach

Except for the northeastern part of British Columbia where hardwoods are a very conspicuous component of the available wood supply, presently available inventory data indicate that softwood volumes far exceed hardwood volumes on a province-wide basis. However, there is optimism about the role of hardwoods in British Columbia forestry:

> Hardwoods are considered the "Cinderella trees" of the 1990s in the southern interior of British Columbia. They have long been cut, burned, and sprayed to create coniferous forests of high quality. Recently, however, there have been concerns that this expensive eradication policy is a mistake. Not only is the demand for hardwoods growing, but concerns have developed over the negative aspects of growing coniferous monocultures. Indeed, hardwoods will likely play a crucial role, both ecologically and socially, in the health of our future forests (Simard and Vyse 1992).

Therefore, this review is based on the assumption that hardwoods are strategically important in the province in terms of ecosystem processes, multiple-resource uses, biodiversity, and forest health, as well as their overall position in the province's available wood supply. Hardwoods in British Columbia, like hardwoods elsewhere in North America, have certain ecological roles that distinguish them from softwood species occurring in the same ecosystems. The focus on hardwoods, however, does not minimize the importance of management of mixed stands. This is a complex subject that is alluded to but not specifically addressed by this review.

There are different ways to synthesize research needs related to hardwood or mixedwood stands. One way is to focus on ecosystem processes in which one or more different hardwoods are involved. An example is current research on the influence of hardwoods on root diseases affecting softwoods, in which both red alder and paper birch, in different biogeoclimatic zones, are objects of study. There are also other softwood-hardwood management questions (i.e., those dealing with competition and nutrient relations) that are common to two or more combinations of conifer-deciduous species mixes.

The other way to synthesize hardwood-related research needs is by species. This is the approach used here, partly because it makes sense taxonomically and genetically, and also because the main hardwood species differ from one another ecologically and silviculturally. The species approach does not prevent research managers from later grouping two or more hardwood species, or two or more kinds of mixedwood stands, under a common project if it makes ecological sense to do so. For example, birch, aspen, and balsam poplar (or black cottonwood) often occur together along with one or more conifers. In such cases, some mixedwood research will automatically need to focus on all of the hardwoods present. The need for such kinds of groupings for research planning purposes is recognized, but a species' focus was considered to be the most efficient way to present information.

Much is already known about the autecology of British Columbia's prominent hardwood tree species. There is also substantial knowledge of silvicultural methods to maintain, increase, or decrease the abundance of hardwoods, although ecosystem-specific silvicultural prescriptions are not as advanced as would be required for intensive hardwood management. This analysis builds upon the ecological and silvicultural knowledge base that already exists—much of it the result of recent B.C. Ministry of Forests and Forest Resource Development Agreement (FRDA) initiatives. Published examples include: management guidelines for black cottonwood, red alder, bigleaf maple, and paper birch in coastal British Columbia (McLennan 1990a; McLennan and Klinka 1990); the 1991 analysis by McLennan and Mamias (1992) of black cottonwood management problems and research needs in British Columbia; ecology and management information for paper birch and black cottonwood in southern British Columbia (Simard and Vyse 1992); management problems associated with hardwoods in northeastern British Columbia (Peterson *et al.* 1989b); pre-harvest aspen control as a silvicultural treatment in the southern interior of British Columbia (Bancroft 1989); the recent problem analysis of impacts of hardwood management on British Columbia wildlife (Enns *et al.* 1993); and several autecological reviews by Coates and Haeussler (1986), Coates *et al.* (1990), and Haeussler *et al.* (1990) which included the province's major hardwood tree species. In addition, there is an unpublished analysis of the paper birch resource in the Prince George Forest Region.[2]

To supplement the reports listed above, information was gathered from analyses done in other jurisdictions for hardwood species that occur in British Columbia, such as those for: red alder in the Pacific Northwest (Gedney 1990; Harrington 1990); aspen and balsam poplar in the prairie provinces (Peterson and Peterson 1992); aspen in Ontario's boreal mixedwood forests (Whitney and McLean 1981; Davison *et al.* 1988); balsam poplar (Zasada and Phipps 1990); black cottonwood (DeBell 1990); bigleaf maple (Minore and Zasada 1990); and paper birch (Perala and Alm 1990a and b; Safford *et al.* 1990).

[2] Rose,C.L. 1991. A preliminary analysis of birch growth and yield in the central interior of British Columbia. Prep. for B.C. Min. For., Prince George, B.C. Unpubl. draft.

This component of the strategic analysis does not discuss hardwood ecological relationships in the individual forest regions, forest districts, TSAs, or TFLs in British Columbia. There are many ecological features and concepts involving hardwoods that are applicable wherever hardwoods are dominant components of ecosystems. However, there are differences in the role of hardwoods in different biogeoclimatic zones, subzones, or variants. Those ecologically based geographic differences are emphasized here.

3.2 Silvical Overview of British Columbia's Main Hardwoods

Information recently assembled by Haeussler *et al.* (1990) was a key source for the following species descriptions because that reference described ecological characteristics in a standardized way for each tree species. Other recent reviews that complement the work of Haeussler *et al.* (1990) include:

- Red alder: Bancroft *et al.* (1990), Harrington (1990), Plank *et al.* (1990)
- Aspen: DeByle (1990), Massie *et al.* (1990), Navratil *et al.* (1990), Perala (1990), Rauscher *et al.* (1990), Navratil and Chapman (1991), Peterson and Peterson (1992)
- Balsam poplar: Zasada and Phipps (1990)
- Birch: Perala and Alm (1989, 1990a and b), Safford *et al.* 1990, Densmore and Page (1992), Simard and Vyse (1992)
- Black cottonwood: DeBell (1990), McLennan (1990a and b), McLennan and Klinka (1990), McLennan and Mamias (1992), Simard and Vyse (1992)
- Bigleaf maple: Minore and Zasada (1990)

3.2.1 Red alder (*Alnus rubra*)

Red alder is a medium-sized deciduous tree up to 35 m tall. It is the most abundant hardwood occurring along the northwest Pacific Coast. In British Columbia, it is found along the entire length of the coast, including Vancouver Island and the Queen Charlotte Islands. It is restricted to within 200 km of the coast and only occurs inland in the Coast Mountains along major river valleys such as the Fraser and Skeena (Fowells 1965; Harrington 1990). Red alder is abundant in the Coastal Western Hemlock (CWH) and Coastal Douglas-fir (CDF) biogeoclimatic zones and occurs at low elevations in the Mountain Hemlock (MH) zone. It primarily grows in low coastal valleys, ranging from sea level to approximately 1200 m.

This species is found on a wide variety of soils and substrates ranging from well-drained gravels and sands to poorly drained clays or organic soils. The best stands are found on deep, well-drained loams, sandy loams, or silt loams of alluvial or marine origin (Fowells 1965; Harrington 1990).

In most situations, red alder grows as a single-stemmed tree. Under low light conditions the crown is narrow, but in full light and in the absence of competition, branches spread out from near the base to produce a broad, rounded crown.

Red alder exhibits rapid early growth (Harrington 1990). Of its associates, only black cottonwood and bigleaf maple sprouts can grow as rapidly as alder during the juvenile stage. Where moisture is adequate, a seedling can grow to 1 m or more in the first year. Chester (1988) described first-year height growth as averaging between 14 and 40 cm.

Maximum annual height growth occurs at a very early age. Red alder near Haney reached 9 m in height and 9.5 cm in diameter by age nine (Kunzli 1985). Growth slows after the juvenile stage, with the decrease beginning much earlier on poor sites. Maximum annual productivity occurs between the ages of 10–15 years (Zavitkovski and Stevens 1972).

Various reports and summaries (Atterbury 1978; Chester 1988) have compared the potential growth of red alder and conifers. On good sites, red alder trees are taller than Douglas-fir for the first 30 years and taller than western hemlock for the first 40 years. Tree volume is greater than that of Douglas-fir for at least 60 years and greater than that of western hemlock for the first 40 years. However, early mortality causes them to have significantly lower volume per hectare than coniferous stands after age 40. Stand density management guidelines have been derived for red alder by Hibbs (1987).

Red alder flowers between late February and early May depending on latitude and climate (Kenady 1978). In coastal Alaska, flowering is in April and May (Viereck and Little 1972). Separate male and female catkins are produced on the same plant. The female catkins develop into small cones containing small, winged nutlets (Brayshaw 1978). Cone ripening takes place between August and November. Seed dispersal begins shortly after ripening and continues through fall and winter (Kenady 1978). On the south coast of British Columbia, seeds disperse between November and February and germination occurs in May.

This species will rapidly invade clearcut areas especially if disturbance has created areas of exposed mineral soil (Hosie 1973; Kenady 1978). Red alder begins to produce seed between 6 and 8 years of age with optimum production occurring at about age 25. It produces ample seed every year with bumper crops every 3–5 years. Dissemination of seeds is primarily by wind.

Red alder can be regenerated intentionally from coppices, seed, or seedlings (Ahrens *et al.* 1992). It sprouts vigorously from the root collar or stump when young. Sprouting vigour is greatest on trees 1–4 years old; stands less than 6 years old are the best choice for coppice regeneration (Chester 1988). Once alder reaches age 15, its capacity for vegetative reproduction is greatly diminished, and few trees will produce sprouts that live for more than 2 years (DeBell *et al.* 1984). The average number of sprouts per cut stem increases as stump height is increased up to 60 cm. In general, sprouting is maximized on stumps taller than 10 cm and shorter than 60 cm. Stumps with the cut surface facing south or west have the least mortality and are most likely to sprout, presumably because of light interception. There is evidence that level-cut stumps have fewer sprouts than angled stumps, possibly because water is slower to drain off, causing faster decay. Red alder does not sucker from the roots (Harrington 1984).

Red alder is generally one of the first trees to become established on burned-over areas (Hosie 1973), primarily by seedlings. Red alder's nitrogen-fixing capabilities allow it to establish quickly and grow on sites where burning has created a nitrogen deficiency. Fire is rarely a damaging agent to established pure stands because of their extremely low flammability. In fact, red alder has been planted to act as a firebreak to protect adjacent conifers (Harrington 1990).

This hardwood is a major competitor in young conifer plantations throughout its range in British Columbia. Competition problems are prevalent with Douglas-fir, since it is the most frequently planted conifer where alder occurs in the Vancouver Forest Region and is also shade intolerant, and therefore highly sensitive to light competition. Alder also competes seriously with Sitka spruce in the Prince Rupert Forest Region. Alder seedlings that establish in disturbed areas following harvesting form the primary source of competition. Sprouts that develop from cut stems are a lesser source of competition for young conifers. Red alder competition can also seriously hinder natural regeneration of conifers. Studies of red alder succession in the Oregon Coast Range show that natural regeneration under red alder is very rare. Alder stands often succeed to communities dominated by salmonberry or vine maple rather than to conifers (Carlton 1988).

Interactions between red alder and coniferous crop trees involve trade-offs between the negative effects of competition and the beneficial effects of soil fertility (Binkley 1984). For conifers to benefit from nitrogen fixation, red alder could be regenerated after conifers are well established. Red alder can successfully grow and fix nitrogen under thinned Douglas-fir stands, but it suffers heavy mortality and only minimal nitrogen fixation when grown under dense Douglas-fir stands (Helgerson *et al.* 1984). Additional aspects of alder's nutritional role are discussed in Section 3.4.2.

3.2.2 Bigleaf maple (*Acer macrophyllum)*

Bigleaf maple is now an object of considerable research interest (Nadkarni 1984; Fried *et al.* 1988; Fried *et al.* 1990; Zasada *et al.* 1990). This maple is a large tree, 15–25 m tall at maturity, with a broad, spreading crown. The fruit is a winged samara with paired, hairy seeds (Hosie 1973; Minore and Zasada 1990). Bigleaf maple is confined to Vancouver Island and the adjacent mainland coast as far north as Sullivan Bay at approximately 50° N latitude (Hosie 1973; Krajina *et al.* 1982). It penetrates inland up the Fraser Canyon to Lytton. It occurs only in the CDF, CWH, and sub-continental Interior Douglas-fir (IDF) bio-geoclimatic zones, and is most abundant on southeastern Vancouver Island and adjacent areas of the CDF zone. Bigleaf maple is a low-elevation species and rarely occurs above 300 m in coastal British Columbia (Minore and Zasada 1990), but it has been observed at elevations above 350 m on southeastern Vancouver Island (Packee 1976).

Maple's best growth is on alluvial sites and at the base of colluvial slopes (Fowells 1965; Packee 1976), but it may also be found on morainal and marine soils, and often appears as a pioneer species following landslides. It is characterized by rapid growth for the first 40–60 years of its life. Maturity is reached at about 150 years and mature trees average about 25 m in height and 45 cm in diameter (Fowells 1965). Under low light conditions, bigleaf maple develops a narrow crown and a long, limb-free bole. Under open-grown conditions its crown is broad and round (Hosie 1973).

This hardwood is considered to be a very serious competitor with Douglas-fir on some of the most productive growing sites. It does not aggressively seed-in to clearcut sites, however. The primary source of competition is from already established plants, especially those trees cut during harvesting. Bigleaf maple sprouts easily outgrow conifers, and because a single plant has the capacity to establish over a large area, the potential stocking by desired species can be greatly reduced (Brand 1984). No other individual of any plant species provides as much competition to Douglas-fir as a single sprouted stump of bigleaf maple. Sprouting can be stimulated by cutting stems (Minore and Zasada 1990) and by burning that top-kills the tree (Kelpsas 1978). Sprouts can grow 2–4 m in height in the first growing season. Height growth is controlled by the number of sprouts and the size of the original stump. There can be 50–60 sprouts per stump and within 30–40 years the clump can cover an area as large as 100 m^2 (Lauterbach and Warren 1982). In contrast, early seedling growth is much slower than sprout growth because the seedling does not have an established root system to provide carbohydrate reserves. Seedlings established under a canopy of other species may have extremely slow rates of growth until released by removal of the overstorey. Suppressed trees are extremely persistent and can die back and resprout repeatedly under overmature conifer stands.

Bigleaf maple first begins to produce flowers at about 10 years of age. Seed crops are produced every year. Open-grown trees begin to produce seed earlier in life and have larger seed crops than those growing in the shade. Seeds are dispersed throughout the fall and winter. Dispersal is primarily by wind, but small mammals and some birds may also be involved. Bigleaf maple sprouts vigorously from dormant buds at the base of the stem following top-kill or cutting of the parent tree (Fowells 1965; Brand 1984; Pendl and D'Anjou 1984). It does not produce suckers from rhizomes or roots and there are no reports of natural layering. Bigleaf maple already established on a site can respond to canopy removal with vigorous growth. Cut stumps sprout to produce a wide-crowned, multi-stemmed shrub.

Grime (1979) noted that in Oregon bigleaf maple has a regeneration strategy involving a bank of persistent seedlings. These establish themselves under young coniferous or mixed stands, then persist in a stunted or etiolated condition until a disturbance creates conditions favourable for more rapid growth. Seedlings of bigleaf maple are rarely found in Oregon clearcuts. There is some uncertainty whether this is because of site and seedbed conditions, or because deer browse is so severe that seedlings only become established at later stages of stand development when deer are less abundant (Fried *et al.* 1988).

3.2.3 Black cottonwood (*Populus balsamifera* ssp. *trichocarpa*)

Black cottonwood is found throughout southern and central British Columbia from the Coast to the Rocky Mountains. It is absent along the outer coast and does not occur on northern Vancouver Island or the Queen Charlotte Islands. In northern British Columbia, it is present adjacent to the Alaska panhandle but it is replaced by balsam poplar inland (Brayshaw 1978; Krajina *et al.* 1982). Black cottonwood differs from balsam poplar in having wider leaves and a three-valved rather than a two-valved fruit (Hosie 1973; Brayshaw 1978). There are many intermediate forms between this subspecies and ssp. *balsamifera* where the ranges of the two overlap in the north (Brayshaw 1978).

This species is found in all biogeoclimatic zones except the Spruce-Willow-Birch (SWB) and Alpine Tundra (AT). Although black cottonwood primarily grows in valley bottoms, it occurs from sea level to the lower limits of the MH zone on the coast (Packee 1976) and has been recorded as high as 2100 m in elevation in the Selkirk Mountains (Fowells 1965; DeBell 1990). Black cottonwood is characteristically associated with river banks, gravel bars, or low-lying land, but it also grows on the loams, clays, and rich humic soils of upland sites. The largest trees grow at low elevations on deep alluvial soils, while the poorest growth is on newly deposited gravel (Fowells 1965; DeBell 1990).

Black cottonwood achieves the largest size of any deciduous tree in British Columbia, and, given the proper site conditions, cottonwoods are also the fastest-growing (McLennan and Mamias 1992). The species exhibits rapid juvenile growth that outstrips that of its competitors, allowing it to establish and maintain a dominant position in a stand (Packee 1976). Exceptional trees can reach 13.7 m in height and 18 cm in diameter in 7 years. By age 27, black cottonwood can exceed 36 m in height and 80 cm in diameter. Maturity is normally reached in 60–70 years, but good growth can be maintained for as long as 200 years. Black cottonwood outlives red alder where these two species occur together.

In cutover areas, large numbers of sprouts are produced from cut stumps. With the possible exception of red alder, vigorous cottonwood sprouts are the fastest-growing plants on recently harvested coastal alluvial sites on the Skeena River.

The flowers of black cottonwood appear from late March or early April through to late May on the coast; they can appear as late as mid-June in some areas of the Interior. Fruits are ripe within a month of flowering, and in some cases seed dispersal can be as early as late May. Black cottonwood first produces seed at approximately 10 years of age. Good seed crops are produced annually (DeBell 1990). The timing of seed dispersal coincides with the timing of flooding in many coastal rivers, a circumstance of relevance to foresters involved with regeneration silviculture on coastal floodplains. Work by Beaudry *et al.* (1990) on the lower Skeena River floodplain has shown that when the goal is to replace unmerchantable stands of red alder and willow with high-value Sitka spruce and black cottonwood, small-scale topographic differences that control deposition of new alluvium are very influential in the distribution of mineral soil seedbeds.

Seedling establishment is the primary means of reproduction of black cottonwood in the Cariboo Forest Region (Perry 1983) and probably throughout British Columbia. Sprouting from the stump is the most common form of vegetative reproduction in black cottonwood, although minor root suckering also occurs (Roe 1958). Black cottonwood is also known to regenerate from broken stem or root fragments incorporated in moist mineral soil.

Black cottonwood is a severe competitor with conifers because of its rapid height growth and early dominance of forested sites. Competition is most severe on extremely productive bottomland sites and will continue for the length of the rotation. Cottonwood plants may be extremely dense in the first few years of growth, but self-thinning will normally take place by age five as weaker trees are quickly suppressed by the more dominant plants (Roe 1958). It is a valuable crop tree because of high mean annual increments. The short possible rotations (20–30 years for sawlogs and 6–7 years for pulp) reduces the risk of losing the plantation to erosion on alluvial soils. It can be regenerated relatively easily and it establishes rapidly, so that sites vulnerable to erosion are rapidly stabilized.

This hardwood is not found as an understorey species beneath mature forest canopies. Following harvesting, seeding-in occurs from residual or nearby trees. Black cottonwood is highly susceptible to fire and even light burns can cause considerable injury (Fowells 1965).

3.2.4 Balsam poplar (*Populus balsamifera* ssp. *balsamifera*)

Balsam poplar has a long straight trunk and an open crown, reaching 35 m in height and 60–80 cm in diameter. The bark is grey and deeply furrowed. No geographic varieties of balsam poplar are described in British Columbia (Taylor and MacBryde 1977).

However, balsam poplar hybridizes extensively with the closely related black cottonwood (*P. balsamifera* ssp. *trichocarpa*) and may hybridize with *P. tremuloides* in some areas (Hosie 1973; Hultén 1974). Balsam poplar is found across Canada but is replaced by black cottonwood through most of British Columbia, where it is restricted to areas adjacent to, or east of, the Rocky Mountain Trench (Krajina *et al.* 1982). It extends westward in northern British Columbia to the Stikine Plateau. Balsam poplar is abundant in the Boreal Black and White Spruce (BWBS) zone, less common in the SWB zone, and occurs sporadically in some eastern subzones of the Sub-boreal Spruce (SBS), IDF, and Interior Cedar–Hemlock (ICH) zones (Krajina *et al.* 1982). Balsam poplar grows from sea level in Alaska to 1650 m elevation in the Rocky Mountains (Fowells 1965; Zasada and Phipps 1990). However, it is primarily a lowland species (Hosie 1973; Zasada *et al.* 1981).

Balsam poplar is most commonly found on moist upland and alluvial bottomland sites. It exhibits its best growth on moist, rich bottomlands with deep soil. Where it occurs together with black cottonwood, the cottonwood generally inhabits the alluvial sites, and balsam poplar the uplands. Balsam poplar rarely grows on dry, exposed sites.

Like other hardwoods, this species is characterized by rapid early growth that allows it to establish and maintain dominance above other vegetation. Rapid growth can be maintained for the first 40–50 years by which time it can reach heights of 25 m and diameters of 45 cm. Balsam poplar is relatively short-lived in the southern parts of its range but can live as long as 200 years in Alaska (Foote 1983; Zasada and Phipps 1990). On good sites, balsam poplar will outgrow aspen.

Catkins flower between April and June before the leaves appear. The seed matures very early, from mid-May to mid-June when the leaves are about two-thirds grown. Seed dispersal occurs immediately after the seeds are mature. Balsam poplar first flowers between 8 and 10 years of age (Schopmeyer 1974) and subsequently produces a good seed crop every year (Lutz 1955).

Balsam poplar will regenerate vegetatively from root suckers as well as from stump sprouts and buried branch pieces (Lutz 1955; Zasada *et al.* 1981). Callus sprouts usually originate at the top of a cut stump, or from where a stump has been damaged during harvesting. Suckers also develop from exposed roots. Suckering occurs less often in gravelly soil than in silty soils and is greatest where the organic layer has been removed, exposing mineral soil. Branch parts must be well buried in the soil to produce aerial shoots (Zasada *et al.* 1983).

Seedling germination will likely occur on areas of exposed mineral soil (Lutz 1955; Zasada *et al.* 1981). Removal of the overstorey canopy from a site in Alaska resulted in very large increases in balsam poplar growth (Walker and Chapin 1986). Of the tree species in the northern boreal forest, balsam poplar is perhaps the most resistant to destruction by fire (Lutz 1955). Like aspen, balsam poplar is stimulated to produce root suckers following fire. In Alberta, the majority of suckering occurred during the second season following spring burning of a 15-year-old stand (Bailey and Anderson 1979). Density after 5 years was greater on burned areas than on unburned areas. Additional information on the ecology and management of balsam poplar has been assembled by Peterson and Peterson (1992).

3.2.5 Aspen (*Populus tremuloides*)

Aspen is the most widely distributed native tree in North America (Brisette and Barnes 1984). Three varieties are recognized in British Columbia. The variety *vancouveriana* is found on Vancouver Island and adjacent coastal areas, var. *aurea* occurs in the Cariboo Forest Region and extends east to the Rocky Mountains, and the typical var. *tremuloides* is widely distributed throughout the British Columbia mainland (Taylor and MacBryde 1977; Brayshaw 1978). Aspen is particularly abundant in the central and northeastern parts of the province, especially in the BWBS, SBS, and IDF biogeoclimatic zones, where it forms extensive stands (Brayshaw 1978; Krajina *et al.* 1982). Aspen extends from valley bottoms to approximately 1200 m in the British Columbia interior and is occasionally found near sea level on the coast.

This species can inhabit a wide range of sites, including shallow rocky soils, loamy sands, and wet clays, but it is predominantly a species of well-drained uplands. Best growth is on moist but well-drained and porous, loamy soils; rockiness greatly limits stand development (Steneker 1976; Burns 1983; Perala 1990).

Aspen is characterized by rapid early growth and a relatively short lifespan. Although individual trees may live as long as 200 years, stands generally reach an advanced state of decay between 55 and 90 years. It most often occurs in cutover or recently burned areas as small clumps of trees, each consisting of large numbers of root suckers (Schier and Campbell 1978). Vigorous suckers may grow as much as 2 m in their first year, but subsequent height growth will average 30–60 cm annually (Steneker 1976). Seedling growth is much slower. Fowells (1965) reported that growth in the first year averages 30 cm, while in Alaska, 3-year-old seedlings reached a maximum height of 27.5 cm (Zasada *et al.* 1981).

Flowering takes place before the leaves appear in early spring (usually April or May). The fruits mature as the leaves expand and are normally ripe during May or June, about 4–6 weeks after flowering. Seed dispersal takes place shortly after ripening is complete, typically in the first few weeks of June. Aspen begins to flower between 10 and 20 years of age. Female trees produce an adequate seed crop annually with good seed crops every 4–5 years. The tiny cottony seeds can be carried several kilometres by wind (Fowells 1965; Maini 1972). Reproduction does occur from seed (Maini 1972) but is generally considered uncommon, because the short period of seed viability rarely coincides with moist environmental conditions (Barnes 1966). However, Peterson *et al.* (1989b) indicated that seedling establishment may be more important in relatively cold northern soils than is generally believed.

The dominant form of regeneration in aspen is through suckers or adventitious shoots that develop from the extensive lateral root system of each clone (Steneker 1976; Schier 1981; Schier *et al.* 1985). The importance of aspen's occurrence as clones, rather than as genetically different individuals in a stand, has been emphasized for mensurational sampling design (Zahner and Crawford 1965), for silvicultural management (Steneker and Wall 1970; Steneker 1976, Peterson and Peterson 1992), and for sampling to estimate stem decay on a stand basis (Hiratsuka and Loman 1984).

Aspen is considered to be a serious competitor with coniferous trees throughout most of the interior of British Columbia, especially in the BWBS zone, where it is particularly well established. Most aspen competition results from the suckers of trees already established before harvesting rather than from seedlings. The numbers of young suckers produced can be immense. A single tree in Alaska reportedly produced 36 230 suckers within 3 years (Lutz 1955). Aspen density and the rapid growth of young suckers provide young conifers with severe competition for root and crown space (Lees 1966). Suckers have the advantage of an established root system and always grow more rapidly than coniferous seedlings when open-grown (Jones 1974).

Root sucker formation is generally stimulated following overstorey removal. Even where there are only a few scattered aspen residuals in a conifer stand, aspen root suckers will generally dominate regeneration after harvesting as long as aspen root density is adequate (Schier *et al.* 1985). In the Penticton Forest District, 1-year-old suckers were reported to average 40 cm in height on moisture-deficient sites and 95 cm in height on sites with moisture available all year (Noble–Hearle 1989). Sucker densities in the first year after harvest can reach 225 000 stems per hectare, but regardless of the first-year density, stands self-thin and usually stabilize in the range of 20 000–25 000 stems per hectare (Peterson *et al.* 1989a).

Aspen is adapted to an environment with recurring fires. Aspen is considered beneficial where burning or other forms of disturbance have reduced soil nutrient levels, because it returns significant amounts of nutrients to surficial layers through its litter (Fowells 1965; Krajina *et al.* 1982). High-severity fires kill aspen, promote prolific sprouting, and maintain the seral aspen stage (Brown 1985; Jones and DeByle 1985). Low-severity fires thin aspen stands; aspen suckers and fire-tolerant conifer species (e.g., Douglas-fir and ponderosa pine) fill in canopy gaps. Suckering is common on burned sites in the SBS zone and is particularly prolific on dry sites that have abundant aspen before harvest (Hamilton 1988; Hamilton and Yearsley 1988). Repeated burning is thought to promote suckering and result in denser stands (Fowells 1965), but the regenerative capacity of aspen roots is not unlimited (Perala 1990). A study by Buckman and Blankenship (1965) revealed that repeated spring burns eventually caused a significant reduction in sucker density. Jones and DeByle (1985) suggest that frequent fires may adversely affect site quality for aspen.

In a study that examined the effect of repeated harvesting at rotations ranging from 1 to 20 years, Stiell and Berry (1986) found that the shortest rotation at which sucker production can be physiologically maintained is about 10 years. Aspen stands of present or potential value occur on many not satisfactorily restocked (NSR) and noncommercial brush areas in the province. Some of these stands may be best managed for pure hardwood or mixedwood production. Nutrient losses due to harvesting will be minimized if rotations are greater than 60 years and if whole-tree harvesting occurs during the leafless season, so that the foliage component of the nutrient pool is not removed from the site (Peterson *et al.* 1989b).

3.2.6 Paper birch (*Betula papyrifera*)

Paper birch is probably the most variable tree species in Canada. Many geographic varieties have been described, some of which are difficult to recognize. It also hybridizes extensively with other birch species. Recognized varieties in British Columbia include: the common var. *papyrifera*, which occurs across Canada and is found in the interior of British Columbia; var. *commutata*, the coastal form found in the Fraser Valley, on southern Vancouver Island, and scattered along the coast; and var. *subcordata*, which results from the crossing of paper birch and water birch (*B. occidentalis*) (Dugle 1966; Taylor and MacBryde 1977; Brayshaw 1978). This summary deals primarily with var. *papyrifera*.

Paper birch is found throughout British Columbia but is sporadic on the outer coast, absent in the Queen Charlotte Islands, and only found on the southeastern portion of Vancouver Island (Calder and Taylor 1968; Brayshaw 1978). Paper birch is common in most low- to medium-elevation biogeoclimatic zones in the Interior. It is common in the BWBS, SBS, IDF, and ICH zones, less common in the CWH, CDF, Ponderosa Pine (PP), and Bunchgrass (BG) zones, and absent from the Engelmann Spruce–Subalpine Fir (ESSF), MH, and AT zones. It is most abundant in warm, moist Interior valleys and is found over a wide range of elevations but primarily occurs at low to moderate elevations. It does not occur in subalpine forests.

This species occurs on a wide variety of parent materials and on soil textures ranging from gravelly sands to loams and organic soils. It is most abundant on rolling upland terrain or on alluvial sites but it is also found on open slopes, rock slides, bogs, and swamp margins. Best growth occurs on well-drained sandy or silty soils or on soils derived from limestone (Fowells 1965; Hosie 1973; Brayshaw 1978; Krajina *et al.* 1982; Marchant and Sherlock 1984; Safford *et al.* 1990).

Paper birch grows to 30 m tall and is often multi-stemmed. It does not exhibit the rapid early growth that characterizes other hardwood species such as black cottonwood and red alder. Paper birch seedlings average 10 cm in height after the first growing season (Fowells 1965) and can reach a maximum of 40 cm on favourable sites in full sunlight (Marquis 1966). Grant and Thompson (1975) reported that 3-year-old birch in British Columbia average 32 cm in height. Growth of sprouts is considerably more rapid than that of seedlings. Sprouts can grow up to 60 cm in the first year and are twice as tall as seedlings after 4 years.

Birch is considered a short-lived species. Trees mature and cease height growth at 60–70 years and few live longer than 140 years. Paper birch stands are characterized by a lack of birch in the smaller age classes. Dense stands are found in nature, but little ingress of birch occurs once the stands are established (Foster and King 1986). Paper birch does not reproduce well in established forests and therefore only occurs in later stages of forest succession where gaps are created in the canopy following a disturbance such as a blowdown (Hibbs 1982; Tang and Kozlowski 1982).

The reproductive ecology of paper birch has been well summarized by Perala and Alm (1989, 1990a) and by Densmore and Page (1992). Female catkins release large quantities of small, wide-winged fruit (Hosie 1973; Brayshaw 1978). It begins bearing seed at about 15 years of age, with the optimum seed-bearing age being 40–70 years. Paper birch trees produce good seed crops every 2–4 years. Seeds are winged nutlets that are dispersed by wind and water. Although the seed is light and travels easily, most of the seed falls within 100 m of the parent tree (Bjorkbom *et al.* 1965; Zasada 1971; Schopmeyer 1974; Archibold 1980; Safford *et al.* 1990).

Paper birch will sprout from the root collar and stump following cutting or fire (Fowells 1965; Hyvarinen 1968; Klinka and Scagel 1984). Prolific sprouting will occur when trees are young, but sprouting vigour decreases with age. Sprouting may occur at the base of standing live trees that have been subjected to increased exposure by disturbance. While vegetative reproduction is important for the persistence of individual trees following disturbance, regeneration from seed is the most important means of reproduction of the species (Lutz 1955).

Although birch is sometimes considered to be an aggressive species (Watson *et al.* 1980), it is not as serious a competitor as aspen in the central Interior (Revel 1983) and is too scattered on the coast to be a significant competitor. Vigorous growth and abundance of birch can cause localized threats to the survival and development of spruce seedlings in the Interior (Arlidge 1967). In the wetter ICH subzones of the Kamloops Forest Region, birch usually does not pose problems for regeneration establishment but may affect growth and survival years after conifers are established (Mather 1988). Recent work by Simard (1990) indicated that low densities of birch, when growing with Douglas-fir, may have positive effects by limiting the spread of *Armillaria* root rot.

Following harvesting or disturbance, abundant seeding-in of paper birch will normally occur where seed trees are left standing and a suitable seedbed has been created. The sprouting vigour of mature trees cut during harvesting is variable and may depend to some extent on site conditions. Following canopy removal in the IDFmw and ICHmw subzones near Salmon Arm, height growth of birch was noted to be initially slow (30 cm/yr), but after 2 years the growth rate rapidly increased.

The bark of paper birch is thin and very flammable, making this tree highly susceptible to fires of even moderate intensity (Lutz 1955; Safford *et al.* 1990). Sprouting is common on trees damaged or killed by fire (Hosie 1973), but sprouts are less frequent on middle-aged and old trees than in young stands (Lutz 1955). Paper birch thrives in an environment with a regular fire history, and regeneration is frequently more common on burned sites than on unburned areas (Behrend and Patrick 1969). In the Kamloops Forest Region, broadcast-burned sites have significantly less birch stems than mechanically site-prepared areas (Mather 1988).

3.3 Biogeoclimatic Framework for Hardwood Data

This section summarizes the occurrence of British Columbia's main hardwood species in the province's biogeoclimatic zones and their presence in the most productive ecosystem associations of several example biogeoclimatic zones or subzones.

3.3.1 Relative abundance of hardwoods in the province's biogeoclimatic zones

As shown in Figure 1, balsam poplar and black cottonwood (if taken as one species) occur with a relatively uniform frequency in each of the 10 listed forested biogeoclimatic zones. The same is true for paper birch. Bigleaf maple and red alder have the most restricted distribution of the five hardwoods summarized in Figure 1, with maple reaching its greatest frequency in the CDF zone and alder in the CWH zone. Aspen is as geographically widespread as birch, reaching its greatest frequency in the BWBS and SBS zones in the northeastern part of the province. A more inclusive summary of the relative abundances of British Columbia's hardwoods by biogeoclimatic zone is shown in Table 3.

To place the six species that are the focus of the present analysis in ecological perspective, Table 3 lists all 13 of British Columbia's hardwoods that can reach tree size.

The frequency of hardwoods on the five-class soil moisture gradient (Figure 1) shows them skewed towards the wetter half of the gradient. Of the 26 tree species ranked by Klinka *et al.* (1990), only tamarack occurs on wetter soils than balsam poplar and black cottonwood; and only the poplars, tamarack, black spruce, and Alaska yellow-cedar grow on wetter soils than red alder.

The main hardwood species have their greatest frequency on the most productive (rich and very rich) sites along the soil nutrient gradient (Klinka *et al.* 1990). Paper birch is more likely to grow on sites of somewhat lower nutrient status. All of the six hardwoods listed in Figure 1 are shade intolerant or very shade intolerant, a circumstance of importance to silvicultural management and regeneration of these species.

The four main hardwood species are mentioned as potential components of only nine of 48 representative site associations in the 12 forested biogeoclimatic zones reviewed by Meidinger and Pojar (1991) (Table 4). This listing is obviously a substantial underestimate. However, it does draw attention to the fact that hardwoods are not prominent species in many site associations in the province. This is partly because site associations, by definition, represent relatively stable late-successional conditions and all of the hardwoods considered here are prominent in earlier seral stages.

3.3.2 Relation of hardwoods to wildlife habitat classes

In the 92 habitat classes (52 forested and 40 nonforested) used by the B.C. Ministry of Environment, Lands and Park's Wildlife Branch in British Columbia (Fenger 1990), hardwoods are recognized in the name of 11 (about 21%) of the 52 forested habitat classes, as listed below:

1. black cottonwood riparian
2. boreal white spruce - trembling aspen
3. Sitka spruce - black cottonwood riparian
4. sub-boreal white spruce - trembling aspen
5. trembling aspen copse
6. western hemlock - paper birch
7. western redcedar - black cottonwood riparian
8. western redcedar - paper birch
9. white spruce - balsam poplar riparian
10. white spruce - black cottonwood riparian
11. white spruce - paper birch

Species	Climatic gradient: MH	ESSF & MS	BWBS	SBS	SBPS	IDF	ICH	PP	CDF	CWH	Soil moisture: very dry	dry	fresh	moist	wet	ranking	Soil nutrient: very poor	poor	medium	rich	very rich	ranking	Shade tolerance: very shade-tolerant	shade-tolerant	moderately shade-tolerant	shade-intolerant	very shade-intolerant	ranking	Potential for natural regeneration: in the shade	in the open	Spatial requirements
Balsam poplar & black cottonwood	○	○	•	•	•	○	•	○	•	○		○	•	●	○	25			○	•	●	18				○	●	22	L	H	H
Trembling aspen		•	●	●	•	•	•	○	○	○	○	•	●	●	○	13		○	•	●	●	18			○	•	●	16	L	H	H
Red alder									•	●	○	•	●	●		22		○	•	●	●	18				○	●	18	L	H	H
Bigleaf maple						○			●	•			•	●	○	14			○	•	●	25			○	●	•	13	L	H	H
Paper birch		○	•	•	○	•	•	○	○	○	○	•	●	•	○	9		○	●	●	•	13				○	●	22	L	H	H

Distribution along the climatic gradient (in the forested biogeoclimatic zones); Distribution along the soil moisture gradient; Distribution along the soil nutrient gradient; Shade tolerance; Potential for natural regeneration.

● very frequent • frequent ○ less frequent □ absent

L low
M medium
H High

FIGURE 1. Selected silvical characteristics of the main hardwood tree species in British Columbia, as summarized by Klinka *et al.* 1990. Klinka *et al.* originally grouped 26 softwood and hardwood tree species in their table. The numerical rankings shown in the moisture gradient, nutrient gradient, and shade tolerance columns refer to the species' comparative position along gradients. A ranking of 1 refers to the species adapted to the driest soils, nutrient poorest soils, or exhibiting the greatest shade tolerance; a ranking of 26 would apply to the species adapted to wettest soils, nutrient richest soils, or exhibiting the least tolerance to shade.

TABLE 3. Occurrence classes (relative abundances) of British Columbia's 13 hardwood tree species within each of the province's 14 biogeoclimatic zones (Meidinger and Pojar 1991)

Angiosperms	BG	PP	IDF	ICH	MS	SBPS	SBS	BWBS	SWB	MH	CDF	CWH	ESSF	AT[b]
Acer macrophyllum (bigleaf maple)	-	-	+	-	-	-	-	-	-	-	++	++	-	-
Alnus rubra (red alder)	-	-	-	-	-	-	-	-	-	-	+++	+++	-	-
Arbutus menziesii (arbutus)	-	-	-	-	-	-	-	-	-	-	++	+	-	-
Betula neoalaskana (Alaska paper birch)	-	-	-	-	-	-	-	++	-	-	-	-	-	-
B. occidentalis (water birch)	+	+	+	(+)	-	-	(+)	+	-	-	-	-	-	-
B. papyrifera (paper birch)	+	+	++	++	+	-	++	++	-	-	+	+	-	-
Cornus nuttallii (western flowering dogwood)	-	-	+	-	-	-	-	-	-	-	++	++	-	-
Populus balsamifera ssp. *balsamifera* (balsam poplar)	-	-	-	-	-	-	+	++	+	-	-	-	-	-
P. balsamifera ssp. *trichocarpa* (black cottonwood)	+	+	+	++	+	+	++	+	-	-	++	++	+	-
P. tremuloides (trembling aspen)	+	+	+++	++	++	+	+++	+++	+	-	+	+	+	
Prunus emarginata (bitter cherry)	-	-	+[c]	++[c]	-	-	+[c]	-	-	-	++	+	-	-
Quercus garryana (Garry oak)	-	-	-	-	-	-	-	-	-	-	++	(+)	-	-
Rhamnus purshiana (cascara)	-	-	-	++[d]	-	-	-	-	-	-	++	+	-	-

[a] Occurrence classes: +++(abundant); ++(common); +(present but uncommon); (+)(very rare); -(absent).
[b] Tree species occur only in krummholz form in the Alpine Tundra zone.
[c] *P. emarginata* occurs in these zones, but only rarely as a (small) tree.
[d] Rarely as a small tree.

TABLE 4. Hardwood species associated with various site associations in British Columbia's biogeoclimatic zones

Biogeoclimatic zone	Site association	Associated hardwood species
Ponderosa Pine (PP)	Douglas-fir – water birch – Douglas maple	aspen or black cottonwood in mature seral or young climax stands
Interior Cedar-Hemlock (ICH)	Western redcedar – western hemlock – devil's club – lady fern	black cottonwood
Sub-boreal Pine-Spruce (SBPS)	Lodgepole pine – juniper – feathermoss	aspen in young, seral stands
	Lodgepole pine – kinnikinnick – *Cladonia*	aspen in young, seral stands
	White spruce – horsetail – glow moss	aspen is a component of mature stands occasionally
Sub-boreal Spruce (SBS)	Hybrid spruce – huckleberry – highbush cranberry	aspen and paper birch are frequent components of seral stands
Boreal white and black spruce (BWBS)	White spruce – aspen-step moss	seral stands are dominated by aspen, with occasional balsam poplar
	Black spruce – lingonberry – knight's plume	aspen often dominates seral stands
Spruce – Willow – Birch (SWB)	White spruce – grey-leaved willow – scrub	aspen is a minor component in mature birch stands

The degree to which hardwoods figure in the nomenclature of wildlife habitat classes is only a general indication of their value in the province's wildlife habitats. The list above omits red alder and bigleaf maple, possibly because maple rarely occurs in sufficient abundance to be characteristic of any one kind of habitat class. The absence of red alder in the name of any habitat classes probably reflects its lack of occurrence in exceptionally large continuous areas as with 'trembling aspen copse' or the various riparian habitat types named above.

3.4 Synopsis Of Hardwood Roles in Ecological Processes

Hardwoods serve several important ecological roles. They are commonly viewed as a nurse crop for other commercially important tree species. They have nutrient cycling characteristics that differ from conifers. Although not well documented, hardwoods are thought to exert different microclimatic and hydrologic influences than do conifers. Hardwoods are prominent early colonizers of disturbed sites and in this context they provide rapid carbon fixation in their period of fast juvenile growth. At the other end of their life cycle, hardwoods have a relatively early release of carbon because most stands break up at younger ages than coniferous stands. Hardwoods are relatively resistant to airborne pollutants because they carry a receptive surface area of foliage for only part of each year. Several hardwood species are important for stabilization of soil erosion and protection of aquatic habitats in alluvial and riparian ecosystems. Hardwood-dominated ecosystems are also important contributors to the overall genetic and biological diversity of the province's forests.

3.4.1 Hardwoods as nurse crops

Shepperd and Jones (1985) defined a nurse crop as any stand of trees or shrubs that fosters development of another species, usually by protecting the second species during its youth from frost, insolation, or wind. The role of black cottonwood, paper birch, and aspen as nurse crops for conifers has been discussed by various investigators. The concept of nurse crop is less frequently applied to alder, but the nutritional benefit that red alder provides to Douglas-fir when these two species occur together can be considered as one aspect of the nurse crop concept.

Aspen is commonly referred to as a nurse crop because of the shade it provides other tree species that are not easily established in full sunlight. The recent study by Kabzems and Lousier (1992) addressed the question of whether aspen aided in the establishment of white spruce. In the Fort Nelson area the most obvious benefit of an aspen canopy is temperature and moisture amelioration during white spruce germination and seedling establishment. The description by Ebata (1989) of pest concerns during backlog reforestation in British Columbia provides another example of aspen's potential as a nurse crop. Root rots are a concern for spruce regeneration on many backlog sites, but sites that contain pure aspen generally do not require treatment for *Tomentosus* root rot because aspen is not a known host.

Simard (1990) indicated that the retention of a low density of paper birch can reduce the spread of *Armillaria* root rot in Douglas-fir stands. Other investigators have suggested that birch provides nurse crop functions by improving soils through enhanced nutrient cycling, by protecting conifers from frost (particularly on low-lying sites), and by increasing stand windfirmness on shallow soils (Perala and Alm 1990b). Birches improve soils by cycling nutrients efficiently (see Section 3.4.2), conveying oxygen to the root profile, and improving soil structure and permeability (Perala and Alm 1990a). The literature reviewed by Perala and Alm (1990b) suggests that the value of birch to conifers is confined to the seedling stage. However, the *Armillaria*-related nurse crop functions described by Simard (1990) are of relevance far beyond the seedling stage.

McLennan and Klinka (1990) described an approach for coastal areas that uses a nurse tree regeneration method where the shading effect of rapidly growing black cottonwood saplings suppresses the vigour of shade-intolerant shrubs, thus providing improved growth conditions for shade-tolerant conifers such as western redcedar.

Another way to view the nurse crop concept is to accept that it includes all of the beneficial effects of noncrop vegetation listed by Walstad *et al.* (1987). These beneficial effects include;

1. prevention of soil erosion on disturbed or unstable sites;
2. uptake, storage, and recycling of nutrients that might otherwise be lost from the ecosystem;
3. improvement of soil physical and chemical properties through the addition of organic matter and nutrients;
4. improvement of excessively hot, dry, or cold microclimatic conditions through shade or mulching effects;
5. protection of tree seedlings from browsing animals; and
6. reduction or elimination of diseases in desired tree species.

Management implications

The nurse crop role of hardwoods, as portrayed by several examples above, is of importance to silviculturists mainly during the seedling regeneration phase of stand management. Beyond the regeneration phase, competition from hardwoods is predominant over their initial nurse crop role.

Research needs

The ecological basis for the nurse crop concept needs to be defined more precisely for each of British Columbia's main hardwood species if managers are to plan regeneration and productivity enhancement around the nurse crop idea.

3.4.2 Roles in nutrient cycling and maintenance of site productivity

Differences in nutrient content and litter characteristics between deciduous and coniferous trees were first documented many decades ago, but one of the first detailed nutrient-cycle descriptions was that by Ovington (1958a and b) on development of woodland conditions under different tree species. Shortly after, a detailed synthesis was prepared by Rodin and Bazilevich (1967). In the 25 years since then, the literature on forest nutrient cycling has increased greatly, as indicated by the detailed review of biogeochemistry of temperate forest ecosystems prepared by Kimmins *et al.* (1985). From the well-developed literature on this subject, this section selects only a few examples of data sources that deal specifically with the nutrient cycling of British Columbia's key hardwoods.

Deciduous tree species have evolved patterns of nutrient use that differ from conifers. In coastal areas, decomposition and nutrient mineralization occur mainly outside the growing season, thus influencing nutrient use (Lassoie *et al.* 1985). Therefore, substantial amounts of nutrients can be immobilized in the large standing biomass and deep forest floor of Pacific Northwest forest ecosystems. This favours tree species that use nutrients efficiently placing hardwoods at a disadvantage compared to softwoods. Lassoie *et al.* pointed out that softwoods have less than half the nutrient requirements of most hardwoods, partly because they retain multi-year age classes of foliage, thereby reducing coniferous nutrient demands for foliage replacement. Carlyle (1986) concluded that conifers tend to dominate on nitrogen-poor sites because they are more efficient than deciduous species in their use of this nutrient.

Of British Columbia's main hardwood species, red alder is the best understood in terms of its influence on site fertility and productivity, mainly because of alder's ability to increase soil nitrogen through symbiotic N fixation (Comeau and Sachs 1992). However, red alder forests and their removal have important influences on the distribution and movement of not only N but also P, Ca, Mg, K, and site fertility in general (Van Miegroet and Cole 1988; Van Miegroet *et al.* 1990). Substantially more nutrients are tied up in aboveground biomass and in the forest floor in alder stands than in adjacent Douglas-fir stands on the same site. Consequently, harvesting alder can lead to a greater base cation removal per unit of biomass removed when compared to Douglas-fir.

This recent alder research is a good example of the ecological importance of hardwoods in modern silviculture. For example, the work by Van Miegroet *et al.* (1990) indicates that alders planted in N-rich sites previously occupied by alder grew slower than alders planted in areas previously occupied by Douglas-fir. This suggests a change in site conditions caused by prolonged alder occupancy. Recent research in adjacent conifer and alder-conifer stands in Washington and Oregon indicated that the relatively lower pH in the upper soil in alder-conifer stands may result in substantially higher concentrations of Al in soil solutions (Binkley and Sollins 1990). Cole *et al.* (1990, 1991a, 1991b) also documented how changes in soil properties resulting from alder's N fixation could decrease site productivity for second-rotation alder stands. Their research in western Washington, as well as that by Brozek (1990), indicated that alder's influence in decreasing soil and soil solution pH leads to increased Al concentration and lowered P availability. Second-rotation alder on former red alder sites had 33% less height growth and 75% less aboveground biomass accumulation at age 5 than was the case for first-rotation alder (Cole *et al.* 1990, 1991a, 1991b).

It is tempting to assume that harvesting hardwoods generally leads to a greater nutrient export per unit of biomass harvested than would conifer removal from the same site. In a given climatic region, deciduous trees usually do contain more nutrients per unit biomass than conifers (Marion 1979). However, Johnson (1983) indicated that this is not always the case and that generalizations about nutrient content per unit of biomass of coniferous versus deciduous species may have little meaning. Johnson emphasized that this subject must be addressed at the individual species level, not at the level of coniferous versus deciduous. For example, aspen has relatively high Ca concentrations in its bark, whereas its companion, spruce, has a high Ca concentration in the foliage (Johnson 1983). Therefore, the actual nutritional effects of whole-tree harvesting may not be much different between aspen and spruce. The species differences may be of practical importance only if the forest manager is choosing between retention or removal of foliage or bark from the harvest site.

There are differences in denitrification rates between conifer and hardwood ecosystems. The main difference is that many conifers appear to possess an adaptive advantage over hardwoods in environments where nutrients, water, or length of growing season are limiting. Conifer litter is of lower mineralizable quality than is hardwood litter. Furthermore, the underlying mineral soil in conifer stands is often more acidic than litter and soils of hardwood forests (Davidson *et al.* 1990). Denitrification represents a potential loss of N from forest soils as well as a source of N oxides to the atmosphere. This process has not been closely examined in forest ecosystems of the Pacific Northwest but Vermes and Myrold (1992) did obtain estimates from Oregon study sites that included four red alder stands. In these 8–78-year-old stands, denitrification rates ranged from 0.09 to 5.4 kg N per hectare per year. These researchers, noting that McClellan (1987) had found greater denitrification potentials in floodplain soils than in upslope soils, cautioned that the N losses from their four upland study sites may be lower than they would be on sites near stream channels.

Management implications

The recent research by Cole *et al.* (1990, 1991a, 199b) is important because it demonstrates that although N_2 fixation associated with red alder enhances the N status of a site, changes in soil solution chemistry caused by the presence of alder may negatively affect the productivity of the second-rotation forest. While N_2 fixation by alder results in site improvement for Douglas-fir plantations, it may be detrimental to the productivity of second-rotation red alder. Results from this study led to two hypotheses about the mineral nutrition and management of red alder. First, the negative effect that alder has on the future productivity of alder probably occurs before the establishment of the second-rotation forest, and is initiated during the 50-year development of the original stand. This could be partially responsible for the short lifespan of this species. Second, a recovery from the natural stresses caused by alder may be a long-term process depending on whether toxicity from Al concentrations or nutritional deficiency is the primary cause for the observed decline in productivity.

If repeated harvesting of red alder on short rotations is contemplated in British Columbia, forest managers should realize that there could be decreases in site productivity for second- or subsequent rotation alder stands.

Research needs

Alder management in British Columbia will require more detailed information on the effects of P availability, soil acidity changes, Al toxicity, cation availability, or competition with other vegetation on the lowering of second-rotation alder productivity. Studies should also be undertaken, in co-operation with United States researchers, to determine the causes and implications of decreased alder productivity. Overall, nutritional changes that result from the presence of hardwoods before and after harvesting requires further investigation. From comparative studies of adjacent conifer and alder-conifer stands, Binkley *et al.* (1992) stressed the difficulty in estimating N fluxes accurately and they have proposed a co-ordinated international project to examine methods to predict tree-available N.

Davidson *et al.* (1990) and various other investigators indicated that the most important factor in predicting N loss from denitrification is site fertility. Therefore, generalizations about conifers versus hardwoods depend on the relative degrees to which conifers occur more often than hardwoods on infertile sites. This is an additional reason for more detailed quantification of the relative abundance of hardwoods and softwoods in ecosystem units in each biogeoclimatic zone and subzone. Research is required to define the ecosystems in which a silvicultural choice between hardwood or softwood species may be an aid to long-term management of N supply—a major determinant of forest biomass production. The most productive ecosystems in each biogeoclimatic zone should be examined first.

3.4.3 Hardwood influences on microclimatic and hydrologic relationships

In general, hardwood forests experience higher levels of solar radiation than coniferous forests (Monteith 1975). This is significant for site-specific silvicultural prescriptions because higher forest floor temperatures in hardwood stands in early spring compared to coniferous stands result in higher rates of root growth, higher respiration rates in roots and micro-organisms, more rapid litter decomposition, and greater evaporation from soil and litter. Partly because of these microclimatic contrasts, there is usually a more abundant shrub and herb layer in deciduous forests than there is beneath a coniferous canopy This difference is relevant to silvicultural prescriptions designed to manage competing vegetation. Overall, hardwood forests intercept less water and are able to deplete soil water faster and to a greater depth than coniferous forests.

The fact that hardwoods lose all of their foliage annually determines their hydrological properties more than any other factor. There are differences in hydrological characteristics of deciduous and coniferous forests (Hinckley *et al.* 1981). Both leaf area index and seasonal duration of leaf retention in deciduous forests are about half the values of those in coniferous forests. Canopy storage capacities range from 1.0 to 2.1 mm of water per unit area of land in conifer forests, and are about 1.0 mm in hardwoods during the summer, but only 0.5 mm in winter. Interception losses in conifers range from 20 to 85% of total precipitation and from 10 to 50% in hardwoods when their leaves are out (Hinckley *et al.* 1981). In winter, interception in hardwood forests averages less than 10% and stemflow is generally greater in hardwood trees than in conifers (Rutter 1975; Benecke 1976). Aspen forests also allow more ground water recharge than do conifer forests, primarily because of lower seasonal water losses to interception and transpiration by aspen as compared to conifers (Perala and Russell 1983; Gifford *et al.* 1984; Perala 1990).

One hypothesis that may require further testing in British Columbia forest ecosystems is that deciduous forests could decrease in strategic importance if one assumed a trend to increased incidence of drought conditions associated with climate change. Lassoie *et al.* (1985) described several physiological contrasts between Pacific Northwest conifer and deciduous forests, including the suggestion that conifers may have an advantage over hardwoods during drought. For example, conifer needles exchange heat with the atmosphere better than broad leaves, thereby maintaining needle temperatures nearer to ambient temperatures This reduces the needle to air vapour-pressure gradient, which is especially important during periods of drought-induced stomatal closure. The relatively large foliar surface areas of conifer forests can collect enough condensation in summer to add water to the soil through fog drip. Deciduous tree species are also suggested to be inferior to conifers in internal water storage reservoirs, which can be used to moderate the effects of drought. Furthermore, the relatively small-diameter tracheids of softwoods limit cavitation during periods of high-water stress, thereby maintaining the water conduction continuity that is critical in times of drought (Lassoie *et al.* 1985).

The most comprehensive long-term forest hydrology studies, such as those at the H.J. Andrews Experimental Forest in Oregon (Hicks *et al.* 1991) and Carnation Creek on Vancouver Island (Hartman 1982; Chamberlain 1988), refer to the increase in hardwoods following harvesting, especially in the riparian zone. However, these studies did not set out to document differences in water yield with hardwood versus softwood forest canopy. In the Oregon study, no subsequent increase in water yield was observed after one silvicultural attempt to reduce hardwoods (Hicks *et al.* 1991). The H.J. Andrews researchers speculated that hardwoods are likely to use more water than conifers in summer for equivalent leaf areas, but that hypothesis was based on data from aspen in the Rocky Mountains where higher stomatal conductance has been demonstrated in aspen than in subalpine conifers (Kaufman 1984). In the Carnation Creek studies, the choice of streamside treatments did involve hardwoods in the sense that in some cases there were no alder seed tree treatments; in others alder seed trees were "hacked and squirted" with Tordon®, and in still others small alder trees were felled (Dryburgh 1982).

Management implications

Pre-harvest silvicultural prescriptions are normally not based on canopy differences between deciduous and coniferous species. Therefore, the meteorologic and hydrologic differences that result from canopy differences have little immediate practical significance for silviculturists. The main management implications of the features outlined above will be in those cases where deliberate and specific canopy manipulation is planned for purposes of influencing rainfall interception and water yield.

Research needs

Research in the Carnation Creek study site was not intended to quantify differences between coniferous and deciduous species. Therefore, this remains a subject not yet specifically studied in relation to British Columbia hardwood stands. The few forest hydrology studies that have long-term data were not focused on specific differences between coniferous and deciduous species in relation to hydrologic effects. This is a research need for British Columbia's main hardwoods, involving questions such as:

- What are the roles of snow interception and melt rates in deciduous versus coniferous stands?
- What are the overall implications of deciduous versus coniferous cover on soil water?

- What are the overall implications of subsurface and overland flow in hardwood versus coniferous stands?

- What are the implications for stream water quality, quantity, and temporal patterns in deciduous versus coniferous stands?

3.4.4 Hardwoods as colonizers of disturbed sites through rapid natural regeneration

The silvical descriptions of British Columbia's main hardwoods showed that all six species possess two key characteristics: (1) adaptation for rapid regeneration of disturbed sites or forest openings by one or more of natural seeding, root suckers, or root-collar sprouts; and (2) rapid early growth of seedlings, suckers, or sprouts.

The six hardwood species that rapidly invade large disturbed areas (with bigleaf maple doing so less effectively than the other five) are of strategic importance for several reasons. First, they provide a rapid re-greening of harvested areas, which much of the public finds aesthetically displeasing. Second, although not well quantified for different ecosystems in British Columbia, the rapid re-establishment of a woody plant cover after harvesting and other disturbances probably helps reduce precipitation-induced soil erosion. Third, hardwood regeneration influences wildlife habitat more rapidly than conifer growth, through early creation of vertical structure and an early abundance of browse and forage species.

Management implications

The vegetative reproduction and rapid growth of hardwoods can be of management importance because of their potential remedial role in soil stabilization, erosion control programs, and wildlife habitat enhancement.

Research needs

Autecological characteristics are well documented for the British Columbia hardwoods that are rapid invaders of disturbed sites. This review did not identify any priority research needs for this aspect of hardwood ecology.

3.4.5 Hardwood influences on CO_2 exchange and climate change

In a world seeking to slow the rate of human-caused CO_2 release, there is expected to be increased interest in hardwoods simply as reservoirs of stored carbon. There are two important features of British Columbia's hardwoods in this context. The first is that they do not have long lifespans when compared with their companion conifers. Carbon stored in mature hardwoods is not a very secure reservoir because respiratory losses associated with decaying wood, whether standing or on the ground, result in a significant release of carbon long before stands reach the ages typically reached by coniferous stands. Along with decay, insects and fires also contribute to carbon release.

The second important feature is that hardwoods commonly have exceptionally rapid growth rates in the first one or two decades of stand development. The high rates of standing crop accumulation and high amounts of standing crop per unit volume of growing space, documented in Alberta and Saskatchewan by Peterson *et al.* (1982), indicate that in their early years these species are very effective at capturing atmospheric CO_2. Data from the prairie provinces indicate that within 10 years from the date of stand establishment most tree and shrub species that characteristically occupy disturbed sites can achieve standing crop densities (dry weight of aboveground standing crop/m^3 of stand space) at least equal to those of mature forest stands.

These two characteristics—rapid carbon fixation in the early phases of stand development and rapid release of carbon with stand breakup between 100 and 200 years of age—must be considered when estimating the relative merits of hardwoods and softwoods for the carbon sink. In general, fast-growing species such as hardwoods are expected to be the favoured beneficiaries of enriched CO_2 levels in the atmosphere (Pollard 1985). The main point of this prediction is that, in the long term, regardless of changes in the degree to which hardwoods can be used in pulp, fibre and wafer products, managers of the forest land base are likely to have more deciduous woody biomass to deal with, whether or not it was part of their silvicultural plans. There is little documentation to date of likely responses of specific hardwood species to assumed climate changes. Those who have studied this subject indicate that drought rather than cold has been the principal selective agent in the evolution of the deciduous habit (Stebbins 1972).

A study has recently been initiated by the B.C. Ministry of Forests Research Branch to investigate impacts of harvesting, prescribed burning, and other management strategies on carbon budgets and long-term productivity in boreal hardwood, mixedwood, and conifer forests (P. Comeau, BCMOF Research Branch, pers. comm.). Related research in Minnesota and Michigan (Alban and Perala 1992), revealed that soil carbon stayed relatively constant throughout a chronosequence of pure aspen stands ranging from 0 to 80 years. Soil carbon was not affected by harvesting of aspen. The Lake States data indicated that aspen grown on 40-year rotations on good soils will withdraw more carbon per year than old-growth forests. Johnson's (1992) review supported the finding that harvesting of aspen, if unaccompanied by burning or erosion, does not change soil C.

Management implications

One hypothesis—that the relatively rapid development of a canopy by early-successional hardwood stands (e.g., dense stands of aspen suckers) serves as an early capturer of CO_2 in the post-harvest period before a significant softwood canopy develops—is not yet adequately tested or quantified. There are also other unanswered questions, such as the long-term benefits of hardwoods versus softwoods as net carbon sinks. For this question, one possible hypothesis is that because most of British Columbia's hardwoods decay rapidly, their role as carbon sinks is limited. Until such questions are better researched, there are no immediate management steps to recommend for the silvicultural manipulation of hardwoods and related carbon budgets.

Research needs

Persuasive information on the relative net benefits of hardwoods versus softwoods in relation to net carbon assimilation is not yet available. This raises the question of whether there are relevant differences between conifer and deciduous species for estimates of global changes in greenhouse gases. It is possible that the total biomass carried on the land base is more important than the conifer-deciduous distinction. Continued data collection is needed to address this uncertainty.

The two species that have received the most research attention in relation to carbon storage are red alder (Comeau and Sachs 1992) and aspen (Alban and Perala 1990, 1992), with the latter based on studies in the Lake States. Aspen appears to be the hardwood selected to receive more attention in this subject through Research Branch Project BC-FR14 (P. Comeau, BCMOF Research Branch, pers. comm.). It is recommended that the main objective of such research be a focus on the site conditions and management practices in northeastern British Columbia that might distinguish aspen's role in carbon storage.

3.4.6 Hardwoods as recipients of airborne pollutants

The difference in response of deciduous species and conifers to airborne pollutants and salt damage have been documented in studies of urban, industrial, and roadside environments. It was well known even in the last century that conifers were generally more susceptible to damage from air pollution than were broadleaved species. Good (1991) cited the Edinburgh publication *The Forester* by Brown and Nisbett (1894) in which this deciduous-conifer distinction was noted. Where de-icing salt is heavily used on highways, both salt spray and salt contamination of soils can influence the health of roadside trees. Dobson (1991) states that *Populus alba* was the species with the overall greatest tolerance to the effects of de-icing salt, among 46 deciduous trees and shrubs observed. *Populus canescens* was the third most tolerant. *Betula pendula* was intermediate in its tolerance to de-icing salt and *Alnus incana* was moderately susceptible.

The abundance of deciduous tree species and shrubs, almost to the total exclusion of conifers, in a substantial radius around Trail, B.C., suggests that hardwoods may be better adapted than conifers to cumulative effects of past air pollution from smelting facilities. Field sampling is needed in this area to help quantify the degree to which the present prominence of hardwoods is a result of the introduction of species resistant to airborne pollutants or a consequence of some inherent resistance, probably related to annual loss of all foliage, in the native deciduous species. However, relationships may not be that simple. For example, studies by Addison *et al.* (1984) indicate that under fumigation with 0.34 ppm SO_2 (Canada's maximum acceptable limit), deciduous trees and shrubs were much more sensitive than conifers. They suggested that the difference may be because SO_2 can enter broad leaves more easily than needles. Although deciduous species could not be ranked among themselves, after exposure to SO_2, decrease in net CO_2 assimilation rate was significantly more rapid in aspen, paper birch, willow, and green alder than it was in jack pine, white spruce, or black spruce.

Management implications

Hardwood tree species may react differently than conifers to inputs of airborne sulphur, heavy-metal compounds, and roadside salt compounds. These differences are of management importance in pollution-prone areas where managers have a choice in selecting the best-adapted species in reclamation and revegetation programs.

Research needs

More detailed comparative information is needed on the differences between British Columbia's hardwood and softwood species in response to airborne pollutants.

3.4.7 Hardwoods as stabilizers in alluvial and riparian habitats

Hardwoods figure prominently in valley-bottom, alluvial, and streamside (riparian) communities. Their occurrence in valley-bottom and riparian areas is of major significance because, as Newton (1989) pointed out, riparian zones in coastal areas of the Pacific Northwest include some of the most productive temperate forest ecosystems in the world. Newton concludes that the production potential of these rich sites is achievable, but is seldom achieved, because ecologically based management is generally not carried out in riparian zones for various reasons.

In Oregon, Gregory *et al.* (1990) described how problems arise if the traditional assumption is made that stocking in riparian forests closely resembles that of upslope forests. A practical question is how productive are riparian forests for wood production in relation to upslope forests? In light of the common perception of productive streamside forests, it is surprising that few inventories of riparian forests are available. An equally important question is why riparian forests experience such high rates of mortality compared to upslope forests, aside from the obvious mortality of riparian trees from flooding and soil erosion during flooding.

The abundance of hardwood tree species in alluvial areas of southwestern British Columbia is not a recent phenomenon. A compilation of vegetation descriptions from surveyors' records from 1858 to 1880 in the delta of the Fraser River (North *et al.* 1979) indicates that hardwoods were prominent in 13 of 17 forested types that North and co-workers recognized. Four of the 13 were deciduous woodland types with various combinations of bigleaf maple, alder, and cottonwood; three types were scrub forest involving only alder; and six were coniferous forest types involving one or more of alder, cottonwood, and maple. Fringes of the main arm of the Fraser River, Annacis Island, and steep side slopes or ravines of the upland lying to the east of Burns Bog were the main areas of hardwood prominence in the mid- to late 1800s. There was some human disturbance to forest vegetation before 1858 that could have encouraged early-successional hardwoods. However, the island, river fringe, ravine, and steep slope concentrations of hardwood-dominated types indicate that even in pre-settlement times, alder, maple, and cottonwood filled an important soil stabilization role in ecosystems that are naturally prone to erosion without human disturbance.

Pacific Northwest forest researchers, such as Franklin (1992), have emphasized recently that development of management approaches requiring integration of economic and ecological values is especially important in riparian zones because of the many linkages between terrestrial and aquatic ecosystems. Much attention has been given to riparian zone management (Walters *et al.* 1980; Johnson *et al.* 1985; Salo and Cundy 1987; COPE 1989; Bancroft *et al.* 1990; Lousier and Bancroft 1990; Bunnell *et al.* 1991; Rood and Mahoney 1991; Thomson 1991; Rautio and Bunnell 1992). However, relatively little of that attention deals with the ecology of mixed-species stands of trees (Cannell *et al.* 1992) or with management of pure hardwood stands for the prime purpose of riparian zone protection. One example of the latter is intensive use of poplars in Iowa to create a woodland buffer between stream edges and adjacent cropped land (Licht 1992).

In Oregon, alder has limitations for riparian zone protection. Beack (1989) states that alder "typically lives for 50 to 60 years then rapidly decays and drops to the forest floor." Hence, if conifers are harvested at age 45 in a riparian zone, leaving alder as the primary shade trees, the alder may fulfill its protective role for only 10–15 years. For this reason it is preferable to leave a mixture of conifers and alder to shade streams where such options are available.

To date, most studies and operational trials of vegetation dynamics in managed coastal riparian areas have dealt with conifer-dominated ecosystems (Hibbs *et al.* 1991). Recent research has documented the effectiveness of riparian buffer strips of hybrid poplar (*Populus trichocarpa* x *P. deltoides*) and red alder for reducing nitrogen and herbicide concentrations from ground water draining adjacent agricultural lands (Entry and Emmingham 1991). A related question is the role of hardwoods in managing municipal effluents. The strategic importance of hardwoods will increase as there is more use of fast-growing tree species for biomass production on lands irrigated by municipal effluents. The potential for this method of biomass production has been described for hybrid poplars in British Columbia by Carlson (1992) and is a forest land use of gradually increasing economic significance.

Management implications

Numerous coastal Pacific Northwest reports dealing with riparian zone management indicate that red alder, black cottonwood, and bigleaf maple have very important roles in silviculture prescriptions for these highly productive ecosystems. The Oregon case noted above, suggesting retention of conifers and red alder in mixed stands for riparian zone protection, is an example of how existing information can be silviculturally applied.

Research needs

The main hardwood research needs in relation to riparian zones involve integrated resource management and the role of hardwoods in maintaining forest health. These were two of the four priority areas defined in Project B11 of the British Columbia Hardwood and Vegetation Management Technical Advisory Committee (FRDA II). Riparian silviculture is an area where advancements are needed. Fortunately, such advancements are within reach, partly because the reproductive ecology of riparian vegetation is fairly well known (Zasada and Tappeiner 1989).

3.4.8 Hardwoods as contributors to the genetic and biological diversity of British Columbia's forests

Hansen *et al.* (1990), described the heightened interest in ways to maintain and enhance biological diversity as the harvesting of wood proceeds. However, by summer 1992 the Vancouver Forest Region had not completed the drafting of biodiversity guidelines, and incremental silviculture guidelines were under revision. Suggestions on how to maintain important wildlife habitat features in managed second-growth forests are now sufficiently advanced that they can be used in pre-harvest silvicultural prescriptions.[3] Present suggestions will potentially involve hardwoods in the following ways:

- retention of safe snags and green trees in all cutblocks;
- regeneration of stands with a mixture of tree species when ecologically appropriate;
- retention of a hardwood component in the stands during vegetation management; and
- promotion of a mixed-species stand including a hardwood component during spacing and thinning, if ecologically appropriate for the site.

The main argument for maintaining biodiversity is that it is not always possible to identify which individual species are critical to ecosystem sustainability, nor which species may be economically most important in the future (Burton *et al.* 1992). It is therefore prudent to maximize flexibility by promoting a wide array of species.

Management implications

Biodiversity guidelines, currently under development by the B.C. Forest Service, will have important implications for the choice and use of hardwoods in silvicultural plans. There are also important genetic and biodiversity considerations for hardwood plantations. For example, native hardwood populations are important pools from which to increase the genetic variability of otherwise genotypically uniform clonal material if plantations of cottonwoods or other hardwoods become a more widely used method of biomass production.

Research needs

Management for biodiversity requires silvicultural steps that promote not only multiple tree species but also stands with a variety of canopy structures. Hardwoods are a key element in such management regimes but specific ways to accomplish these goals are not yet well developed for British Columbia's main hardwood species.

3.5 Some Silvicultural Aspects of Hardwood Management

An ecological feature of hardwoods that influences all of the silvicultural subheadings reviewed below is their relatively short lifespan compared to softwoods. This section therefore begins with a summary of hardwood data related to lifespans, ages of maturity, and some suggested rotation lengths.

3.5.1 Summary of some hardwood maturity ages and rotation lengths

The relatively short lifespans of the province's hardwood species have an important impact on management regimes, especially for rotation lengths and techniques for maintaining a diverse forest structure. Therefore, an important silvicultural question is at what ages are the key hardwood species considered to be mature? The question has various answers because the definition of maturity varies with context such as: inventory classification, merchantability, stands that have reached

[3] August 22, 1992. Memorandum to established licencees and consultants, K.J. Ingram, File 955-3-1, based on recommendations by D. Seip.

the age of culmination of mean annual increment, pathological rotation age for species susceptible to stem decay, or biological maturity based on estimates of average longevity. The following examples indicate the divergence of estimates at which British Columbia's hardwoods are considered to be mature:

- Paper birch – estimates of maturity range from 50 to 80 years, although some birch can live to over 200 years (Safford *et al.* 1990; Simard and Vyse 1992).

- Black cottonwood – estimates range from 60 years in the Willamette Valley, Oregon, to over 200 years in British Columbia (Thomas and Podmore 1953). McLennan and Mamias (1992) indicated that canopies of black cottonwood begin to break up after 70–90 years.

- Bigleaf maple – estimates are from 150 years (Fowells 1965) to 200 years (Minore and Zasada 1990). Under intensive management, rotations of 50 years or less have been suggested (Kerbes 1968).

- Red alder – matures at 60–70 years, with maximum ages around 100 years (Harrington 1990). In Oregon, Baack[4] gave alder an even lower maturity age, noting that alder typically lives for 50–60 years then rapidly decays and drops to the forest floor.

- Aspen and balsam poplar – estimates of maturity range from 35 to 100 years depending mainly on the definition used. As summarized by Peterson and Peterson (1992), aspen stand break-up commonly begins at age 60. In terms of culmination of mean annual increment, 75 years is often mentioned as an appropriate aspen rotation age, although pulpwood can be produced at rotations from 35–45 years. Early Alberta stem decay specialists mentioned a pathological rotation age of 40–50 years for aspen. Perala (1990) referred to pathological rotation ages of 55–60 years in the Lake States, and 80–90 years in Alaska and the western parts of aspen's range; for balsam poplar, Alaskan data indicate that mature stands of this species typically occur on alluvial sites 80–100 years after establishment. There are suggestions of geographic variation in aspen lifespan based on the observation by Perala (1990) that deterioration of aspen stands begins earliest at the southern limits of its range and is a relatively slower process in the western part of aspen's range.

Management implications

The ages of maturity summarized above are generally greater than those used by the B.C. Ministry of Forests for inventory purposes and they should not be confused with operational definitions of potential rotation periods. The March 1992 version of *Operational Cruising Requirements in the Vancouver Forest Region*[5] defined an average age greater than 40 years as mature for coastal deciduous species, compared with 120 years for coniferous species. Scott Paper expects to harvest unmanaged black cottonwood stands at 40–50 years, with rotations ranging down as low as 15 years if there is intensive management involving site preparation, planting, and brushing.

Research needs

The cottonwood example above indicates that there is relatively good information available for this species. However, more detailed information is needed on the definition of maturity for other hardwoods, in managed and unmanaged stands, and in relation to the presence or absence of conifers.

---

[4] Baack, D. 1989. Oregon hardwoods. Report prepared for Western Hardwood Association, Portland, Oregon.

[5] Vancouver Forest Region. Unpubl. memo.

3.5.2 Acceptability of hardwoods as advance regeneration

Advance regeneration appears before any special measures are undertaken to establish new forest growth (Smith 1986). In that context, do British Columbia's main hardwoods have a strategically important role? In general, no, because five of the six main species have the characteristic of rapid and abundant regeneration after disturbance rather than in the understorey of stands of harvestable age. The exception is bigleaf maple because, unlike the other five, it is not a pioneer species that rapidly invades disturbed areas. However, it is often present in undisturbed stands and is able to sprout vigorously after disturbance. Maple seedling establishment is most likely to occur in Douglas-fir stands after the start of natural thinning. Increases in light from 0 to 20% of that in the open result in increases of 0–60% in maple survival, but additional increases in light are not beneficial (Minore and Zasada 1990). Bigleaf maple was classed by Krajina *et al.* (1982) as low to moderate in shade tolerance. The presence of bigleaf maple in undisturbed stands and its potential for rapid growth indicates that it can respond quickly to gap formation or overstorey removal, but it does not aggressively invade clearcuts, despite the vigorous stump sprouting after harvesting.

Aspen is also somewhat different from the other main British Columbia hardwoods in the context of advance regeneration. In general, it does not fit the definition of advance regeneration because it normally does not have a significant amount of biomass present before harvest. It does, however, have the ability to exist as a root system capable of sucker production in conifer-dominated stands that contain very few aspen stems in the understorey. Although it is very intolerant of shade throughout its life (Perala 1990), North American and European aspen can maintain a viable clonal root system in what appear to be pure coniferous stands with only a very low density of short-lived suckers present on the forest floor at any one time (Peterson and Peterson 1992). The long-term maintenance of scattered suckers and an aspen root system capable of producing many suckers when overstorey conifers are removed is a form of regeneration that happens without any advance silvicultural measures except the harvesting of overstorey conifers.

If rapid formation of aspen suckers is equated with advance regeneration, one question that boreal mixedwood managers will have to face is the degree to which aspen suckers occurring in regeneration survey quadrats are now countable as an acceptable species, in contrast to the former practice of meeting stocking standards with coniferous species only.

For the other main hardwoods in British Columbia, shade tolerance, as it relates to the potential for advance regeneration, can be summarized as follows:

- Zasada and Phipps (1990) indicated that balsam poplar showed all the characteristics of an early successional species—low shade tolerance, rapid juvenile growth, prolific seed production, relatively short lifespan, good self-pruning, and replacement by more shade-tolerant species. For these reasons it is classified as very intolerant of shade.
- Black cottonwood is shade intolerant and does not grow in forest understories. The extreme shade intolerance limits management of black cottonwood in mixtures with conifers (Simard and Vyse 1992).
- Paper birch is shade intolerant and hence usually only lasts one generation in natural succession. It is a common component of climax forests, however, where gaps have been created by blowdown or root rot (Simard and Vyse 1992). Among its hardwood associates, only aspen is more shade intolerant than birch (Safford *et al.* 1990).

- Of the 26 northwestern tree species that Minore (1979) listed in order of decreasing shade tolerance, red alder was listed as 21st, with only several dry-zone species (*Pinus contorta, Larix occidentalis, Pinus ponderosa, Juniperis occidentalis,* and *Quercus kelloggii*) being less shade tolerant than red alder. Harrington (1990) indicated that red alder requires more light than any of its tree associates except black cottonwood.

Management implications

Except for the great capacity of aspen and balsam poplar to regenerate by root suckers after overstorey removal, and for birch, bigleaf maple, and alder to regenerate by root-collar sprouts when the parent tree is removed, the province's main hardwoods are not strategically important as advance regeneration. Their importance lies instead in the rapidity with which they can establish a green cover and woody biomass on a forest area after harvest or other disturbance.

Work to date on advance regeneration (Herring and McMinn 1980; McCaughey and Ferguson 1988; Weetman and Vyse 1990) reveals a predominant focus on conifers, and especially subalpine fir and Pacific silver fir, as candidates for acceptable advance regeneration. The Weetman and Vyse summary listed no hardwood species as 'usually acceptable' in any of 11 biogeoclimatic zones. Only aspen ranked as a 'sometimes acceptable' hardwood for acceptance as advance regeneration, and then only in the BWBS zone. Aspen was considered to be 'rarely acceptable' as advance regeneration in the IDF, ICH, Montane Spruce (MS), and SBS biogeoclimatic zones; the same rating was given to poplar in the ICH and SBS zones. White birch was considered to be 'rarely acceptable' in the ICH zone.

Research needs

Recent analyses of hardwoods in northeastern British Columbia (Peterson *et al.* 1989b) revealed a tendency for existing mensurational data to overestimate ages and to underestimate hardwood stand height classes and site indices based on height data. If the Ministry of Forests wishes to continue the use of traditional mensurational indices as a measure of the relative importance of any given hardwood species, data improvements are clearly needed. Field handbooks, which provide forest mensuration data for ecosystems within any given biogeoclimatic zone, traditionally present site indices for only coniferous species. Evaluation of the overall importance of hardwoods will be hampered until they too can be used as a measure of site index. In many sites hardwoods are the only species present and therefore are the only means by which to express site index.

Forest researchers in British Columbia, and the Pacific Northwest in general, have not given much attention to hardwoods where they occur as a minor but uniformly and widely distributed component of forest stands. The current inventory system, intended as a broadly based planning tool for timber supply estimates, does not provide detailed information on hardwoods that have low abundance over widespread areas. In our view, it would be unrealistic to change the forest inventory system to provide such detail. However, it is important during local silvicultural surveys to recognize the presence of scattered hardwoods in forest stands, even if they are not very abundant and even if not viewed as advance regeneration in the sense that some conifer species are. These scattered hardwoods are often significant in terms of wildlife values, local biodiversity, and forest health.

The present analysis could not quantify the overall provincial importance of hardwoods that are low in numbers but ubiquitous; the subject is only mentioned here in the context of future research and reporting needs. Hardwood presence is now recorded in most silvicultural surveys of young stands, so some information is available from Ministry records. More detailed reporting is needed where hardwoods occur as inconspicuous but widely distributed components of ecosystems.

3.5.3 Re-establishing the same hardwood types after harvesting old-growth or young natural stands of hardwoods

Hardwoods have not figured prominently to date in the consideration of an old-growth strategy in British Columbia (B.C. Ministry of Forests 1992; MacKinnon 1992). Minimum ages to qualify as old growth are suggested for eight coniferous species in the coastal forest types and for 13 coniferous species in Interior forest types; no hardwoods are listed. However, the public review draft report on British Columbia's old-growth strategy does acknowledge that forests dominated by deciduous trees "may also have old-growth stages that should be recognized." The draft urged a re-examination of policies and procedures for planning, harvesting, and silvicultural activities to accommodate:

- increased use and acceptability of a deciduous component;
- snag management; and
- use of the full spectrum of partial-cutting systems, including green-tree retention.

The potential increase in importance of hardwoods is evident in the first goal listed above, but management steps to protect snags and to increase green-tree retention will also have management implications for hardwoods.

Weetman and Vyse (1990) recommended methods for re-establishing hardwoods after harvest of old growth and young natural stands on the coast and in the northern Interior (Table 5). To re-establish hardwoods back to the same forest type as before harvesting, the clearcut method is recommended in nearly all cases, except for the use of coppice (vegetative reproduction from stump sprouts or root suckers) for cottonwood harvested from young natural stands on the coast and for aspen harvested from young natural stands in the Interior. When the recommended regeneration method is clearcutting with natural regeneration (CCN), there is automatically some inherent coppicing for those hardwood species that naturally regenerate by root suckers or stump sprouts. In the case of aspen, it is known that the proportion of stump sprouts to root suckers can be relatively high when young aspen stands, under 25 years old, are harvested; when older aspen are harvested, natural regeneration is often exclusively by root suckers.

Management implications

The regeneration methods listed by Weetman and Vyse (1990) (Table 5) are known to work if the goal is to re-establish the same forest type as before, but could deviate from the present focus on clearcut or coppice methods if the forest type is to be changed. This may increasingly be the case as silvicultural practices intensify. In those circumstances, there could be some involvement of seed-tree, shelterwood, or selection methods where hardwood regeneration is concerned.

To date, the planting of hardwoods has not been a very widespread practice. Paper birch has been planted experimentally by Simard in the Kamloops Forest Region, and aspen and birch are currently planned for planting elsewhere in the British Columbia interior (T. Newsome, pers. comm., Nov. 1992). However, these limited planting efforts are indicative of the present situation, in which nursery production planting programs are not geared to large-scale regeneration of hardwood species.

Research needs

The regeneration ecology of the main hardwood species is well known and requires no specific additional research. If nursery production of hardwood seedlings and subsequent out-planting are to be expanded, the main research needs will be in relation to diseases, insects, and other factors that limit seedling success in the nursery and on planting sites.

TABLE 5. Recommended, feasible, and not feasible regeneration methods to re-establish hardwood forest types (after Weetman and Vyse 1990)

	Regeneration method[a]		
Forest type	**Recommended**	**Feasible**	**Not feasible**
A. To re-establish the same hardwood forest type when old growth is harvested			
Coastal			
cottonwood	CCP	CCN, ST, CO	SW, SE
red alder[b]	CCP	CCN, ST	SW, SE, CO
Interior			
aspen	CCN	—	CCP, ST, SW, SE, CO
white birch	CCN	ST	CCP, SW, SE, CO
mixedwoods	CCP	—	CCN, ST, SW, SE, CO
B. To re-establish the same hardwood forest type when young natural stands are harvested			
Coastal			
cottonwood	CO	—	CCP, CCN, ST, SW, SE
red alder[b]	CCP	CCN, ST	SW, SE, CO
Interior			
aspen	CCN, CO	—	CCP, ST, SW, SE
white birch	CCN	ST	CCP, SW, SE, CO
mixedwoods	CCP	—	CCN, ST, SW, SE, CO

[a] CCP = clearcut with planting; CCN = clearcut with natural regeneration; SE = selection method; ST = seed-tree method; SW = shelterwood method; CO = coppice method.

[b] For alder, Weetman and Vyse (1990) listed CPP as not feasible and CCN as recommended. That rating is changed in the table above, based on a reviewer who suggested that CCP be the recommended method for alder regeneration, with CCN considered feasible. Up to now, the only commercial regeneration of alder in the Pacific Northwest is by Weyerhauser using planting; their experience is that natural regeneration of alder tends to be patchy, creating difficulties in establishing desired densities.

3.5.4 Fire relations of hardwoods

In general, the three boreal hardwoods (aspen, balsam poplar, and paper birch) have different fire relations than alluvial-site black cottonwood and coastal alder and maple. All three boreal hardwoods can be destroyed by fire, but balsam poplar is probably the most resistant (Larsen 1980), partly because of its thick bark and the high water content of its stem. In contrast, young birch or aspen are readily killed by fire because of their thin bark. Of more significance for silvicultural planning of burned-over areas is that all three boreal hardwoods are post-fire invaders par excellence—aspen and balsam poplar mainly by root suckers, and paper birch both by seeding and root collar sprouting (Simard and Vyse 1992).

Alluvial-site black cottonwood and coastal alder and maple are less commonly associated with large burned areas than are the Interior upland-site hardwoods. If cottonwood, alder, or maple stands are burned, and if the desire is to encourage the return of these same species, the goal is not as automatically achieved as it is for the hardwoods that occur on uplands in the Interior. The response of coastal hardwoods to fire is governed by the intensity of fire (severe, moderate, or light). Alder bark is thin but sufficiently fire resistant to prevent damage in light fire situations (Worthington 1957). The lack of flammable debris in alder stands has led to its use in some instances as a firebreak for adjacent conifers (Worthington *et al.* 1962; Harrington 1990), a role also fulfilled by aspen in some circumstances in the western United States (DeByle and Winokur 1985).

Severe fires can kill bigleaf maple stems and canopies but it usually sprouts back vigorously. Light to moderate fires can stimulate black cottonwood and balsam poplar sprouting while severe fires may reduce sprouting. DeBell (1990) considered black cottonwood highly susceptible to fire damage, whereas mature balsam poplar can withstand mild to moderately intense fires as the thickness of the bark increases with age, but fissures in the bark may make the cambium susceptible (Zasada and Phipps 1990).

The general responses of the main hardwood species to burning have been noted by Hawkes *et al.* (1990) and Haeussler (1992) and are summarized as follows:

Bigleaf maple	low-severity fires stimulate vigorous basal sprouting; maple may be killed by severe fires
Red alder	mature trees are usually killed by fire; young alder will sprout after low-intensity burns
Paper birch	young to mature trees will sprout after most fires, but can be killed by severe burns; overmature trees sprout poorly, if at all
Balsam poplar	produces suckers and root-collar sprouts after most fires, but vigour is decreased by severe fires
Black cottonwood	sprouts after low-severity fires, but is usually killed by medium to severe fires; thick bark of this species enables older trees to survive surface fires.
Aspen	suckers are profuse after most fires; high-intensity fires often have little negative impact

Management implications

Fire is relevant to the management of British Columbia's hardwoods in two main contexts: (1) if the frequency and areal extent of the province's fires increase (or decrease) over the long term will the province's biomass of hardwoods increase (or decrease)? and (2) if hardwood stands are destroyed by fire and if the goal, for whatever reason, is to re-establish hardwood stands on the burned sites, will the task be easier than it would be for re-establishment of conifers after fire? For the forest manager, answers to these questions will vary by biogeoclimatic zone within the province, and also by site association within each zone and subzone.

Research needs

A recent report by Quintilio *et al.* (1991) stressed that in comparison to the wealth of information available on other aspects of aspen ecology, there is still not much empirical fire behaviour data in relation to documented burning conditions. For example, they recorded experimental burns in which there was a notable lack of post-burn suckering. Several hypotheses were offered for this unexpected lack of regeneration, but further data collection from study sites in aspen-dominated sites in northeastern British Columbia is required.

The call for additional empirical fire behaviour data also applies to birch and balsam poplar in the interior of the province, but is probably not needed for management of the coastal hardwoods.

3.5.5 Hardwoods as competing vegetation

In British Columbia, 22 major complexes of competing vegetation have been recognized on harvested sites and plantations (Newton and Comeau 1990). These complexes include more than 30 tree, shrub, grass, rush, herb, and fern species that have the potential to interfere with conifer growth. Every one of the six hardwoods considered in this review is among these major complexes of competing vegetation.

Brush problems in British Columbia have been well documented by Boateng (1984) and others. In many cases the "brush" involved is one or more of the hardwood tree species that are now economically important. The degree to which dollars continue to be spent on eradication of hardwood tree species that in certain circumstances yield economic benefits is, in our view, part of the strategic evaluation of this resource. Continued attention to wood quality of the available hardwood standing crop must also be part of any such evaluation.

The available information on how to control hardwoods in ecosystems where they are viewed as weeds is so vast that it cannot be adequately reviewed here. Some key references in recent years that pertain to British Columbia's main hardwood species are: Pendl and D'Anjou 1984; CRAFTS 1987, 1988; Boateng and Ackerman 1988; Baker 1989; Bancroft 1989; Casteel 1989; DeBell and Turpin 1989; Drouin 1989; Presslee 1989; Thompson 1989; Cole and Newton 1990; D'Anjou 1990; Haeussler *et al.* 1990; Holmsen 1990; Pendl and D'Anjou 1990; Pollack and LePage 1990; Wall 1990; Cole and Newton 1991a and b; Figueroa 1991; Quintilio *et al.* 1991; Farnden 1992; Hart and Comeau 1992; Comeau *et al.* 1993. This is in addition to the information and sources noted in such review articles as: DeBell 1990; Harrington 1990; Minore and Zasada 1990; Perala 1990; Safford *et al.* 1990; and Zasada and Phipps 1990. In the prairie provinces, there is an even greater array of researchers who have specialized in ways to remove aspen to improve forage for livestock and wildlife. This diverse literature has been summarized by Peterson and Peterson (1992).

A synopsis of the effectiveness of different methods of control for British Columbia's main hardwoods is provided in Table 6. The review by Hart and Comeau (1992) suggests that manual brushing of British Columbia's main hardwood species is generally not effective.

TABLE 6. Effectiveness of various treatments for controlling British Columbia's six main hardwood species

Cottonwood (and balsam poplar)	
Manual brushing[a]	sprouts may grow 1.5–3 m in height in one growing season; stems may increase 25 times in number
Girdling[b]	*Balsam poplar*: kills parent stem; reduces but does not eliminate suckering/sprouting; *Cottonwood*: effectiveness variable; 100% control of sprouting in some cases
Mechanical site preparation[c]	provides suitable seedbed for the large annual seed crops; stem and root fragments readily regenerate
Burning[d]	*Cottonwood*: sprouts after low-severity fires; severe burns may reduce sprouting vigour; moderately sensitive to fire. *Balsam poplar*: suckers and sprouts after most fires; vigour decreased by severe burns; highly resistant to fire
Herbicides[e]	*Cottonwood*: cut-stump, triclopyr or glyphosate, early foliar to senescence; basal bark, triclopyr, early foliar to dormant; *Balsam poplar*: stem injection, glyphosate, all seasons; soil application, hexazinone, dormant
Bigleaf maple	
Manual brushing	sprouts may grow between 2 and 3 m in two growing seasons; stems may increase up to 50 times in number; forms multistem clumps that cover large areas
Girdling	control duration is 0 years from girdling
Mechanical site preparation	damaged stems sprout; seedling establishment rare.
Burning	severe burns can kill plants; low-severity fires stimulate vigorous basal sprouting; moderately sensitive to fire.
Herbicides	cut-stump, triclopyr, early foliar to senescence; basal bark, triclopyr, late foliar to dormant

TABLE 6. (continued)

Aspen	
Manual brushing	sprouts and suckers grow 1.5–3 m in one growing season; five times increase in sprouts after cutting
Girdling	as effective as herbicides, less costly, but may require longer time between treatment and harvest than herbicides; girdling kills parent stem and reduces but does not eliminate suckering
Mechanical site preparation	promotes suckering; intense deep scarification can reduce suckering; negligible seeding-in occurs
Burning	suckers or sprouts profusely after most fires (young trees only); density can be dramatically increased; high-severity fires often have little negative impact; highly resistant to fire
Herbicides	foliar, triclopyr, early to late foliar; soil, hexazinone, early foliar; stem injection, glyphosate, all seasons; cut-stump, 2,4-D amine, late foliar to late summer
Combined herbicides and burning[f]	Aerial spraying of aspen in June with 2,4-D ester followed by prescribed fire the next April was more effective than 2,4-D alone; prescribed burning in May followed by aerial spraying of 2,4-D ester was also effective
Birch	
Manual brushing	sprouts vigorously; can regrow to 40–70% of pre-treatment height in one growing season; sprouts rapidly following cutting
Girdling	effective girdling difficult to achieve in some cases
Mechanical site preparation	stimulates seeding-in, especially on mixed organic and mineral seedbeds; expect more seeding-in than after burning or no site preparation; damaged stems sprout
Burning	stimulate seeding-in; seed mainly establishes on exposed mineral soil and not on burned LFH; young-mature trees sprout after most fires but can be killed by severe fires; moderately resistant to fire
Herbicides	foliar, triclopyr, late foliar to late summer; cut-stump, 2,4-D amine, late foliar to late summer; stem injection, glyphosate, all seasons

TABLE 6. (continued)

Red alder	
Manual brushing	effective if: alder >5 years old; cut at height of <20 cm; cut during prescribed window; vigorous sprouter; 1.5–3 m growth in one growing season; cutting effectiveness highly sensitive to timing and more effective on older trees (>4–15 yrs)
Girdling	more effective on older trees (>4–15 yrs)
Mechanical site preparation	invades exposed mineral soil; expect increased invasion after treatment
Burning	burns can reduce stump sprouting; seedlings establish on exposed mineral soil; mature trees usually killed; young trees often sprout following low-severity burn; sensitive to fire
Herbicides	foliar, 2,4-D ester, all seasons; foliar, triclopyr, late foliar to late summer; cut-stump, 2,4-D amine, late foliar to late summer; cut-stump, glyphosate, or triclopyr, early foliar to senescence; stem injection, glyphosate, all seasons; basal bark, triclopyr, late foliar to late summer

[a] Manual brushing efficacy, based on a single treatment, is derived from Farnden (1992) and Hart and Comeau (1992).

[b] Girdling efficacy is derived from Farnden (1992); for aspen, additional information is derived from Bancroft (1989).

[c] Mechanical site preparation efficacy is derived from Coates *et al.* (1990).

[d] Burning efficacy is derived from Haeussler (1992) and Coates *et al.* (1990).

[e] Herbicide efficacy in this table is derived entirely from Comeau *et al.* (1993) indicating only the highest rated (most effective) treatment, with information always presented in the same order (method of application, herbicide used, season of application). Rate of application is not recorded here but is provided in Comeau *et al.* (1993). Although not recorded above, other efficacy ratings are found in D'Anjou (1990), Otchere–Boateng (1990), and Farnden (1992). Other sources of herbicide information for individual species are: Bancroft (1989) and Bowes (1991) for aspen; Figueroa and Nishimura (1992) for bigleaf maple; and Figueroa (1991) and Newton and Cole (1991) for alder and birch.

[f] Information on combined use of herbicides and burning is presented only for aspen and is derived from Bailey and Anderson (1979) and Bailey *et al.* (1985).

Management implications

Vegetation management is strongly linked to reforestation success and future wood supplies. Hardwoods figure prominently in that linkage, partly because hardwoods, along with many shrubs and herbaceous species, are more prolific seed producers and have more efficient seed dispersal than most conifers (Wagner and Zasada 1991). Furthermore, hardwoods possess a greater variety of vegetative reproductive methods than do conifers. As hardwoods take on increasing value for biomass production, wildlife habitat, biodiversity enhancement, soil stabilization, and site protection they will be viewed less as "weed species" to be eliminated by vegetation management techniques.

Research needs

Although much attention has been given to vegetation management as a silvicultural step, plant competition is still a confusing subject because there are two markedly different operational definitions of competition (Grace and Tilman 1990). The first stresses the total competitive effect of a species or of an entire community on another species. This definition does not adjust for differences in the biomass of competitors removed, and thus does not measure the intensity of competition per unit neighbour biomass. The second operational definition of competition commonly used is the intensity of competition per unit biomass.

Because of the prominence of hardwoods in many of British Columbia's highly productive lowland ecosystems, the two definitions of competition outlined above are of more than academic interest. For example, Grace and Tilman (1990) point out that researchers who assert that competition is greater in more productive habitats are likely referring to the definition based on "total competitive effect." In contrast, plant competition specialists who assert that competition should be about equal across a range of productivities are referring to the intensity of competition per unit neighbour biomass. It is recommended that stands in which alder, birch, and aspen provide obvious competition to conifers be selected for additional research to assess whether competition from hardwoods varies substantially by site productivity. The two operational definitions of competition suggested by Grace and Tilman (1990) should also be tested and compared at several sample sites.

3.5.6 Opportunities for intensive management on very productive sites

Among the key British Columbia hardwood species, techniques for high-intensity management are most highly developed for black cottonwood (Massie 1990; Dunlap *et al.* 1992). Black cottonwood, balsam poplar, and aspen are the hardwoods commonly viewed as suitable for short-rotation management, but red alder, paper birch, and bigleaf maple may also be candidate species.

For aspen and balsam poplar, there are not yet strong incentives for short-rotation management because of the abundance of unused stands of older age classes available for harvesting, even though many existing stands are now too old to be decay-free. When it becomes economically viable to harvest these boreal hardwoods on short rotations there is good background information available from short-rotation trials by Berry and Stiell (1978), Perala (1979), and Zsuffa (1979, 1991).

There has been considerable interest in red alder because of its rapid initial growth rate, as shown in recent work by Comeau and Sachs (1992) and earlier studies by Zavitkovski and Stevens (1972).

To date, there is no evident interest in short-rotation management of paper birch or bigleaf maple. The key reason is that paper birch has its main value in stems of size for lumber or plywood production, and bigleaf maple has few, if any, uses for small-sized young stems.

Management implications

The strategic importance of British Columbia's hardwood cannot be accurately quantified until there are better data on the degree to which the province's most productive forest ecosystems are dominated by hardwoods. However, as hardwoods reach their greatest frequency on sites with good moisture and nutrient supply (Figure 1), one can hypothesize that the province's hardwoods are actually more important than generally recognized. They are now a relatively unused but abundant resource on very productive sites where the goal has traditionally been to encourage coniferous wood of higher current economic value. Hardwoods have a strategically important role on highly productive sites, partly because they are often there already.

Experience in the Lake States is predictive of what could happen in northeastern British Columbia and western Canada through a diversified wood industry based on coppice management of aspen. It is evident that the coppice system works best on the better soils where aspen can quickly grow to good diameters before there are volume losses from stem decay. Soils that are very wet or very dry are best regenerated back to conifers. Smith (1986) summed up the Lake States aspen coppice system this way:

> Aspen regeneration from root suckers depends mainly on being sure to cut all the trees down, preferably during the dormant season. As with other sprouting species, the regeneration step is simple and almost magically automatic.

More recent experience in western Canada indicates that aspen regeneration is not always automatic. Navratil *et al.* (1991) pointed out that on the most productive boreal mixedwood sites aspen regeneration can often be inhibited by invasion of alder (*Alnus crispa*) and willow, a thick duff layer, a rise in the water table after harvest, low soil temperature, increase in balsam poplar competition, or soil compaction.

Whether current attempts to manage forests in ways that encourage more biodiversity are called "new forestry," "new perspectives in forestry," or some other label, hardwoods are expected to have an increasing profile in preharvest silvicultural prescriptions. In this context, hardwoods have a potential role in short-rotation forestry because of their rapid growth in post-disturbance conditions and their relatively short lifespans compared to their companion softwood species.

Research needs

There is not yet very precise data on desirable stocking levels for hardwoods. Furthermore, a range of questions related to incremental silviculture, including spacing and pruning, has also not received attention.

It is not known if the coppice management of aspen in the Lake States is transferable to aspen-dominated ecosystems in northeastern British Columbia. Because of site and climatic differences, there may be fewer options for high production, short-rotation aspen management in northeastern British Columbia than in the Lake States.

Intensive management of red alder will require more detailed information on growth and yield, as well as stand management guidelines. A study of the geographic variation of several silviculturally important features of red alder is only recently underway in British Columbia (Table 32). The B.C. Forest Service is a member of the Oregon State University hardwood co-operative that is dealing with several alder-related research projects. Production of reliable alder planting stock in nurseries is a relatively recent development.

3.5.7 Silvicultural challenges of managing hardwoods in mixedwood stands

Foresters have long tried to judge which combination of two tree species will give the greatest total yield over a particular time interval, but useful information for practical application is still limited. Except for the recent work by Comeau and Sachs (1992) on red alder–Douglas-fir combinations, and by Simard (1990) on paper birch–Douglas-fir combinations, detailed information on optimal combinations of deciduous-conifer mixes is not available. This dilemma is described in detail by Leary (1985) and poses challenges for managers of hardwoods. To date, the most detailed research on deciduous-conifer interactions has been with red alder. Related to the work by Comeau and Sachs, data collection on experimentally manipulated stands of red alder and Douglas-fir is a current and active area of research (Shainsky *et al.* 1992; Shainsky and Radosevich 1992).

Little work has been done on silvicultural combinations of alder and western hemlock. Most attention has gone to total conversion of alder stands to either Douglas-fir or hemlock. In western Oregon, thinnings in a 14-year-old alder stand were combined with underplanting of western hemlock. There were two purposes to this program. First, the underplanting can shorten the conversion period to a conifer stand that is more valuable than the alder; and second, the thinning of alder to final crop-tree spacing increases the marketable volume while freeing up site resources necessary to support the conifers planted in the understorey (Emmingham *et al.* 1989). These investigators concluded that it is biologically possible to establish a viable hemlock stand beneath thinned alder. Stubblefield and Oliver (1978) also emphasized the silvicultural opportunities available from reconstruction of mixed alder-conifer stands.

As foresters show increasing interest in alternatives to clearcutting, the strategic importance of hardwood species is apt to change significantly. For example, a review of past partial-cutting practices in the Prince Rupert Forest Region (Weetman *et al.* 1990) revealed that where large basal area removals of conifers were made in stands with a significant aspen or hardwood component present, hardwood-conifer mixedwood stands have often developed. With increasing economic acceptance of a greater variety of tree species and lower qualities of stem raw material, the hardwoods resulting from various silvicultural systems will take on an increasingly important role.

Rose (1991) cited several problems in characterizing birch in mixedwood stands in the Prince George Forest Region. The first is that mixed stands could not be reliably identified from forest cover maps. Second, some mixed stands that appeared to have a substantial hardwood component actually contained mostly decadent birch. Serious rot and decay were particularly prevalent in birch on clayey soils. There is also a very large variation in spacing and density of birch when one is attempting to establish comparative mensurational plots. Research by Simard (1990) indicated that although maximum Douglas-fir performance is achieved when all neighbouring birch are removed, such treatment is operationally impractical. Her research suggested that retaining a low density of birch at the expense of a small reduction in Douglas-fir growth may have positive effects on site productivity, ecosystem diversity, and the spread of *Armillaria* root rot. A practical alternative to the ecological thresholds is an operational competition threshold, namely a birch density at which 90% of maximum Douglas-fir performance is achieved. In Simard's study, the operational competition threshold increased from 340 to 2100 birch stems per hectare as site quality decreased.

There is considerable Scandinavian experience on the effects of hardwoods on softwood growth in mixedwood stands (Hagglund and Peterson 1985; Frivold and Mielikäinen 1989). Studies have shown that birch mixed with conifer stands can have a positive influence upon both stand health and long-term soil development. However, birch can also be a competitor with conifers and most Scandinavian studies indicate that the total volume yields of mixed birch-softwood stands are about equal to those of pure softwood stands. The optimal birch proportion during the first 50 years of the rotation is estimated to be between 20 and 60% by volume in Finnish research. This suggests that after 50 years the birch proportion should be greatly reduced by thinning (Frivold and Mielikäinen 1989).

Management implications

The move from a "conifer-only" era to one of mixedwood management will involve more varied kinds of silvicultural prescriptions. For example, recognition of hardwoods as part of the operating forest land base will require ecosystem-specific silvicultural prescriptions to maintain, decrease, or increase the proportion of hardwoods relative to softwoods. However, in the foreseeable future deliberate mixedwood management is likely to involve only a small part of the total provincial forest land base. In places where pure aspen, cottonwood, or alder management is undertaken, or where there is acceptance of minor components of hardwoods in coniferous plantations, silvicultural prescriptions will be less complex.

Research needs

The silvicultural techniques described by Emmingham *et al.* (1989), which involved underplanting hemlock beneath thinned alder, should be tested in coastal ecosystems and also on a larger scale than was done in the study area near Astoria, Oregon. Also, Comeau and Sachs (1992) suggest that additional field studies are required (in a variety of pure and mixed stands) to obtain the data necessary for calibration verification, and validation of their red alder–Douglas-fir growth modeling.

Peterson *et al.* (1989a and b) have described the main management challenges, opportunities, and related research needs for aspen and balsam poplar in boreal mixedwood stands.

4 MULTIPLE USE POTENTIAL OF HARDWOODS IN BRITISH COLUMBIA

Integrated resource management is a concept embraced by the various sectors of resource management in British Columbia (Forest Resources Commission 1991), but there have been difficulties in translating these ideas into practice (Young 1990). Perhaps the main stumbling block to including other resource values into the forest management equation has been the lack of awareness of how to proceed from the start. Hardwood harvesting for profit is relatively new in this province and opportunities to accommodate the needs of other sectors of the hardwood resource into the planning process are far greater than they have been for coniferous forest utilization. A thorough knowledge of what the existing resources are in a potential hardwood management area will assist greatly in the planning process. However, while the importance of hardwoods to recreation, wildlife, and fisheries resources is generally recognized, specific information such as recreational use levels in hardwood stands, wildlife species use in hardwoods, or even geographic reference points for hardwood resource use potential is either unavailable at a small scale or poorly defined. This section summarizes wildlife, fisheries, and recreational uses that may occur within those TSAs with a recognized hardwood management potential. It also provides some indication of the sources of uncertainty, data gaps, and the research and management needs that may be required to further the hardwood management planning process.

4.1 Study Approach

The inventory statistics supplied by the B.C. Ministry of Forests Inventory Branch were examined and printed using the Provincial Summary Reporting (PSR) system (Orca Consulting Group Inc. 1991) as a guide. These values represent hardwood data for the province from the ongoing forest inventory process, and are generally up to date (March 1992). The inventory type groups with deciduous as either a leading species or a secondary species were of primary concern (Appendix 2b) in the assessment. Most of the multiple resource use evaluation was centred on TSA summaries (B.C. Ministry of Forests

1992a) of mature, deciduous leading species by area, by volume, and by age categories. Net backlog NSR was also considered (B.C. Ministry of Forests 1990b) in the assessment for selected TSAs. A very generalized map (1:2 000 000) of the geographic distribution of leading species, site, and age classes was also available for review (Bill Chalk, pers. comm., 1992).

These data were compared to biogeoclimatic ecological classification (BEC) mapping (B.C. Ministry of Forests 1988a), selected examples of biophysical mapping (Demarchi and Lea 1989), semi-primitive and primitive area mapping (B.C. Ministry of Forests 1992b), and the inventory of undeveloped watersheds of British Columbia (Ministry of Forests Recreation Branch 1992). In the absence of wildlife and fisheries mapping at similar scales, general references such as Campbell *et al.* (1990), Cannings *et al.* (1987), McTaggart-Cowan and Guiguet (1973), and others were used. Consideration of fisheries biota was restricted to streamside or riparian fisheries habitat. A brief review of the literature on riparian forestry practices and fisheries habitat provided some of the fisheries habitat information. Because of the paucity of raw data summaries for fish species distribution and habitat needs, personal communications with resource managers throughout British Columbia were found to be particularly valuable.

Recreational use of hardwoods was difficult to quantify and describe because of a lack of reference material dealing directly with hardwood use for recreation in British Columbia. Therefore, personal communications with recreation officers within the B.C. Ministry of Forests and other sources were used.

4.2 Overview of Multiple Resource Use Potential for British Columbia's Hardwoods

The hardwood inventory is expressed by leading species in volumes and areas present in the province by regional or general provincial area and TSA (Section 2). Potential locations for hardwood use were then ranked and discussed in terms of immediate use or longer-term (annual) potential.

Hardwood age range distribution data are particularly relevant for multiple resource use considerations, especially for wildlife. These data for selected TSAs are plotted in a set of figures presented in Appendix 2b (Figures 2.1–2.10), and related in TSA summaries in Appendix 2d. The data are derived from the Provincial Summary Reporting System printouts dated March 2, 1992. An example of the data summaries is provided in Appendix 2a. These data represent coverage of hardwood-dominated inventory type groups and inventory type groups on all ownerships on an area basis for selected TSAs. Only those TSAs with a significant component of hardwood are described here, although hardwoods occur throughout the province. We have concentrated on TSAs with an economic potential for development, although minor elements of hardwoods in a stand may be critically important to wildlife in some areas. The figures in Appendix 9 illustrate the database for ownerships outside the TFLs, and are frequently an underestimate of the deciduous resource of individual TSAs (most notably the Arrowsmith TSA where substantial stands of mixedwood bigleaf maple and alder exist in older harvested areas).

The figures in Appendix 2b are presented here only to indicate the distribution of inventory type groups by age class in the "hardwood TSAs." The Fraser TSA summary bar graphs have a high diversity of mixedwood types, and as such have a high diversity of wildlife, fish, recreational usage, and cultural importance. Stevens (pers. comm., 1992) indicated that a large proportion of B.C. Ministry of Environment, Lands and Parks (BCE) listed species occur in the lower drainage of the Fraser. It is also the largest human population centre, with considerable recreational use of forests. The Arrow was chosen for display because the inventory type group data tends to represent the Nelson Forest Region. Deciduous forests usually occur as a mixedwood in these TSAs with few large, pure stands.

The forests of the Nelson Forest Region have a relatively high diversity of tree species, including several deciduous species. There are important pure cottonwood stands in the Nelson Region TSAs (G. Woods, pers. comm., 1992; D. Jones pers. comm. 1992) but they often occur in privately held lands or in TFLs and are not included in these graphs. Also of note is that aspen in deciduous stands is roughly equal in area to aspen in coniferous mixedwood and that age classes tend to be in the mature to overmature class.

Many of the age classes for deciduous-conifer inventory type groups are greater than 61 years throughout those TSAs with a relatively high deciduous volume or area. In some cases, the age classes are actually older than the leading species can biologically achieve. For example, the Nelson, Bulkley, Fraser, and Kamloops TSAs all have deciduous (mainly aspen, with the exception of the Fraser, where alder occurs primarily) leading species combined with a conifer species covering a relatively large land base, but these areas are predominantly over age class 61–80. The previous section identifies 60 as the age of maturity for aspen, so the age of the stand may refer to the conifers in the stand and not the leading species, although the rules of inventory do not allow this (A. Britneff, pers. comm., 1992). If this is true in some cases, and if the stand inventory statements for 1992 are projections from earlier data, then some of these stands may no longer have the standing crop of deciduous wood indicated by the graphs in Appendix 2b. Presumably, the regenerative capability of deciduous species will prevail in these stands. However, from a multiple resource use perspective, the standing crop of mature, cavity-nesting substrate (e.g., birch and aspen of a large size and greater than 27 cm dbh) may already be limited in stands where breakup has occurred but is not reflected in the present inventory.

In those inventory type groups where a deciduous is the leading species and other deciduous species are co-dominants, the standing crops may have already reverted to an earlier successional stage, as emergent juveniles take over the old-aged parent stand. Peterson and Peterson (1992) noted 18-year-old juveniles under a 120-year-old stand of aspen at Lesser Slave Lake. This situation may be relevant for inventory data in the Fort Nelson TSA.

Overall, the stand coverage in the Arrow TSA is small when compared to other TSAs in British Columbia, but it may be highly significant to fish and wildlife and to recreational users of these stands. The Kamloops TSA is the only TSA in the Kamloops Forest Region to be represented in Appendix 1b, although the Okanagan also has significant birch stands in the northern Interior Cedar–Hemlock zone (S. Simard, pers. comm., 1992). Aspen is the main deciduous species (by area) of this TSA (also noted in Simard and Vyse 1992) although birch is considered by Simard to be the most important economic species because of its greater volume. The potential for aspen to produce a higher volume has never been tested, however. The fir-deciduous inventory type group is skewed to favour age classes greater than 61 years, whereas in most TSAs illustrated age classes have a somewhat normal distribution.

The exceptions are an even representation of various ages of conifer leading (pine, spruce, fir) deciduous inventory type groups of the Williams Lake TSA. Aspen is the most common species of the Williams Lake TSA, occurring both as mixedwood and as pure stands. However, the inventory statistics for this TSA illustrate that about 30 000 ha of aspen-deciduous are classed as greater than 81 years. Darryl Barron (pers. comm., 1992) thought that most of the hectarage occurred at low to mid-elevations in the Horsefly area. The Quesnel TSA appears to have only birch in pure stands, the rest are mixedwoods with aspen (and probably birch) evenly distributed with respect to age class. These stands occur in greatest abundance on the Quesnel River and in the Quesnel uplands at low elevation. The Interior has an oblique band of upland, probably fire-originated aspen, and associated interior hardwood species, most notably birch. This band starts north of Kamloops and follows the Fraser across to east of the Alkali Lake country and north extending up as far as Hazelton. The Quesnel stands are an eastern extension of this band. Ray Coupé (pers. comm., 1992) refers to these stands as occurring within the transition belt between the wetter forest types of the eastern Shuswap and Quesnel Highlands and the drier western portion of the Chilcotin Plateau.

The Kispiox TSA, at the northern reach of the hardwood band mentioned above, has a large aspen resource with mostly mature to overmature age classes, especially where it occurs in pure stands. The Kalum TSA, although important from an industrial perspective, is not represented in Appendix 26 because the primary hardwood resource is not on publicly held lands. The Bulkley TSA is dominated by aspen and aspen-mixedwood inventory type groups. There is a relatively wide distribution of age classes of aspen with conifers, although older age classes are more common.

The Prince George TSA is large and has a substantial deciduous element, dominated by aspen and birch. In comparison to other TSAs, the age classes are better represented in earlier stages. This may reflect the fire history and harvesting in this TSA, particularly in the SBS zone. Pure birch, mixed aspen-deciduous, and mixed aspen-conifer stands cover large areas. Again, the age class of the oldest stands of pure deciduous is probably a function of projections from inventory statistics and should be adjusted in the field to reflect the true age of the stand. Because of its large deciduous inventory, the Prince George TSA is grouped with others (such as the Fort Nelson TSA) of greatest economic potential, and therefore of greatest interest for the multiple-resource use of these stands.

The northeastern portion of the province including the Dawson Creek, Fort Nelson, and Fort St. John TSAs all have substantial, currently marketed deciduous forests. In the Dawson Creek TSA, the pine mixedwood types frequently occur in a younger age class than spruce, as do the cottonwood stands. Cottonwood-coniferous types are limited in area in comparison to others, and as these are most likely to be riparian they have special significance to multiple-resource use. Dawson Creek's greatest areas of deciduous are the aspen-deciduous types, the majority standing in an overmature state, although there is considerable area covered with age class 41–60. Many of the older stands may be two-aged. In recent field work conducted throughout the three northeastern TSAs (Enns and Siddle 1992), of approximately 500 field sites in pure deciduous, mature stands, 45% had juvenile deciduous trees composing up to 14% of the understorey.

The Fort St. John TSA has many harvestable stands of deciduous forest not held by the Crown, and therefore not graphed. For those that are, a comparatively large (89 000 ha) area is in younger age classes of mixed pine and deciduous, and large areas of (relatively) young aspen-deciduous inventory type group. The Fort Nelson TSA and Fort St. John data graphed in Appendix 2b indicate a large concentration of trembling aspen–dominated stands, which constitute more than 50% of the forest inventory compartment. The Fort Nelson TSA does not appear from the graphs to have the largest concentration of hardwoods. However, polygons mapped from *draft* inventory distribution maps (B. Chalk, pers. comm., 1992) indicate that large but fragmented stands exist to the north of Fort Nelson on the Fort Nelson and Liard rivers. Although the Cassiar has some of the highest values for hardwood-occupied lands, the species and volumes were not identified as having economic potential and so they are not included in the figures presented in Appendix 2b.

As these figures and some of the analysis provided prior to this section indicate, potential hardwood markets are not uniformly distributed throughout the province. Further, ecological factors such as soils, physiography, stand histories, and climate are also variable, and their effect on hardwoods is poorly understood. Multiple-resource capability in hardwood forests, or forests with deciduous trees as dominant or co-dominant species also varies from TSA to TSA. Some variables important to the discussion of multiple-resource use are difficult to quantify economically. These include wildlife populations, which have no recognized economic value and no information base. Also, there are regional differences in human demography, aesthetics, and cultural heritage. However, these variables are important in discussions of multiple-resource use of hardwood forests and potential conflicts between hardwood management and multiple-resource use of hardwood or hardwood-mixedwood stands.

A consideration of the importance of net backlog not satisfactorily restocked (NSR) land in TSAs may have some relevance in the discussion of hardwood importance to integrated resource management, because some of these stands may eventually be re-classified as one of the type groups discussed here. Some of the TSAs with relatively high NSR areas coincide with those identified above as having a high relative area of hardwood inventory type groups, namely Prince George, Dawson Creek, and Fort St. John. The NSR data is tabulated in Appendix 2c.

Although there may be errors in age class calculations (especially at the ends of the distribution of mixedwood age classes), over-averaging of inventory statistics and projections from pre-existing inventory, lack of field checking, and classification ambiguities, the B.C. Ministry of Forests Inventory Branch data still provide a useful and accurate depiction of hardwood distribution and abundance for the province. The main failing of this study is its lack of examination of the detailed mapping available for those areas where hardwood species are the predominant forest trees for entire compartments of the inventory. Even if time was available for that exercise, however, it would not bring us any closer to an understanding of the relationship between hardwoods and fisheries, wildlife, recreation, native cultural importance, and aesthetics. Data for these fields are either missing completely at the inventory scale of mapping (with the exception of special projects), or they present very generalized information.

4.3 Assessment of Wildlife-Hardwood Interactions

4.3.1 Current developments

The importance of hardwoods to wildlife on a provincial scale has been reviewed by Enns *et al.* (1992) and for localized regions within British Columbia by Pojar (1992), Lance and Phinney (1992)[6], and others. There are very few provincially based publications that can be used by resource managers, so several projects have been initiated. These, and some other relevant projects are summarized in Table 7.

The topics of major concern to wildlife managers regarding hardwood management are centred primarily on birds, with some current interest in B.C. Environment–listed large mammals. Table 7 also outlines the current trend in management concern for two areas of hardwood harvesting: the coastal cottonwood resource and the northeastern trembling aspen resource.

4.3.2 Use of hardwoods by wildlife species in TSAs

A summary of important habitats for bird families in hardwood stands is provided in Table 8. TSAs are not always identified as being important for one family or another, but elements of habitat that may be common to groups of TSAs are briefly identified. Appendix 3 provides a more detailed list of these birds by species, as well as a list by deciduous tree species of hardwood-using birds, mammals, reptiles, and amphibians.

[6] Lance, A.N. and M. Phinney. 1992. Bird diversity and abundance following aspen clearcutting in the BWBS BGC zone. Project B28 Unpubl. rep. B.C. Min. For. Res. Br., Victoria, B.C.

TABLE 7. Current research projects focusing on multiple-resource use of hardwoods

Project supervisors/authors	Species of concern
Hamilton, A. N.	Grizzly bear, conifers and cottonwood, and associated understorey species, such as Devil's club, red elderberry, *Ribes* spp.
Jones, D., Neil, D.	All species: harvesting in riparian areas. Silvicultural Systems Working Group Projects—Penticton and Cranbrook
Lance, A.M., Moss,	Wildlife management in mixedwood forests: a problem analysis
Lance, A.M., Phinney, M.	Bird species composition and abundance versus aspen abundance
Darling, L.	Birds of the northeastern B.C.: includes birds of managed and nonmanaged deciduous stands
Pojar, R.	Birds of the Prince Rupert Forest Region in aspen stands
Enns, K., Siddle, C.	Distribution, abundance, and habitat utilization of several species of eastern songbirds in aspen and mixedwood stands of northeastern B.C.
Seip, D., Savard, J.P.	Biodiversity in coastal forests, including some deciduous stands
Farr, Bunnell, F.	Eagle use of cottonwood in coastal riparian areas
Neal, R.	Alternative silviculture in riparian areas

TABLE 8. Bird families (bracket = no. of species) and hardwood stand feature of interest. Distribution with respect to TSAs is noted, where appropriate.

Bird family	Hardwood stand features of interest	Distribution
Emberizidae: warblers, cowbird, ovenbird, chat (12)	Old-growth aspen, mixed aspen and spruce, mixed birch and spruce (Enns and Siddle 1992)	Limited distribution in specific habitats in Ft. St. John, Dawson Creek and Ft. Nelson TSAs
Anatidae: waterfowl (6)	Some species have a requirement for other keystone species who prepare their habitat for them. Examples include Pileated Woodpecker and Common Flicker; use of their cavities is common, if not critical	Southern Interior TSAs, and southern Coastal TSAs
Ardeidae: herons (3)	Slough-edge thickets or cottonwoods; nesting habitats poorly known	Coastal and southern Interior TSAs, esp. Arrowsmith, Sunshine Coast, Soo, Fraser
Columbidae: pigeons and doves (2)	Red alder and cottonwood used for nesting	Southern and Coastal TSAs
Paridae: chickadees (4)	May rely on cavities in hardwoods provided by other species (i.e., secondary cavity-nester) in willow or aspen	Southern and Interior TSAs
Phasianidae: grouse and pheasant (4)	Exclusive use of trembling aspen in mid-seral stages, and brushy birch woodlands	TSAs with birch and aspen; Fraser, but mainly interior TSAs
Picidae: woodpeckers (10)	Large-stemmed trembling aspen with variable heart-rot component, or mature cottonwood for cavities	All interior TSAs where large hardwood stems are a main forest component: Ft. St. John, Dawson Creek, Kalum, Okanagan, Kamloops, Arrow, Quesnel, Williams Lake

TABLE 8. (continued)

Bird family	Hardwood stand features of interest	Distribution
Sittidae: nuthatches (2)	Partially decayed cottonwood for cavity nesting	Interior and Coastal TSAs with cottonwood as a frequent leading species: all TSAs where they occur
Trochilidae: Calliope and Rufous Hummingbird (2)	Reliance on keystone species; use of sapsucker feeding holes in deciduous species, as well as nesting in deciduous trees (may be under-estimated) (Campbell *et al.* 1990)	South-central TSAs and Coastal TSAs
Troglodytidae: wrens (3)	Some secondary cavity nesting in deciduous trees, foraging in deciduous thickets is common	Interior and Coastal seral stages, e.g., Fraser, Soo, Sunshine Coast (not exclusive)
Tyrannidae: flycatchers (2)	Shrub (esp. alder) thickets	Interior and Coastal seral stages, e.g., Fraser, Soo, Sunshine Coast (not exclusive)
Tytonidae and Strigidae: owls (7)	Mixedwood and deciduous forest habitats and edges are important for nesting and for hunting	Eastern Vancouver Region and most Interior region TSAs
Vireonidae: vireos (5)	Habitat poorly defined (as in Emberizidae) but requires shrubby deciduous forests at middle maturity	Limited distributions, northeastern TSAs

Although Table 8 is highly generalized, it indicates some of the habitat features needed by birds with some element of hardwood forest use. It is significant that entire groups of birds have deciduous habitat requirements. The table also documents preferential use and does not include species that use hardwood trees incidentally or occasionally.

The above table also indicates that the Emberizidae (warblers), the Picidae (woodpeckers), the Accipitridae (hawks/raptors) and the Anatidae (waterfowl) have the most obvious reliance on some elements of hardwood forests. Many of these needs are poorly defined, especially for the vireos, the woodpeckers and the warblers. The woodpeckers have additional significance because they provide cavities for a wide variety of smaller birds and mammals. For example, some species of economically important waterfowl require Pileated Woodpecker cavities for nest sites, as do the chickadees. Many, if not most species of birds probably have some need for deciduous habitat. This habitat requirement may not be completely known, however, due to a past emphasis on coniferous habitat use.

Obviously there are mammals, reptiles, and amphibians with a requirement for hardwood forests. However, ungulates have the greatest affinity for deciduous forests as a group. Roosevelt and Rocky Mountain Elk, White-tailed and Black-tailed Deer, Moose (Westell 1954, Reynolds 1969), and Columbia Black-tailed Deer (Bunnell 1990) all use seral stages of hardwoods in various times in the lifecycle from natality in Rocky Mountain Elk to critical winter and early spring forage range in the deer family.

Grizzly bear and black bear are recognized as having distinct requirements for early to mid-seral stages of riparian forest. The shrub components of these stands are of primary importance as forage, making shrub vegetation management of mixedwood stands as a forestry practice a concern of wildlife habitat managers. Mixedwoods, especially types where spruce and cottonwood occur, provide some of the most productive grizzly bear habitat (Hamilton *et al.* 1991).

Furbearers also have requirements for hardwood forests. These species include marten, ermine, bobcat, fisher, snowshoe hare, and others that either use hardwood forests as habitat or depend on prey that use hardwood forests (see Section 4.3.4 for a discussion of trapline species). Other species with requirements for hardwoods in British Columbia include the three bat species: fringed myotis, Townsend's big-eared bat and Keen's long-eared myotis.

The exact requirements for mixedwood forest types and their use patterns are not clearly defined for a number of the more infrequently studied species of British Columbia. Some of these include the Pacific water shrew, northern long-eared myotis, southern red bat, Townsend's chipmunk, Pacific jumping mouse, western small-footed myotis, porcupine, and mountain beaver.

Specific elements of hardwood stands may be critically important to some species. For example, some reptiles and amphibians use mature hardwood stand litterfall and debris. Sandy soils in trembling aspen stands are used for aestivation by painted turtles and sensitivity to disturbance during this period is high.

The B.C. Ministry of Environment, Lands and Parks has produced a series of lists of wildlife species in need of research and/or management attention (B.C. Wildlife Branch 1993). Many of the listed species have a requirement for some element of deciduous forests. Table 9 provides a summary of these species and the required deciduous elements. This list is expected to change; therefore, listed species are placed in the table regardless of their present status. Further to Table 7, some species of birds are included as a specific examination of habitat management requirements.

TABLE 9. B.C. Environment listed species and associated hardwood habitat elements

Species	Associated habitat elements
Great Blue Heron	most common coastal nest trees are red alder
Green-backed Heron	most nests built in red alders; preferred breeding habitats are thickets or woodlands of willows or alders along shores of sloughs, lakes, and slow-moving rivers
Black-crowned Night-Heron	preferred Interior habitat is freshwater marshes with dense willow and birch
Common Goldeneye	breeding habitat includes lakes in aspen parkland
Barrow's Goldeneye	breeding habitat includes lakes in aspen parkland; trembling aspen and black cottonwood are common nest trees
Bufflehead	breeding habitat includes lakes in aspen parkland; most common nest tree is trembling aspen; black cottonwood and poplar also used (min. dbh 38 cm)
Osprey	large trees near water are important habitat component; nest trees are often deciduous
Bald Eagle	uses mature aspen as nest trees in aspen-dominated ecosystems
Blue Grouse	summer range for females with broods includes open grassland associated with scattered coniferous or deciduous trees, or adjacent to dense aspen groves or coniferous forests
Ruffed Grouse	exclusively nests in trembling aspen, breeds in dense pole saplings, with a herbaceous understorey
Sharp-tailed Grouse	preferred year-round habitat is open lowland adjacent to brushy or open woodlands, including aspen parkland
Band-tailed Pigeon	almost exclusively use red alder for nesting; occurs in coastal red alder, trembling aspen, and black cottonwood stands
Lewis' Woodpecker	large (>30 cm dbh) black cottonwood trees used for 30% of nests
Williamson's Sapsucker	requires large (>30 cm dbh) aspen for nesting and roosting
Pileated Woodpecker	breeding habitat is upland mature forests; exclusive nesting in trembling aspen in the Interior; requires large (>50 cm dbh) trees for nesting and roosting
Western Bluebird	habitat use in open woodlands and pasture-land edges
Black-throated Green Warbler	preferred breeding habitat is aspen and mixedwood forests (includes other spp., i.e., Canada and Connecticut) (Enns and Siddle 1992)
Brewer's Sparrow	nest habitat includes dense clumps of birches

TABLE 9. (continued)

Species	Associated habitat elements
Pacific Water Shrew	primary habitats are shrub to pole stages of red alder
Southern Red Bat	distribution and habitat use poorly understood; use of alluvial and lacustrine cottonwood
Northern Long-eared Myotis	uses hardwoods for daytime roosting
White-tailed Jackrabbit	uses aspen copses in dry grasslands
Nuttall's Cottontail	use of vegetation in dry aspen copses
Beaver	use aspen extensively for dam and lodge construction; willow is primary food source
Townsend's Chipmunk	use of deciduous riparian habitat in alder on Fraser River
Pacific Jumping Mouse	uses buds of hardwood trees as a source of food
Bobcat	habitat needs include riparian habitats with cottonwood (i.e., areas with high productivity and relatively high small mammal density)
Fisher	secondary use of deciduous nesting cavities
Ermine	habitat requirements include open deciduous forests for hunting
Long-tailed Weasel	habitat requirements include deciduous, especially aspen copses and aspen-dominated stands
Moose	preferred browse species (willow, poplar, alder, birch, and maple) are of early successional hardwood forests
Roosevelt Elk	habitat includes deciduous seral stages where elk feed on stems as well as bark
Rocky Mountain Elk	preference for recent burns with abundant seral birch and aspen
White-tailed Deer	habitat requirements include foraging in seral trembling aspen and black cottonwood forests
Sitka Black-tailed Deer	use of hardwood seral stages includes winter forage on shrub species commonly in coastal red alder, trembling aspen, and black cottonwood stands
Mule Deer	use of various seral stages of birch and trembling aspen, as well as riparian cottonwood
Black Bear	habitats include early seral to mature aspen stands for foraging and feeding on small mammals
Grizzly Bear	foraging occurs in seral and maturing stages of cottonwood and red alder with rich shrub understories

Although some elements of hardwood stands are critical for the habitat integrity and survival of the species discussed in Table 9 (above), this does not prepare managers adequately for what species may be present in TSAs or how to integrate wildlife habitat management. The main patterns in wildlife use of hardwood-dominated inventory type groups, or of TSAs, cannot be described in detail because there have been very few specific efforts to quantify wildlife habitat use along these lines. To assist managers, an assessment of wildlife use patterns in hardwoods by TSA was compiled using a generalized overlay of the 1:2 000 000 biogeoclimatic map on the TSA map. Inferential sources such as Meidinger and Pojar (1991) were used to derive some general patterns of wildlife in hardwoods for individual TSAs and TSA groups.

A checklist of selected TSAs with a combination of diverse wildlife populations and habitat, as well as hardwood availability is provided below. Some of the wildlife species are listed for these selected TSAs but not all. Some of the details described may be more prevalent in some TSAs than in others.

Fort Nelson TSA – has extensive mature aspen and roughly 1/16 the number of hectares in an immature state, as well as abundant cottonwood and birch in a mainly mature state.

Wildlife species using early to mid-seral to mature forests in uplands and riparian areas, in both mixed and pure deciduous stands include species of rare warblers such as the Canada, Bay-breasted, Palm, Mourning, and Cape May Warblers, the Ovenbird, a high diversity of woodpeckers, most of British Columbia's ungulates, the northern water shrew, black bear and the Sharp-tailed, as well as the Ruffed Grouse.

Fort St. John TSA – has roughly half the aspen (and considerably less birch and cottonwood) as in the Fort Nelson TSA, with similar proportions in immature states; however, climatic differences may contribute to a higher species diversity.

There is generally a higher diversity of wildlife species that use hardwoods in this TSA than in the other two northeastern TSAs. Densities of rare warblers may be higher in this TSA due to better habitat and longer summer seasons.

Dawson Creek TSA – does not have the area of immature aspen that the Fort St. John TSA has, which is important for many species (Table 9), but has a significantly higher mature cottonwood component.

Because of the cottonwood availability at older to mature stages, especially in riparian areas, the diversity of wildlife species is high, particularly in areas with variation in habitat types. Wildlife species or groups of note include rare warblers, grey wolf and ungulates, smaller mammals including lynx, marten, ermine, red squirrel, black bear, Northern Goshawk, Broad-winged Hawk, and a variety of passerine and nonpasserine birds, especially woodpeckers.

Mackenzie TSA – mature aspen is of note in the Parsnip and the Findlay and along the eastern shore of Williston Lake and the western slopes of the Misinchinka Ranges, but is minor in comparison to the above TSAs. Also, early seral stages and diversity of hardwood species is comparatively low. However, mixed stands are extensive and important.

Species of note include Grey-cheeked Thrush, moose, Pileated Woodpecker and Osprey, as well as several nonpasserine birds. Snowshoe hare, porcupine, wolverine, grey wolf, and ungulates are also dependent on some aspects of these stands for either forage or prey.

Prince George TSA – mature aspen and mixed woods are common throughout the TSA but appear to be most prevalent at the southern boundary with the Quesnel TSA.

Moose and carnivore-rodent prey groups are important in this TSA.

Cassiar TSA – has almost 2 million ha of mature aspen, most of it in the lower reaches of the Stikine, Unuk, Taku, and Alsek river drainages.

Wildlife of the deciduous-dominated stands of the Cassiar TSA include grizzly bear, river otter, grey wolf, Semipalmated Plover, Northern Shrike, Northern Goshawk, Northern Hawk-owl, Common Redpoll, mountain beaver, Swainson's Thrush, western toad, wood frog, Marbled Murrelet. The wildlife value of the shrub lands of the SWB should also be considered; this includes moose, Northern Waterthrush, and Arctic Tern, while the upland areas include habitat for caribou and passerine birds, especially raptors.

Quesnel, Williams Lake and the 100 Mile House TSAs – are grouped together because of the similarity in hardwood-using wildlife populations. When combined, they have 1.5 million ha of mature aspen alone. The smallest coverage is in the 100 Mile House TSA, at roughly 370 000 ha. The stands are widespread in both upland and riparian areas.

Wildlife species with an affinity for hardwood forests in these TSAs include black bear, moose, mule deer, white-tailed deer, beaver, and muskrat. Nonpasserine birds are fairly important including Lewis' Woodpecker, Pileated Woodpecker, Bufflehead, Common Goldeneye, Barrow's Goldeneye, Red-naped Sapsucker, and Wood Duck. Song birds are also important, such as the Bohemian Waxwing, Dark-eyed Junco, Ruby-crowned Kinglet, Boreal Chickadee, and Red-breasted Nuthatch. As in other TSAs, Ruffed Grouse and Sharp-tailed Grouse both depend on these forests, as do lynx and bobcat (for the herbivorous prey commonly found in these stands, e.g., snowshoe hare, deer mouse, and northern pocket gopher).

Kamloops and Okanagan TSAs – Kamloops has 204 000 ha of aspen and roughly half that of birch in mature seral stages. Birch is the most common species of the Okanagan TSA.

These TSAs have a wide variety of dry-land or grassland-deciduous wildlife that rely on the copse hardwoods as well as upland forests and various deciduous-dominated seral stages of coniferous or mixedwood forests. Some of the species that use these stands include white-tailed jackrabbit, Nuttall's cottontail, various small rodents, and their predators including raptors, bobcat, and coyote. White-tailed deer use aspen copses a great deal in these TSAs and moose occur in this type in the northern part of the Kamloops TSA. Sharp-tailed Grouse winter there, as well. Other species include little brown myotis, long-toed salamander, painted turtle, and Wood Duck. There is also distinct use by woodpeckers such as the Pileated Woodpecker, Red-naped Sapsucker, and Downy Woodpecker, as well as birds of prey such as the Long-eared Owl, among many others.

Golden TSA – although only 30 000 ha of mature aspen occurs here, it may be fairly important as it is one of the few midwestern TSAs with substantial hardwood areas.

Wildlife species that use deciduous stands include grizzly and black bear, muskrat, and beaver, as well as Rocky Mountain elk, snowshoe hare, red squirrel, Yellow-bellied Sapsucker, northern alligator lizard, Western Skink, and Pacific treefrog.

Boundary and Arrow TSAs – although the TFLs and private land have most of the deciduous or mixedwood stands, they are substantial in these TSAs. Upland seral aspen and riparian cottonwood are the most common.

Wildlife of these TSAs with an affinity for hardwoods include Black-chinned Hummingbird, Red-naped Sapsucker, Williamson's Sapsucker, and several other species including black bear, mule deer, moose, and Rocky Mountain elk.

Fraser and Arrowsmith TSAs – most of the hardwoods in these TSAs are within TFLs. However, wildlife diversity in these hardwoods is exceptional. The bigleaf maple and red alder stands are most common on uplands and in riparian areas. Cutover areas have a variety of alder seral stages.

The hardwoods of Vancouver Island and the lower Fraser support several unique species with somewhat exclusive use of hardwoods or associated vegetation. These include the Pacific water shrew, Green-backed Heron, Marbled Murrelet, Northern Saw-whet Owl, Wood Duck, and Roosevelt elk. Some species use hardwoods in these TSAs where they might use conifers in others. For example, the Great Blue Heron uses cottonwood for heronries while in the Interior it uses various species of conifers. Ensanita salamander, northern alligator lizard, and northwestern salamander use mature red alder stands. The seral stages are used by Varied Thrush, MacGillivray's Warbler, Orange-crowned Warbler, and Rufous Hummingbird.

4.3.3 Hardwood forest importance to wildlife

While the habitats of the species listed above are very generally defined, the specific needs of these species are difficult to delineate without considerable speculation, or extensive field experience. Some basic habitat values of hardwood stands are as follows:

- high crude protein in spring foliage, especially aspen;
- high diversity and abundance of shrub layers with herbaceous and fruit forage, as well as cover;
- high light infiltration through the canopies compared to coniferous trees, more frequent and episodic litterfall, rapid decay rates of fallen material, higher rates of deadfall (especially into streams);
- high (relative) digestibility and palatability of juvenile tissue;
- associated vegetation complexes of riparian and upland hardwoods often have willow and other species that have comparatively high concentrations of lipid compounds, which are valuable energy sources over winter;
- productivity is usually high: if the stand is early to mid-seral, it generally has sufficient stems of a small enough diameter to provide forage for ungulates; and
- diameter and decay are reliably correlated: size of tree and degree of heart rot tend to be positively correlated to a greater degree than in conifers, and can be predicted with greater confidence as being important for primary cavity-nesting birds, (Yellow-bellied Sapsucker, Flicker, and Pileated Woodpecker) and thus secondary-cavity users.

There are a number of relationships between hardwood stand type and wildlife habitat use that are poorly defined. Many of these were first discussed in Enns *et al.* (1992), but the primary data gaps include the following:

- life histories of hardwood-using wildlife species, distributions in British Columbia, and levels of abundance;
- response to disturbance of most hardwood using species;
- nesting and foraging territories of most hardwood-using bird species;
- optimal tree size for primary cavity nesting birds;
- maturity of stand, species composition, and the effects that physical features, such as slope or proximity to water, might have on patterns of use, and territory sizes;
- importance of seasonal and traditional use of hardwood stands;
- substitution, artificial creation, or enhancement of critical hardwood habitats;
- role of keystone herbivores in hardwood stands and how they are influenced by harvesting; and
- importance of hardwood seral stages in the coniferous ecosystem.

4.3.4 Hardwoods and furbearer trapping

Furbearer trapping is often a main source of income to many people in British Columbia. No review of the importance of hardwoods to wildlife would be complete without a summary of the biology of furbearing species, which may be the most likely wildlife species to be affected by hardwood harvesting.

Fisher *(Martes pennanti)*

Although fisher harvests are small compared to other furbearers, they are susceptible to overtrapping and habitat loss, almost being extirpated in the United States in the 1930s. British Columbia is the northern limit of their distribution and densities are low (Bianci 1989). Fishers prefer edge habitats and riparian areas with a high degree of interspersion. Douglas and Strickland (1987 in Bianci 1989) surveyed Ontario trappers and found that 23% of harvested fishers were in swamp, 21% in old mixed hardwood-softwood, 21% in young mixed hardwood-softwood, 11% in old hardwood, and 6% in old conifer forests. Dens used by fishers can be diverse but natal dens almost exclusively occur in the cavities of large dead trees, usually excavated by other species (Pileated Woodpecker, Northern Flicker). Population densities for British Columbia have been estimated at greater than one per 200 square kilometres, although this number is likely too low (Bianci 1989). In terms of area, but not necessarily productivity, British Columbia has more fisher range than any other province.

The distribution of fisher harvests throughout the province is heavily centred in the Omineca-Peace region where approximately 200 animals were harvested annually from the 1983–84 trapping season to the 1987–88 trapping season. This area encompasses the TSAs of the Prince George Forest Region. The second-highest harvest for that time period occurred in the Cariboo, with annual harvests of 90–150 animals. This area encompasses the Quesnel, Williams Lake, 100 Mile House, Mid Coast, and Kingcome TSAs.

The numbers of fishers present on a trapline depends on habitat quality, reproduction, and the habitat quality of surrounding traplines. Diversity of habitat, including hardwood elements, will improve the quality of a trapline. The effects of clearcutting on fisher may be decreased by limiting the size of cuts, increasing edge area, and maintaining cover on ridgelines, drainage bottoms, and in cutblocks. Leaving wildlife trees in cutblocks can also minimize harvesting impacts on fisher.

Marten *(Martes americana)*

Both the value and the amount of marten harvesting has increased steadily in the last 20 years. The value of the marten pelt is surpassed only by the lynx and in recent years has accounted for as much as 59% of provincial revenue from wild fur. Harvests since 1976 have ranged from 20 000 to 45 000 pelts per year.

Martens live in conifer and mixedwood forests throughout British Columbia, including Vancouver Island and Queen Charlotte Islands. Important habitat elements are shrub cover, mature forest, and adequate prey populations, which are often linked to adequate deciduous habitat. Small mammals make up most of the diet, which also includes birds, berries, and carrion. Most martens do not live more than 5 years because of predation, mice and hare population crashes, and trapping. Trapping is a major cause of mortality, with juveniles being most vulnerable, followed by adult males and adult females.

Over-trapping has not been a problem to date since marten habitat is not easily accessible and because of the province's system of registered traplines. However, martens are easily trapped, so increasing accessibility and pelt prices could lead to population declines. One way of preventing this is to set aside part of the trapping territory as a refuge. Another is to set quotas of about a 20% harvest, calculated from typical winter populations in average and above-average habitats of 50–100 animals per 100 square kilometres (Blood, no date).

Mink *(Mustela vison)*

Mink occur throughout British Columbia but habitat is of the highest quality in the Taiga Plains, where most of the harvest occurs and where considerable hardwood cover also occurs. Riparian forest provides cover, den sites, and additional food for mink hunting away from the water. For inland mink, freshwater fish are an important source of food. Small mammals, birds, snakes, and frogs are also eaten. Inland habitat generally supports 1–6 mink per kilometre of shoreline.

Since mink are largely aquatic, habitat loss is directly due to hydroelectric projects, irrigation, and water pollution. Indirectly, mink habitat may decrease with streamside harvesting or any forestry practice that depletes its main food source of freshwater fish. Mink use streamside vegetation for dens, cover, and prey requirements. While the price of mink pelts has increased over the last 15 years, the provincial catch has declined. Harvests in the 1930s and 1940s were up to 45 000 pelts annually and then began to drop in the early 1960s. Trappers generally harvest 1–12 mink per year. Wild mink now contribute less than 5% annually to the total provincial fur sales. This may reflect competition with ranch mink, and limited access to mink habitat, especially on the Coast. Because of these factors, mink are not very susceptible to over-harvesting.

Muskrat *(Ondatra zibethicus)*

The muskrat is consistently the most valuable furbearer in North America. However, British Columbia's share of the national harvest is 1–2% because of the lack of muskrat habitat. The average muskrat harvest in the province between 1935 and 1945 was 96 500 pelts. This has dropped significantly to 10 000–25 000 pelts in recent years. Without further habitat loss, the muskrat population could withstand trapping intensities of the 1930s and 1940s (Blood, no date).

Some areas with high muskrat densities are the Fraser Valley, Creston Valley, Columbia marshes, wetlands of the Interior Plateau, and the Peace-Liard river system. This includes the following TSAs: Fraser, Fort Nelson, Fort St. John, Dawson Creek, Mackenzie, Prince George, Quesnel, Williams Lake, 100 Mile House, Cassiar, Kootenay Lake, and Boundary. Muskrat habitat includes marshes with emergent vegetation and large floodplains or deltas with riparian forests. Harvesting hardwoods may reduce cover and could lead to water level changes and consequent changes in emergent vegetation unless proper riparian strips are maintained. Muskrats eat aquatic vegetation such as cattail, bulrushes, and horsetail. Muskrat populations may benefit waterfowl by opening up dense vegetation and building dens that are later used as nesting platforms.

Muskrats are short-lived and very prolific, so overcrowding is common and accompanied by increased death by starvation, disease, or fighting. Trapping is one way to control population levels. Trapping as much as 65–75% of a population is not expected to cause a decline (Blood, no date).

Wolverine *(Gulo gulo)*

Wolverines occur over most of British Columbia, with the largest proportion of the harvest coming from mountainous regions such as the Skeena, the Omineca-Peace, and the Kootenay. This includes all of the TSAs of the Prince George, Prince Rupert, and Nelson forest regions. They occur in low densities and require large tracts of land. A diversity of habitats is important for the wolverine since it requires a diversity of prey. A large portion of the diet is leftovers from bear or wolf kills, mainly ungulates and small- or medium-sized mammals. Hardwood forests from seral to mature are important hunting grounds for bear and wolves, and therefore wolverines.

British Columbia has the highest wolverine harvest in North America. In recent years 200–300 wolverines have been trapped annually with pelts valued at $200 each. A harvest of mainly young wolverines indicates a successful breeding year while a harvest of mostly adults indicates low reproduction the previous spring.

Lynx *(Lynx canadensis)*

Habitat requirements for lynx are largely unknown but are expected to be identical to that of the snowshoe hare. Lynx populations fluctuate in 10-year cycles that follow the cycle of the snowshoe hares, which peaks the third year of each decade (B.C. Ministry of Environment, Lands and Parks, no date). The snowshoe hare prefers diverse seral to climax forests with lots of cover and shrubby openings for feeding. In some areas, upland forests of aspen support high densities of hares and lynx. Hardwood harvesting may be beneficial for snowshoe hare forage but may not provide enough cover for lynx. Natal dens have most often been observed in areas with a high degree of blowdown, or in clearcuts with high amounts of slash.

Harvests of lynx are highest in the Peace-Omineca region, and secondarily in the Skeena and Cariboo regions. The TSAs with the most lynx trapping are Fort Nelson, Fort St. John, Dawson Creek, Mackenzie and Robson Valley. Lynx pelts demand one of the highest prices for any furbearer—up to $1000 per pelt. This poses a problem of continued intense harvest pressure in the low years of the population cycle. During the year of the last population peak, 6200 lynx were harvested, fewer than during the previous two peaks.

Beaver (Castor canadensis)

Beaver are the most hardwood-dependent of furbearers. The most productive beaver colonies are those in young stands of poplar or aspen that are used for food as well as the construction of dams and lodges. Aspen of 10–30 years of age provide the maximum amount of usable food. This is quickly overused by beavers after which the colony is abandoned. Forestry activities such as suppression of forest fires has reduced the amount of new or renewed beaver habitat coming into production. Silvicultural practices that eliminate or shorten the deciduous shrub and tree stage of the successional forest also have negative impacts on beavers.

Most of the beaver harvested in British Columbia come from the Omineca-Peace region; the Cariboo region has about half as much harvesting. Beaver is greatly under-harvested in British Columbia. Harvests of the 1980s averaged only 16 000 pelts while the provincial population of 400 000–600 000 is expected to withstand harvesting of 100 000–150 000 annually. Even so, beavers are vulnerable to over-harvesting over small areas because they are easily trapped within their waterways.

The Omineca and Peace River areas are the predominant furtrapping areas. These areas coincide with areas of either realized or potential hardwood harvesting.

4.4 Assessment of the Fisheries-Hardwood Interactions

4.4.1 Current developments

There are few current fisheries research projects that relate directly to the British Columbian hardwood resource, and none that could be related to the TSAs. There are notable areas of applied research, however. One is a second volume of impact analysis from the Carnation Creek study (P. Tschaplinski, pers. comm., 1992), which examines the longer-term impacts of forestry practices on fish habitat. The other is the development of a set of guidelines for the Interior that is similar in scope to the British Columbia Coastal Fisheries/Forestry Guidelines (B.C. Ministry of Forests *et al.* 1992). There are fish inventory mapping projects planned that will cover the province (S. Hawthorn, pers. comm., 1992), but they have not yet been initiated.

The importance of fisheries to British Columbians is almost a fundamental, or "motherhood" issue. For example, it is significant that the federal *Fisheries Act* was some of the earliest pollution legislation, aimed at protecting aquatic habitat for fish, in the absence of legislation for any other medium or species group. Not only do fish provide income and sport but they are also the prey of several species of wildlife, including many with economic importance.

4.4.2 Fish species groups in TSAs

There are about 70 different species of fish in the waters of British Columbia and some are of great commercial importance. Many, such as trout and char, are of great significance to the sports fishery. The distribution of fish in the province is related to their routes of entry described by Carl *et al.* (1977):

1. From the south through the Columbia or Fraser river systems: mountain whitefish, Yellowstone cutthroat, largescale sucker, northern squawfish, peamouth, chiselmouth, red-side shiner, speckled dace, leopard dace, mottled sculpin, torrent sculpin.

2. From the mid-section of the continent through the Great Lakes into the MacKenzie river system, and into British Columbia by the Peace or Liard systems: lake whitefish, white sucker, northern redbelly dace, brook stickleback, walleye.

3. From the lower Yukon River basin or northern Alaska, where areas were unglaciated, into lakes of the upper Yukon River system in British Columbia: lake whitefish, broad whitefish, round whitefish, least cisco, inconnu, Arctic grayling, pike.

4. From the sea: lamprey, sturgeon, salmon, coastal cutthroat, steelhead, Dolly Varden, threespine stickleback, prickly sculpin, Coast Range sculpin.

The species listed in (1) above could be classified as the south-central interior group, with riparian hardwoods and lakeshore hardwoods having the most influence on rearing and adult habitats. The species listed in group (2) are most likely to occur in the northeastern TSAs. The species from group (3) are likely the main Cassiar, MacKenzie, North Kalum, and North Prince George species groups but some of these may also occur in the Fort Nelson TSA. Coastal species are listed in group (4). Table 10 documents the main rivers and TSAs for each of the more economically important fish species in British Columbia.

Table 10 only briefly defines some of the geographic reference points for the main fish species of British Columbia. (Note that fish species distribution is actually remarkably well aligned with forest regions.) Life histories of the salmon species are described in Groot and Margolis (1991), although vegetation of riparian habitats is not discussed.

TABLE 10. Fish species, river habitat, and TSA occurrence

Species	Main habitats	TSA
Chinook Salmon *(Oncorhynchus tshawytscha)*	upper Fraser River, Stikine River, Peace River, and southeast Vancouver Island	Prince George Cassiar Arrowsmith North Coast
Kokanee and Sockeye Salmon *(O. nerka)*	Fraser River, Stikine River, Skeena River, Columbia River, Vancouver Island, Similkameen River, and Rivers Inlet rivers	Fraser Prince George Cassiar North Coast Arrowsmith Strathcona Merritt Arrow Kingcome
Coho Salmon *(O. kisutch)*	Queen Charlotte Islands, Fraser River, Stikine River, and Vancouver Island	North Coast Cassiar Prince George Fraser Strathcona Arrowsmith
Chum Salmon *(O. keta)*	Queen Charlotte Islands, Taku River, Skeena River, and Teslin River	North Coast Cassiar Kispiox Kalum
Pink Salmon *(O. gorbuscha)*	Queen Charlotte Islands, Skeena River, Rivers Inlet rivers, lower Fraser River, and Atlin Lakes rivers	North Coast Mid Coast Cassiar Fraser
Lake Trout *(Salvelinus namaycush)*	in most lakes from Shuswap Lake northward	Cassiar Ft. Nelson Ft. St. John Mackenzie Dawson Creek Prince George Robson Valley Quesnel 100 Mile House Lakes Morice

TABLE 10. (continued)

Species	Main habitats	TSA
Brook Trout *(S. fontinalis)*	many streams and lakes of the southern Interior, southern Vancouver Island, Skagit and Stave rivers	Merritt Okanagan Arrow Boundary Kootenay Lake Arrowsmith Fraser
Brown Trout *(Salmo trutta)*	Kettle River, Cowichan and Little Qualicum rivers	Boundary Arrowsmith
Coastal Cutthroat Trout *(S. clarki)*	Almost all streams and lakes of the Coast, including Vancouver Island and Queen Charlotte Islands	Arrowsmith Strathcona Kingcome Fraser Soo Sunshine Coast Kingcome Mid Coast North Coast
Steelhead Trout *(S. gairdneri)*	Fraser system, Columbia system, Peace River, Thompson rivers, and Skeena system	Prince George Dawson Creek Cassiar Mackenzie Quesnel Williams Lake 100 Mile House Robson Valley Kispiox Kalum North Coast Bulkley
Northern Pike *(Esox lucius)*	Peace-Mackenzie system, Liard-Mackenzie system, and Taku system	Dawson Creek Ft. St. John Ft. Nelson Cassiar Mackenzie
Smallmouth Bass *(Micropterus dolomieui)*	Columbia system, southern Vancouver Island, and Moyie Lake	Arrow Boundary Kootenay Lake Cranbrook Arrowsmith

TABLE 10. (continued)

Species	Main habitats	TSA
White Sturgeon *(Acipenser transmontanus)*	Fraser system, Kootenay Lake and River, Columbia River above Revelstoke, and Okanagan Lake	Fraser Lillooet 100 Mile House Williams Lake Quesnel Prince George Okanagan Kootenay Lake Revelstoke Robson Valley
Arctic Grayling *(Thymallus arcticus)*	Peace-Mackenzie system, Liard-Mackenzie system, and Yukon system	Ft. Nelson Ft. St.John Dawson Creek Mackenzie Cassiar
Round Whitefish *(Prosopium cylindraceum)*	Yukon system, Liard-Mackenzie system, and Chilkat system	Ft. Nelson Cassiar Mackenzie Dawson Creek Ft. St. John
Mountain Whitefish *(P. williamsoni)*	Columbia system, Fraser River, Skeena River, Stikine River, Liard River, and Peace River	Okanagan Arrow Kootenay Lake Fraser Prince George Cassiar North Coast Ft. Nelson
Lake Whitefish *(Coregonus clupeaformis)*	Yukon system, Peace-Mackenzie system, Skeena system, Fraser system, Vancouver Island, and Columbia system	Okanagan Kamloops Prince George Mackenzie Dawson Creek Ft. Nelson Ft. St. John

4.4.3 Hardwood forest importance to fish

The most limiting factor in the assessment of hardwood forest importance to fish of British Columbia is the lack of a complete inventory of fish species abundance and distribution in the province. From a TSA perspective, some areas are relatively well known, such as the Kalum, or many fisheries are known to occur, such as within the Fraser, the Skeena, and the Nass river drainages. The salmonid behaviours and life-history requirements are also well known compared to those of the so-called coarse fish. The importance that streamside and upland hardwood forests have for fish can be summarized as protection of water quality, provision of insect prey through leaf litterfall, coarse woody debris production, streambank and lakeshore stability, and temperature reduction through shading effects. The importance of hardwood species from selected TSAs, or selected known hardwood stands, may be applied simplistically to the economically important species listed above. However, with the exception of some high-potential coastal hardwood harvesting areas, the areas with the greatest commercial interest in hardwoods are the areas with the smallest database for fish. These include the Fort Nelson, Fort St. John, Dawson Creek, and Prince George TSAs. The first- and second-order streams that are likely to be the most severely affected by harvesting are also suspected of having the highest biodiversity of fish *and* vegetation (S. Hawthorn, pers. comm., 1992).

Hardwood forests that contribute to fish habitat lie mainly within riparian zones, although management of upland hardwood forests may have an impact on fish habitat as well. The ways in which hardwood trees and deciduous shrubs in riparian areas contribute to fish habitat are summarized below:

1. Control of sediment loading: many hardwoods on the Coast are seral species that commonly invade following harvesting. Vegetation development can stabilize sediment loading from roads (Swanson *et al.* 1987). Unstable materials in riparian margins can similarly be stabilized. Many of these stands have been mainly hardwood dominated because of river-maintained early succession. However, because of the mainly harvest-related origin of coastal hardwood stands, already destabilized materials may be further eroded by second-pass harvesting of hardwoods. This is a major source of concern for fisheries management. Furthermore, many hardwood stands exist on unstable materials and destabilization of these areas would have similar effects.

   In the Interior, hardwoods originated mainly in response to repeated fires (with some exceptions) and the sediment loading question becomes more related to geomorphology than to anything else. This is important in the northeastern portion of the province (where soils are predominantly lacustrine silts and clays) where siltation following hardwood harvesting is a concern.

2. Stream channel stability is affected, in part, by rooting and deadfall accumulation at streamside (Sullivan *et al.* 1987), regardless of tree species composition. There is a tendency for riparian communities to be dominated by hardwoods because of their tolerance for streamside conditions and because they have a rapid replacement rate in streamside vegetation dynamics. If this stability is not maintained then channels may shift, and infilling of pools and eddies used by fish can occur. Although shifting and infilling is a natural feature of riparian systems, when accompanied by streamside harvesting of hardwoods, the impacts may be greater than temporary displacement and water quality decline.

3. Hardwoods are the primary producers of detritus used by insect and vertebrate prey. The riparian zone produces most of the invertebrate prey for fish through litterfall and subsequent invertebrate food web interactions. When the source of litterfall is removed, the primary production is reduced for a time.

4. Coarse woody debris provides excellent winter habitat for salmonids through the formation of pools for rearing, control of

organic material and storage, and modification of water quality (Bisson *et al.* 1987). It can also help to buttress river banks and act to slow near-bank velocities (Sullivan *et al.* 1987). The species origin of debris is important to production and removal; red alder breaks up and falls over more frequently than coniferous or other riparian species, but also moves off downstream more quickly because of its light weight. Although alder (and presumably other deciduous tree species) is more dynamic in stream debris loading, it does not have the pH depression and leachate loading characteristics that most riparian conifers have (Bisson *et al.* 1987).

5. Temperature control: deciduous vegetation canopies over streams act to maintain lower stream temperatures during summer months.

There are a number of relationships between riparian hardwoods and fish habitat use that are poorly defined. The primary data gaps include the following:

- Life histories of lesser-known fish species, distributions in British Columbia, and levels of abundance.
- Ecology of the more important riparian vegetation complexes as sources of invertebrate prey for fish, and as sources of debris, and how these are affected by harvesting in the riparian zone. The effect of streamside riparian zone enhancement or partial harvesting on fish population dynamics.
- Role played by deciduous vegetation in post-harvesting stream stability.
- Use of understorey vegetation (*Typha latifolia, Rubus parviflorus, Rubus spectabilis*) as indicators of winter habitat to avoid damaging back channels.
- Season of harvesting in some riparian areas and its impact on fish populations.

4.5 Importance of Hardwoods to Native Peoples

4.5.1 Current developments

The most dramatic developments in native affairs are the quest for self-government and the issue of native land claims. These may seem to have little to do with hardwood forests except that hardwoods consistently occur in riparian and floodplain areas that are being identified as having native national significance, and they have a greater likelihood of being part of the traditional native lands than any other land unit in British Columbia. Developments toward land claims in hardwood areas are not clearly defined at this writing, with the exception of the Gitksan and the Treaty 8 concerns, which could affect large areas of the province from the point of view of non-native government control. The Treaty 8 Association now hopes to complete mapping of traditional camping areas at 1:20 000 scale on tributaries affected by hardwood harvesting.

4.5.2 Hardwood utilization by native peoples

The use of hardwoods by native peoples in the realms of medicine, religion, construction, and food is well documented (Turner 1975, 1978, 1979, 1992; Turner and Hebda 1990). Although all natives in the province would have had some interactions with hardwoods found in riparian areas, the peoples of the northeast, the South Coast and Vancouver Island would have been the most dependent on hardwoods because these areas are the major hardwood-producers. Figure 2 illustrates the distribution of the main aboriginal groups. Groups of the northeast, distinguished by language (which would roughly coincide with the Prince George Forest Region), are the Kaska, the Slave, the Sekani, and the Shuswap. Coastal and island tribes (which correspond to the Vancouver Forest Region) are the Comox, Sechelt, Squamish, Halkomelem, and Lillooet (Curran in Turner 1992).

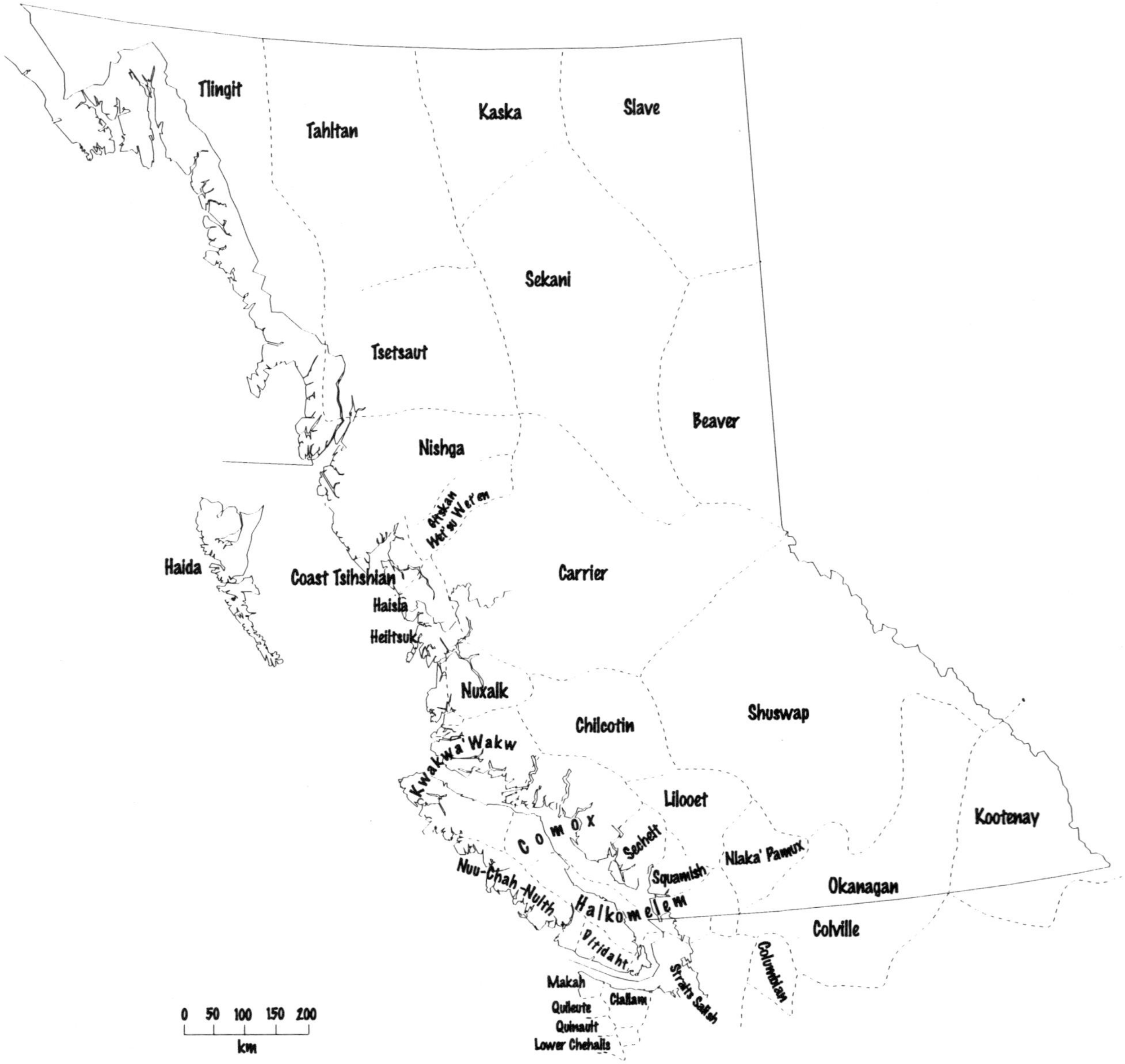

FIGURE 2. Aboriginal groups of British Columbia (from Curran in Turner 1992).

Past uses of deciduous or hardwood trees and associated plants are documented below. Current uses are also briefly described.

Black cottonwood *(Populus trichocarpa)*

Black cottonwood was mainly used by natives for its medicinal qualities, although for peoples of the Interior, cottonwood was a substitute for western redcedar in terms of general utility. Bark and bud products had antibiotic effects, probably because of phenols and glycosides, but they are fatal to humans in excessive amounts. Buds and bark were used in various forms, including infusions, decoctions, poultices and salves, for many general ailments such as sunburn, ringworm, rheumatism, colds, and coughs. Inner bark and cambium were eaten in spring by the Bella Coola, Lillooet and others as a source of food. Use of black cottonwood as a material was diverse.

Roots were used as hearth and drill, as well as thread for sewing. Outer bark served as roofing, while inner bark was used in soap products. Wood was used in dugout canoes, saddles, and hide-scraping blocks. Pillows and mattresses were stuffed with the fruit cotton (Clowater in Turner 1992).

Red alder *(Alnus rubra)*

Although all of the red alder tree was utilized in some form by the native people, the most important function was as a source of dye from the bark. The red or black dye was used on baskets, ropes, wool, hair, buckskins, and tattoos, and to make fishing nets invisible to fish. The wood was used for carving masks and dishes (Turner 1979). Alder wood makes excellent fuel, especially for cooking or smoking salmon because it burns at an even heat and does not impart an unpleasant flavour (Turner 1979). Red alder also had medicinal value. A solution of bark was drunk for tuberculosis, colds, and stomach disorders, as well as being used as a wash for skin sores, eczema, and sore eyes. The bark was also an ingredient in "four-barks" medicine, said to be good as a blood purifier and for various internal ailments (Turner and Hebda 1990). Alder was regarded as having a supernatural persona. In Lillooet mythology, "Alder" was a red-skinned wife of Coyote, who also had "Trembling Aspen" as a white-skinned wife (Lloyd in Turner 1992).

Bigleaf maple *(Acer macrophyllum)*

As a source of food, young maple shoots and sprouted seeds were sometimes eaten by the Thompson, or cooked with meat for flavour (Turner 1975). Sap was used as a tonic or concentrated into syrup. Seeds could be stored over winter and mixed with other food. As material, maple wood was usually carved into small items such as spoons, rattles, and dishes. Inner bark could be woven into baskets and bags. Leaves were used as lining for food containers, but also medicinally, as they were rubbed on boys' faces at puberty so that beards would not grow. Other medical applications of bigleaf maple include the use of the bark as an ingredient in "four-barks" medicine for internal ailments such as stomach, kidney, or digestive tract problems, tuberculosis, and for liver deterioration from too much drinking (Turner and Hebda 1990).

Trembling aspen *(Populus tremuloides)*

Trembling aspen was used mostly for its wood as a construction material and its bark for medicinal purposes. An infusion of bark was drunk for "any" internal ailment, as a contraceptive, and also was an ingredient in "ten-barks" medicine, which was a treatment for tuberculosis and scrofula sores (Turner and Hebda 1990). The upper Thompson used the wood extensively for dugout canoes and fuel while the Kootenays also fashioned hide-covered saddles with aspen wood. Rotten aspen wood is very absorbent and was used by the Carrier as diaper material and to line cradles. The Thompson boiled aspen branches to make a cleaning solution that hunters washed themselves with to disguise their human odour (Turner 1979). Trembling aspen was not used as food but had a place in mythology as the white-skinned wife of Coyote (Lloyd in Turner 1992).

Paper birch *(Betula papyrifera)*

The bark of the birch was as important to the peoples of the Interior as cedar bark was to the coastal people. It was used mainly to make baskets and canoes. Birch bark was also used for wrapping foods for storage, lining graves and covering corpses, splinting broken limbs, binding implements, and as roofing for temporary shelters. Other more unique uses for the bark included snow goggles made by the Tahltan people, moose calls by the Moose people, and toboggans by the Carrier. Birch wood was used to make small carved items such as dishes, cups, spoons, tools, snowshoes, and arrows. As a firewood, birch is superior to aspen, balsam fir, and pine because it burns with a very intense heat. Leaves were steeped to make a soap product (Turner 1992). Shuswap ritual required that girls drink from "a painted cup of birch bark" as part of their puberty ceremony (Boas in Palmer 1975). Birch was not important to native peoples as a source of food.

Hardwood species are still used by many natives and others, although knowledge of traditional uses has diminished. Barks of trees and shrubs have been, and still are, a prominent raw material in native folk medicine (Turner and Hebda 1990). Birch and alder are popular firewoods, birch sap is used to make a mild form of vinegar or a light alcoholic beverage, and bark is still used for a variety of native crafts. Birch trees can be used as an emergency source of water in the forest and a poultice of alder bark can be applied to wounds as an astringent in a wilderness survival situation. Wilderness survival courses often incorporate the traditional native uses of hardwoods. Potential medicinal qualities of hardwoods have not yet been sufficiently researched and may impart substances of great pharmacological importance. The western yew *(Taxus brevifolia)* has gained recent importance in the field of conventional medicine as a potential treatment for cancer. This species was traditionally used with a high degree of confidence by natives in "four-barks" medicine for treatment of internal ailments. Perhaps there are similar lessons to be learned in deciduous forests.

4.6 Importance of Hardwood Resource Management to Natives

Native people have given forests and natural resources special importance. As native people become more involved in forest management within their traditional territories, many have expressed the belief that ways must be found to incorporate spiritual and cultural values into modern forest management practices. Contemporary hardwood and softwood harvesting methods in the 1990s may cause conflicts with native peoples who still follow a traditional lifestyle. Chief Stewart Cameron of the Treaty 8 Tribal Association, Saultau Band, commented that 95% of his Band members earn their income on traplines and Treaty 8 members have expressed the concern that hardwood harvesting would interfere with furbearer productivity. The Lake Babine Band of the Carrier Sekani people depend almost entirely on trapping. They had remained self-reliant within their traditional territories but recent conifer timber harvesting is believed to have negatively affected many of their most productive traplines (Forest Resource Commission 1991). Hardwood and mixedwood removal may have been harmful to marten, beaver, ermine, fisher, river otter, bobcat, raccoon, and snowshoe hare populations. The Band reports they were neither consulted about the impact of timber harvesting nor have they been compensated for their losses. Dean Dokkie, head of the Treaty 8 Tribal Association, is concerned about the lack of consultation with the communities affected by harvesting (Forest Resource Commission 1991).

A Task Force on Native Forestry was set up in 1990 to recommend ways to increase native participation in the forest sector. In an effort to provide economic opportunities, government has encouraged native participation in the forestry industry by training native people in silviculture and providing them with expertise in contracting. Even upon concession of a traditional trapping lifestyle for one of forestry, natives cannot always infiltrate the industry. When the Stuart Trembleur Lake Band initially decided to promote economic activity and employment in the forest industry, the Band had to overcome resistance from the B.C. Ministry of Forests (Forest Resource Commission 1991) because it lacked experience in business and resource management, and funds. In Forest Resources Commission (1991), Chief Pat Alfred of the Nimpkish Band expressed the opinion that:

- Band members have successfully completed forestry programs but then found there was no work for them;

- Bands are not funded to participate in economic development ventures such as forestry;

- Kingcome Village sits across the river from a logging camp but only one out of 200 village people is employed in logging; and

- Native people do not have priority in bidding on forestry contracts.

There is an option for natives in the forestry industry to self-manage forestry ventures. In Forest Resources Commission (1991), Steven Bercek of the Osoyoos Indian Band pointed out that his Band has about 4500 hectares of commercially forested land. The Band had a 5-year management plan prepared under FRDA I that will support a six-person forestry crew year-round with proper management. The Band wants the forest managed for all uses, such as range, recreation, and hunting.

The concerns of natives about commercial use of the hardwood resource are summarized (Forest Resources Commission 1991) as follows:

- potential loss of furbearer habitat in upland and riparian traplines

- harvesting in riparian areas in the northeast will have a detrimental impact on the integrity of lake and streamside tribal communities

- post-harvest silvicultural herbicide treatments of hardwood or mixedwood stands to promote coniferous growth will affect health and ecology

- loss of traditional fishing camps, travel corridors and gathering areas because of riparian harvesting before mapping can describe the location of these areas

- degradation of fisheries because of declines in water quality resulting from harvesting in riparian areas and areas dominated by silty materials

- increased access to areas adjacent to traplines and through traplines

- harvesting in areas not yet discussed in the land claims process

Native leaders believe that, in the northeastern part of the province, Treaty No. 8 stipulates that native hunting and fishing rights supersede all other uses except conservation (R. Whiten, pers. comm., 1992). They also believe that the treaty is being violated in some cases. The opposite view may be the subject of confrontations or, preferably, negotiations in the future. This view holds that native uses of land may not apply where "saving and excepting such tracts (of land) as may be required or taken up from time to time for settlement, mining, lumbering, trading or other purposes (Registrar General of Canada 1899)." The treaty may be open to interpretation on the definition of who, exactly, has the authority to "save and except such tracts [of land]." However, these arguments may be avoided altogether as there is an excellent opportunity for forest resource managers and native leaders to prevent confrontations, especially if hardwood forest-use planning is an open and consultative process from the beginning.

4.7 Aesthetics and Recreational Use of Hardwoods

Deciduous trees, especially trembling aspen and balsam poplar, provide the dominant autumn colours in the boreal regions of western North America. In most cities and towns, and on farms that lie within the aspen parkland and boreal region, aspen that could be considered "amenity trees" are usually residuals from a previous forest. In the western United States, however, aspen are in such demand for landscaping that "rustlers" in the early 1980s removed as many as 40 000 aspen per year in the South Park District of Pike National Forest, Colorado (Buehrer in Peterson and Peterson 1992).

Seasonal colour change, the typical fluttering motion of the leaves, and the abundant penetration of light through the canopy are properties that give aspen aesthetic appeal (Johnson *et al.* in Debyle and Winokur 1985). Its fast growth, medium size, lacy form, self-pruning habit, and relatively easy care are other desirable traits for urban use (Peterson and Peterson 1992). However, the sparse canopy and self-pruning qualities prevent its use as a windbreak (Johnson *et al.* in Debyle and Winokur 1985).

In a survey of urban Edmonton (Peterson and Peterson 1992), *Populus* species were found to be the seventh most common amenity tree. The City of Kamloops rarely uses aspen, choosing to use European species instead. An exception is their extensive use of mountain ash, which is popular because of drought hardiness and rapid growth.

Aspen wood chips are also used for aesthetic purposes, as a mulch for ornamental gardens. A larger market for aspen as an amenity tree may develop if stocks are made more readily available in horticultural outlets, and if they are propagated with such aesthetic characteristics as red autumn leaves instead of yellow, or vertically drooping branches (Peterson and Peterson 1992).

Aesthetics in forestry practices have been under much public scrutiny in recent years. In the United States, private landowners supply 76% of the hardwood harvest (Vodak *et al.* 1985) and as a result they have federal laws governing forest aesthetics (National Forest Products Association 1980). Private land can be owned for reasons other than strictly economic ones (Roberts 1983; Vodak *et al.* 1985). The *National Environmental Policy Act* of 1969 mandates the management of National Forests to assure that "productive and aesthetically pleasing surroundings [be maintained]." The *Rangeland Renewable Resources Planning Act* of 1974 and the *National Forests Management Act* reinforce the government mandate for consideration of amenity resources, specifically identifying aesthetic resources *along* with recreation, wildlife, and wilderness resources. Although there are no similar statutes in Canadian law, there is public and interagency pressure for forest harvest planners to maintain forest aesthetics by varying cutblock shapes and maintaining pleasant viewscapes from roads and other vantage points. This may or may not affect hardwood harvesting to the same degree that it has affected coniferous harvesting in British Columbia, but forest managers are required to "plan the use of the forest and range resources of the Crown, so that the production of timber and forage, the harvesting of timber, the grazing of livestock and the realization of fisheries, wildlife, water, outdoor recreation and other natural resource values are coordinated and integrated, in consultation and cooperation with other ministries and agencies of the Crown and with the private sector" (Revised statutes of British Columbia 1979).

There is a landscape management system to evaluate and inventory scenic landscapes in the province (B.C. Ministry of Forests 1981). Silviculture regulation in British Columbia requires consideration of aesthetics in pre-harvest silviculture prescription (PHSP) as well. The evaluation of scenic quality is coupled with methods to determine the landscape's sensitivity to disturbance and, based on that, varying levels of protection are assigned. The computerized methodologies may not be accessible to timber harvesting operations personnel who do not have adequate computer hardware and software capability, however.

The negative visual impacts of clearcutting deciduous tree species may be less than those of most coniferous tree species being harvested in British Columbia, if time-to-green-up is the primary consideration. Other elements of a deciduous tree harvesting operation may have some advantages, such as the small site sizes (on average) and gentle topography involved. Clearcuts may be noticeable for only a few years because of rapid regrowth of understorey species and abundant hardwood growth. One exception to the generally more positive public opinion of hardwood harvesting is the immediate and sometimes heavy slash loading that occurs in harvesting of overmature hardwood types. Public perception of waste in forestry is putting more pressure on foresters to adopt waste management as part of general forestry practice.

According to the economic analysis presented earlier and the age class data displayed for selected TSAs, slash accumulations may be a common problem, as they already are in some areas of active hardwood harvesting (Enns *et al.* 1992). As discussed earlier, true ages of pure deciduous stands may be different from those depicted in the inventory. After harvesting, scattered deciduous slash may be left to decay within a very few years. The more rapid decay rates of deciduous slash may place hardwood harvesting ahead of conifers in the perception of forest scenic beauty. Hull and Buyoff (1988) determined that dead and down material accumulation was the single most unacceptable feature (aesthetically) of clearcuts, resulting in significant negative impacts on perceptions of scenic beauty of the forest environment. The advanced decay rates will make harvested sites more accessible to hikers, as well as increasing wildlife viewing values from accessibility, high browse species production, and low cover perspectives. Methods to deal with slash accumulation in hardwoods should be developed soon, however.

The recreational patterns of British Columbians are described in a policy framework document (B.C. Ministry of Forests 1989b). Assessments of recreational use were based on recreational user-days and recreational activity-days. Regional differences were found, with the Vancouver Forest Region influencing the overall results of the survey because of its large population. Recreational user-days per person in the forest regions were highest in Prince Rupert and lowest in Vancouver, although Vancouver still had the highest use. Hunting was least popular, except in the northern regions where it was roughly even with fishing. Nature study was found to be most popular throughout all regions, and users were prepared to pay from a few hundred to several hundred dollars in addition to what they already pay to maintain forest recreation. Hunters were willing to pay the most although they were the smallest group. Potential revenue would be highest for wildlife viewing and nature study. The large population of the Vancouver Forest Region has a larger influence on the total potential revenue than all other regions combined.

Deciduous forests, with bright, open subcanopies, are ideal for recreational use in British Columbia. However, aspen stands in particular do not tolerate concentrated use, which leads to destruction or removal of young suckers, and trampling and disturbance of the soil. Snow cover reduces the damage caused by recreational use and the even snow cover in an aspen forest makes for excellent cross-country skiing conditions (Johnson *et al.* in Debyle and Winokur 1985).

The recreational potential of birch, cottonwood, maple, mixedwood, and alder stands can be listed for most of British Columbia as follows:

1. Birdwatching and hiking (common throughout the province), with particular emphasis on organized birdwatching and naturalists groups.

2. Recreational hunting and fishing is the single largest group of recreational activities in the province. Sites are frequently semi-primitive, and often have some seral or deciduous element because of the species being hunted. This is especially important in the northeastern and Prince George TSAs. Semi-primitive areas with a high deciduous forest cover are identified in Appendix 4.

3. In contrast to Item 2, above, wildlife viewing was identified by Ethos Consulting *et al.* (1988, 1991) and Filion *et al.* (1983) as having greater economic importance than hunting, and more universal popularity than any other form of consumptive or nonconsumptive use of the wildlife resource in British Columbia. Because of the high wildlife habitat suitability of deciduous forests, they have an important place in the viewing experience, and in the context of tourism and marketing of tourism, they have exceptionally high values.

4. Fall colour viewing on back roads and high-density hardwood areas. Although this is impossible to quantify, virtually all recreation officers and recreation specialists contacted agreed that this is a common activity in rural and suburban British Columbia. The American eastern seaboard tourism industry advertises fall colour tour packages, with a considerable total economic benefit to the tourism industry. There are areas of the province that have potential for this market: the Elk Valley, the rolling aspen stands near Dawson Creek, the Boundary TSAs, the Bulkley, and parts of the Kalum, especially if combined with wildlife viewing.

5. The most popular recreation areas are situated near water, usually with some deciduous element as a component of the scenery. Although the areas are not chosen specifically for deciduous tree views, these views make up an important component of the majority of recreational opportunities in the province.

6. Firewood cutting is common in Interior birch and aspen stands, and is often considered (sometimes reluctantly) a family outing.

The assessment of recreation has encompassed present patterns of recreational use of hardwoods. There are probably more abundant opportunities for wilderness recreation in hardwoods than are presently available in old-growth coniferous areas.

The B.C. Ministry of Forests Recreation Opportunity Spectrum (1:2 000 000) map was overlain on the Ministry's inventory type group map (B. Chalk, pers. comm., 1992) to identify where forest compartments with greater than 50% of the polygons having hardwood as a leading species coincide with primitive, nonmotorized areas. Appendix 4 provides a comprehensive list of the semiprimitive or primitive deciduous-dominated inventory compartment groups. A short list would include the south Fraser east of Matsqui, the Garibaldi area, polygons near the Quesnel River, Francois Lake, Stuart Lake and the Bulkley Valley, the eastern shore of Williston Lake, and the Beaton, Robson Valley, McBride, and Fraser Lake areas, as well as Kitwanga, Kispiox, and Kalum. The largest concentration of semi-primitive and primitive deciduous-dominated stands exist in the three northeastern TSAs; Fort Nelson, Fort St. John, and Dawson Creek. Of these, the Fort Nelson TSA has the largest hectarage of unused deciduous wilderness without roads.

Recreational potential is still in the policy development stage, although there are several interagency efforts to set aside protected areas in the province, and to decide how backcountry recreation should be managed (Province of British Columbia 1992). Hardwood forests have great potential for early designation as wilderness areas, with few potential conflicts.

5 UTILIZATION AND ECONOMIC BENEFITS

5.1 Estimated Annual Utilization Potential

The estimated annual potential harvest of the hardwood resource by location and species is shown in Table 11 (totaled by location) and Table 12 (totaled by species).

The coastal area is estimated to have a potential annual harvest of about 567 000 m^3, of which 448 000 m^3 is alder. The Interior has a potential of about 6.4 million m^3, of which 5.6 million m^3 is aspen. Overall, the province has a potential annual harvest of about 7 million m^3 for about 20 years, based on current inventory estimates for areas with hardwoods as the lead species and volumes that are mature or near mature. These estimates were derived for broad planning and research purposes. They do not imply that specific allowable annual cuts have been determined by the B.C. Ministry of Forests or that a manufacturing firm would have a designated supply of any specified volume.

5.1.1 Method for deriving harvest estimates

The estimates in Tables 11 and 12 were based largely on current wood flow patterns and were derived by matching TSA and TFL area and volume estimates to adjacent communities or municipalities. In some cases more than one TSA was matched to a community. Wherever possible, a TSA and any TFLs within its boundaries were considered to be a unit (e.g., Williams Lake TSA relates to Williams Lake, McBride-Valemont relates to the Robson Valley TSA).

The 20-year annual harvest was estimated by calculating mature and near-mature volumes. Overmature volumes were not considered because of the quality limitations associated with older hardwoods. A 20-year period was chosen to allow use to become established, as well as to allow enough time to depreciate the capital investment.

The annual estimated harvest was calculated by dividing one-half of the mature volume (m^3) by 20 (year), then for cottonwood and aspen in the Interior, one-fortieth of the near-mature volume was added. For all species, one-eightieth of the near-mature volume was added but only if this amount exceeded the mature volume.

Only one-half of the mature volume was considered because it was assumed that some areas would not be accessible or would have certain constraints, such as being environmentally sensitive. A portion of the immature wood was added because hardwoods can be harvested before 80 years and if growth (growing stock) already exceeds the mature volume any move to a regulated forest would require a larger, not a smaller harvest. Thus, considering accessibility and other constraints, one-half the volume in the age class 61–80 for cottonwood and aspen in the Interior divided by 20 (equal to one-fortieth), or one-half the volume in the age class 41–80 for all other species divided by 40 (equal to one-eightieth), could be harvested without depleting growing stock.

This procedure produces an interim estimate and assumes that mature timber and timber that will mature over the next 20 years will be harvested. It is not an estimate that necessarily relates to sustained yield or to a regulated forest producing a planned timber flow. Timber management, harvest, and allocation plans that identify appropriate harvest levels are still required.

TABLE 11. Estimated annual harvest potential for a 20-year period, by location

Area	Species	Estimated annual harvest[a] (m^3)	Longer-term potential[b]
Coast			
Vancouver	Maple	61 670	good
	Cottonwood	10 125	good
	Birch	7 100	good
	Alder	102 100	good
Powell River	Alder	159 600	good
	Maple	12 500	poor
	Cottonwood	11 200	good
South Vancouver Island	Alder	44 660	good
	Maple	2 875	good
Campbell River	Alder	76 275	good
	Maple	2 975	good
Port Hardy–Port McNeil	Alder	65 600	good
	Cottonwood	10 100	good
Total		566 780	
Interior - Northeast			
Fort Nelson	Birch	139 875	poor
	Aspen	2 400 850	poor
	Cottonwood	179 825	poor
Fort St. John	Birch	32 900	good
	Aspen	647 525	poor
	Cottonwood	42 825	poor
Dawson Creek	Aspen	1 295 675	poor
	Cottonwood	199 050	poor
Total		4 938 525	

TABLE 11. (continued)

Area	Estimated Species	Longer-term annual harvest[a] (m^3)	potential[b]
Interior - North-central			
Prince George–Vanderhoof	Birch	15 225	poor
	Aspen	437 275	poor
	Cottonwood	6 975	poor
McBride-Valemont	Birch	4 650	good
	Aspen	34 375	fair
	Cottonwood	1 850	poor
Mackenzie	Birch	7 575	poor
	Aspen	272 325	poor
	Cottonwood	2 275	poor
Total		782 525	
Interior - Northwest			
Hazelton	Birch	14 000	fair
	Aspen	67 450	poor
	Cottonwood	8 575	poor
Kitimat-Terrace	Cottonwood	4 325	poor
Smithers-Houston	Aspen	29 075	fair
	Cottonwood	5 325	poor
Burns Lake	Aspen	63 775	poor
Total		192 525	
Interior - Central			
Williams Lake	Birch	12 150	poor
	Aspen	75 975	poor
Quesnel	Birch	12 275	poor
	Aspen	160 525	poor
100 Mile House	Birch	5 825	poor
	Aspen	70 825	poor
Total		337 575	

TABLE 11. (continued)

Area	Species	Estimated annual harvest[a] (m^3)	Longer-term potential[b]
Interior – Southern			
Kamloops–North Thompson	Birch	25 125	poor
	Aspen	60 300	poor
	Cottonwood	4 075	poor
Merrit-Princeton	Cottonwood	3 300	poor
Creston-Nelson-Kaslo	Birch	3 150	fair
	Cottonwood	2 875	poor
Castlegar-Slocan-Nakusp	Birch	2 800	good
	Cottonwood	5 450	poor
Revelstoke	Birch	900	good
Salmon Arm–Vernon-Sicamous	Birch	40 720	poor
	Cottonwood	4 575	poor
Kelowna-Penticton-Oliver	Cottonwood	4 575	poor
Greenwood–Grand Forks	Cottonwood	6 375	poor
Cranbrook	Cottonwood	7 275	poor
Total		171 495	
Total Province		6 989 425	

[a] One-half the mature volume divided by 20; plus 1/40th of the near-mature volume in the case of aspen and cottonwood in the interior and 1/80th in the case of all other species if the near-mature volume exceeds the mature volume.

[b] The longer-term potential is a subjective rating based on the volume of timber in the near-mature class that would "move-up" in 20 years to the mature class and support continued harvesting. A rating of "good" means the annual harvest is likely to increase, a rating of "fair" means the annual harvest would likely remain about the same. A rating of "poor" means the harvest might have to be decreased.

TABLE 12. Estimated annual harvest potential for a 20-year period, by species

Region and species		Estimated annual harvest (m^3)
Coast	Maple	80 020
	Alder	448 235
	Cottonwood	31 425
	Birch	7 100
Total coast		566 780
Interior	Birch	317 170
	Cottonwood	489 525
	Aspen	5 615 950
Total Interior		6 422 645
Total Province		6 989 425

Source: Derived from Tables 1 and 2 using the methods described in the text.

5.1.2 Longer-term potential

To assist in the strategic planning process, an estimate of the sustainability of the resource is needed. This longer-term potential is a subjective rating based on the volume of timber in the near-mature class that would "move-up" to the mature class in 20 years and support continued harvesting.

If the volume of the near-mature timber already exceeds the volume of the mature timber reported, the longer-term potential is considered **good** and the annual harvest is likely to increase. If the near-mature timber volume is less than the mature, but only marginally so, the potential is considered **fair** and the annual harvest is likely to remain the same. If the near-mature volume is significantly lower than the mature volume, the area is rated as **poor** and the harvested volume is expected to decrease.

5.2 Products and Markets

A vast array of products can be produced from the province's hardwoods. However, at present only a few are economically viable. The major products listed in Table 13 are being produced from the hardwood species considered in this report. In addition to the major products listed, a variety of lesser products such as wooden toys, carvings, and small sawmill special cuttings are produced by scattered "cottage" industries. Recent production activity in the province is summarized in Appendix 5.

5.2.1 Market statistics

Accurate and consistent data on the production, import, and export of hardwood products are not generally available from traditional sources. This is because hardwoods are combined with all other provinces' data by

Statistics Canada. There have also been fewer than three reporting producers for each product, which has prevented statistical accounting of volumes. This problem is further exacerbated by industry practices in sourcing of raw material—frequently from private lands ("gate wood" or "farmer wood")—and from unreported exchanges or sales of relatively small volumes of raw materials and semi-finished products. In addition, the change in reporting groups by Statistics Canada (e.g., the combination of plywood and veneer categories in 1988) has made statistical evaluation of production levels questionable.

Appendix 6 contains statistics concerning the production and export of Canadian hardwoods. The following section discusses hardwood production and markets in the provincial context. A glossary of forest products terms and abbreviations is provided in Appendix 7.

5.2.2 Markets for products

Logs

Most logs are sold to the hardwood manufacturing sector of the British Columbia forest products industry.

Louisiana-Pacific, with operations at Dawson Creek and Chetwynd, is the largest consumer of hardwoods. The oriented strand board (OSB) mill at Dawson Creek is supported by a pulpwood agreement (AAC 452 000 m^3) but currently relies heavily on aspen from private land. This large mill has the capacity to use over 450 000 m^3 annually. Aspen is the preferred species but some cottonwood (balsam poplar) from the Interior is used. The pulp mill near Chetwynd is also supported by a pulpwood agreement (AAC 452 000 m^3). This mill has an annual capacity of about 450 000 m^3 and produces market pulp from aspen. Currently, the mill uses timber from both Crown and private land.

Canadian Chopstick Manufacturing (Fort Nelson) harvests or purchases large volumes of aspen obtain about 100 000 m^3 of chopstick-quality wood for use in their manufacturing process. The balance of the wood is burned, because of a lack of local markets for residuals and logs. While Canadian Chopstick has recently undertaken trial shipments of lower-grade aspen logs to Korea, this (potentially 350 000 m^3/year) may not prove to be viable because of the intense competition from Russian and Chinese manufacturing plants.

At least three other chopstick manufacturers have ceased operations in the past three years. Chopsticks are no longer produced at Kelowna, Prince George, or Dawson Creek. Similar closures have occurred in other Canadian provinces and northeastern U.S. states.

Norvik Hardwoods of Delta is the next largest consumer of hardwoods. It produces alder sawn products, at a rate of 400 000 m^3/year, with chips as a residual product.

Slocan Forest Products Takama (Fort Nelson) Division is the next largest consumer, using 100 000 m^3 of cottonwood annually for the production of veneer and plywood.

Scott Paper (New Westminster) and Eurocan Pulp and Paper (Kitimat) both consume cottonwood logs. Eurocan's consumption of some 60 000 m^3 is for chip export. Scott uses about 70–75 000 m^3 annually for hardwood pulp, which is used in blended tissue products. They also purchase cottonwood chips. Primex Fibre of Delta consumes up to 30 000 m^3 of cottonwood for the production of chips for export. They have also produced alder chips.

On the coast, West Coast Plywood and Richmond Plywood Corporation consume some 30 000 and 12 000 m^3 per year respectively, of cottonwood logs while Coastland Wood Industries (Nanaimo) has experimented with 6000 m^3 of alder.

Interior veneer and plywood producers process lesser volumes of hardwoods. Atco Lumber (Fruitvale) peels up to 16 000 m^3 of cottonwood annually, and two "thin veneer" producers are consuming lesser volumes. Thompson River Hardwoods (Kamloops) currently consumes 14 000 m^3 of birch and Delvin Fry (Clearwater) will consume up to 30 000 m^3 of aspen per year once their facility commences operation.

TABLE 13. Major products from British Columbia hardwoods

Product	Species	Regions
Logs	Alder	Lower Mainland and south Coast
	Maple	Fraser Valley
	Birch	Fraser Valley and central Interior
	Aspen	South, central, and north Interior
	Cottonwood	Fraser Valley, north Coast, and south Interior
	Balsam poplar	North Interior
Sawnwood	Alder	South Coast
	Maple	Fraser Valley
	Birch	Fraser Valley
	Aspen	North Interior
Veneer-rotary	Cottonwood	Fraser Valley and south Interior
	Birch	Central Interior
	Aspen	North and central Interior
Veneer-sliced	Birch	Fraser Valley and central Interior
	Maple	Fraser Valley
Plywood	Cottonwood	South Coast
	Aspen	North Interior
Chopsticks	Aspen	North Interior
Pulp	Cottonwood	Fraser Valley
	Aspen	Central and north Interior
Pulp Chips	Alder	Fraser Valley
	Aspen	Central and north Interior
	Cottonwood	Fraser Valley and north Coast
OSB/Waferboard	Aspen	North and central Interior [a]
	Balsam poplar	North Interior

[a] Aspen residues and logs from the central Interior region are currently being marketed to Sturdy Wood in Alberta. Additionally, Ainsworth Lumber has committed to the construction of an OSB plant in the central Interior.

Slicing operations consume less volume, and often purchase in cant rather than log forms. Surrey Veneers consumes only 100 m^3 annually of very high quality maple, birch, and alder, while Paul Creek Slicing (Kamloops) consumes up to 2000 m^3 per year of birch.

Lumber and Sawnwood

Except for the domestic consumption of small volumes for pallet and frame stock, the major markets for hardwood lumber and sawnwood are export.

Major domestic consumers of sawnwood are Pacific Pallet (Abbotsford), consuming some 1 million FBM annually, and Stork Craft (Richmond), consuming primarily frame stock for children's furniture. This remanufactured product is largely imported from the United States.

Major export markets for alder and birch sawnwood include the United States, Japan, Italy, and Germany.

Baack[7] (1989) reported that, in 1988, exports of hardwoods from the United States exceeded 155 million board feet, and production of red alder sawnwood from Oregon alone reached 88 million board feet. Some alder lumber from Washington and Oregon is shipped to Canada.

A substantial volume of Oregon and Washington hardwood sawnwood is used domestically. This volume is expected to diminish as log shortages due to environmental restrictions reduce availability. British Columbia's export opportunities should increase if this occurs.

Europe and Asia represent North America's largest export markets. Ekstrom[8] (1992) reported red alder lumber exports of 40 million board feet to Asia and some 14 million board feet to Europe in 1990.

Veneer

Markets for rotary-peeled (1/10" and thicker) cottonwood, alder, and aspen can be found in both the United States and Canada. Major Canadian consumers include both Richmond Plywood and Westcoast Plywoods.

Markets in the United States include a wide variety of softwood and hardwood plywood producers in the Pacific Northwest.

Rotary-peeled (thin) veneer (1/16" and under) is sold only to the United States plants in the Pacific Northwest, and other producing regions use provincially produced veneers as a substitute for both domestic and imported (tropical) veneers in innerplies and "platforms" for hardwood panels. Timber Products Canada, a major broker of green and dry veneer products, estimates the current potential market for British Columbia hardwood veneer at 4–5 railcar loads per week.

Sliced veneer finds markets in the United States, Japan, and Korea, but relatively small volumes are now being shipped. The major constraint to shipment appears to be the availability of materials meeting product specifications.

Chopsticks

The two major markets for aspen chopsticks are Japan and Taiwan. It is estimated that Japan consumes up to 40 million pairs of disposable aspen chopsticks per day. While this market appears enormous, competition is fierce between Korea, states of the former Soviet Union, and North American producers.

---

[7] Baack, D. 1989. Oregon hardwoods. Report prepared for Western Hardwood Association, Portland, Oregon.

[8] Ekstrom, H. 1992. Pacific Northwest hardwoods capture international attention: an analysis of the Washington State hardwood industry. CINTRAFOR, Univ. Wash. Seattle, Wash. Unpubl.

Oriented strand board and waferboard

Oriented strand board (OSB)/waferboard products are used primarily for sheathing products in construction and for crating applications. Relatively small volumes (3.8% of shipments in 1990) are exported to Europe and Japan, with the North American market historically consuming the bulk of production. Since the 1950s, Canada has traditionally shipped about 50% of its production to the United States, and this pattern is expected to continue.

At present, the province has only one OSB plant (Louisiana-Pacific Panel Products, Dawson Creek), but a second (Ainsworth Lumber) is in the final stages of planning. Competition for these plants comes from all other aspen-growing regions of North America, as well as from areas in the southeastern United States that use other fast-growing species.

Pulp

Pulp produced from hardwoods is either used for direct conversion to paper and tissue products (Scott Paper), or for market pulp.

Pulp mills that use hardwoods in British Columbia are listed in Table 14 along with the products produced.

Pulp chips

Current markets for hardwood pulp chips produced in British Columbia are as follows:

Cottonwood	Scott Paper, New Westminster Export to the United States
Red alder	Export to the United States and Japan
Aspen	Domestic use as hog fuel in pulp mills

TABLE 14. British Columbia pulp mills currently consuming hardwoods (Source: R.J. Hyslop files)

Mill/location	Species	End use
Eurocan Pulp and Paper Kitimat	Cottonwood	Export chips
Louisiana-Pacific Canada Chetwynd	Aspen	Market pulp
Fibreco Pulp Taylor Flats	Aspen	Hog fuel
Quesnel River Pulp Quesnel	Aspen	Market pulp (Trial basis)
Scott Paper New Westminster	Cottonwood	Tissue paper

5.2.3 Future market opportunities

Although this report was not intended to provide an extensive survey and evaluation of future market opportunities, the following information was available from references and the consultants' files.

Logs

The major opportunities for increased log purchases are through the expansion of existing manufacturing facilities and the development of new processing facilities. Ainsworth Lumber's proposed OSB plant will use a mix of softwood residuals and aspen roundwood. This proposed mixture will increase the demand for aspen by some 100 000 m^3 annually.

Aside from domestic consumption, some potential exists to market hardwood logs to Southeast Asia. Korea has an annual demand for up to 350 000 m^3 of medium-grade aspen logs for chopsticks, matches, and other splint products. This market is under strong pressure from lower-cost supply in China and the Siberian region.

Sawnwood

Jensen International (1991)[9] reported on the opportunities for increased red alder sales in Europe, particularly in Italy and Germany.

Italy may represent a unique opportunity because its massive furniture industry—a heavy consumer of red alder and birch—has been reliant on supplies from the former Yugoslavia. Given the current conflict and disruption in that region, the Italian industry is seeking a reliable source of quality furniture stock.

Initial contact with these two major European markets may be established through the following trade organizations:

Germany	Zentralvrband des Raunausstater Handwerks Siemensstr. #6–12 W. 5300 Bonn #1, Germany
Italy	Federlegno – Arredo Via Toscana, 10 00187, Rome, Italy

Some opportunity may exist for the manufacture of air-dried aspen planks (1¾" x 6" x 12'). This low value product ($170 US per MFBM) is currently imported from Manitoba by Woodland Container of Minnesota. Shipping costs may limit market potential to local use, but the possibility exists to substitute aspen for higher-value coniferous lumber in some situations (Ryan 1992).

OSB/waferboard

As the softwood plywood industry in both the United States and Canada is further constrained by both economics and raw material shortages, demand and markets for OSB products will continue to expand.

Veneer

Thin rotary-peeled veneers are in high demand in the United States because of shortages of these materials from their own production plants and difficulty in securing safe foreign (tropical) supplies. The current demand for up to five carloads per week (equivalent to 530 m^3 of finished product or 1000 m^3 of raw logs) will likely grow as other supply areas become doubtful suppliers.

Preliminary contact to this potential market may be obtained through a listing of members and consumption from:

Hardwood Plywood Manufacturers' Association
P.O. Box 2789
Reston, VA 22090 USA

[9] Jensen International 1991. European alder market study. Prepared for Washington State Department of Trade and Economic Development. Unpub.

Plywood

Demand for poplar- or aspen-based plywood is not expected to increase significantly in the near future. While some special grades may find niche markets, the balance is not expected to change.

Pulp

Pulp from hardwoods will have to compete on world markets for a share of the available demand. Recycling, reduced use, and increased output from low-cost, fast-growth, short-fibre wood regions is expected to create strong competition.

Pulp chips

Opportunities for pulp chip sales at present are misleading. Although prices have remained high, the economic downturn in Japan has severely constrained shipments and placed pressure on current producers to divert to alternate uses, including hog fuel.

The pulp mills of the Puget Sound region of Washington are expected to increase consumption of hardwood chips as fibre shortages in that state develop, and it is expected that these mills will look to British Columbia for increased supply.

5.2.4 Current and historic market prices

Selling prices for hardwood products are not universally available from published sources. Where prices are available on a historic basis, they are fully reported in this section; where historic prices are not available, current selling prices have been reported.

Logs

Table 15 lists the current price ranges for raw logs as consumed by the British Columbia hardwood industry.

TABLE 15. Current hardwood log price range (July 1992) (Source: R.J. Hyslop files)

Species	Region	End use	$Cdn/m^3
Black cottonwood	Coast	Rotary veneer	40–52
	Coast	Groundwood	40–45
	Interior	Rotary veneer	30–35
Alder	Coast	Sawnwood	38–39
	Coast	Rotary veneer	40–42
	Coast	Sliced veneer	58–60
Birch	Coast	Sawnwood	40–42
	Coast	Sliced veneer	60–62
	Central Interior	Sliced veneer	45
	Central Interior	Rotary veneer	45
Aspen	Central Interior	Rotary veneer	45
	Central Interior	Chopsticks	35–45
	Central Interior	OSB	20–25[a]
	North Interior	Rotary veneer	32–35
	North Interior	OSB	21–21.50
	North Interior	Pulp	21–21.50
Balsam poplar	North Interior	OSB	21–21.50

[a] Projected log prices for Ainsworth Lumber's proposed plant.

Sawnwood

Historic prices for selected grades of red alder sawnwood are shown in Table 16. Table 17 presents the average July 1992 prices for these same grades of alder, birch, and pallet stock. Although historical prices of birch have not been shown here, the current price differential between birch and alder is virtually constant.

TABLE 16. Historic prices for selected grades of red alder sawnwood (annual averages, $US/MFBM) (Source: Hardwood Review – Annual, reported by R.J. Hyslop)

	Grade dimensions (Full sawn[a] – KD[b])		
Year	**4/4[c] Sel/Btr[d]**	**4/4 #1 Shop[e]**	**4/4 #2 Shop**
1985	719	324	225
1986	750	348	234
1987	755	362	235
1988	766	388	247
1989	873	472	277
1990	954	530	313

Table 17. Current prices for selected grades of red alder and birch sawnwood (western) ($US/MFBM)

	Grade (Full sawn[a] – KD[b], S2S[f])				
Species/dimensions	**Sel/Btr[d]**	**#1S[e]**	**#2S**	**#3S**	**Frame[g]**
Alder 4/4[c]	1040	575	325	270	355
5/4	1100	575	370	285	375
6/4	1175	600	435	350	n/a
8/4	1210	620	445	390	n/a
Birch 4/4	955	560	370	270	355
5/4	975	570	380	275	375
6/4	1020	590	410	310	n/a
8/4	1030	600	430	350	n/a
Pallet stock – both species					
1x4	245				
1x6	245				
2x6	255				

(Source: Weekly Hardwood Review, reported by R.J. Hyslop)

[a] Thickness shown is actual size as opposed to nominal size, which is less.
[b] Kiln Dried.
[c] Thickness in quarter inches (i.e., 4/4 = 1 inch).
[d] Selects and Better - composite of best three grades.
[e] Fourth grade (after selects) intended for further manufacture.
[f] Planed top and bottom - two surfaces.
[g] Grade suitable for framing furniture.

Chopsticks

Market prices for chopsticks have been highly variable and competitive in recent years. Pricing, which is based on a case lot of 5000 pairs of chopsticks, depends on the quality and level of distribution within both the Japanese and Taiwanese market systems. Current prices range from $Cdn 40–45 per case, FOB port, Japan.

Veneer

Historic prices of rotary-peeled thick veneer (1/10" and over) are presented in Table 18. Current prices for "thin" (1/16" and less) rotary-peeled veneers and sliced veneers are contained in Tables 19 and 20.

Plywood

Current prices for selected thicknesses and grades of hardwood plywoods are shown in Table 21.

OSB/waferboard

Table 22 lists the historic prices for 7/16" waferboard (FOB Toronto) for 1984–1992 (July). As all Canadian mills sell on a net delivered basis, net mill return must be estimated as delivered price less freight from point of origin.

TABLE 18. Historic green veneer prices for cottonwood/aspen veneer (rotary peeled, mill run, FOB mill) (Source: R.J. Hyslop)

Year	$US/MSF – 1/8" Basis
1981	29.00
1982	22.00
1983	25.25
1984	24.00
1985	22.50
1986	24.50
1987	24.50
1988	28.50
1989	35.00
1990	32.25
1991	31.25

TABLE 19. Current prices (July 1992) for thin hardwood veneers (rotary peeled, mill run, FOB mill)

Species	Thickness(in.)	Dry/Green	$US/MSF
Aspen	1/16	Dry	60.00
Birch	1/32	Green	45.00
Birch	1/32	Dry	61.60

TABLE 20. Current prices (July 1992) for sliced hardwood veneers (FOB mill) (Source: R.J. Hyslop)

Species	Thickness (in)	Dry/Green	Grade	$US/MSF
Birch/Maple	1/32	Dry	AA	115.00
			B	112.00
			C	110.00
			D	71.00
Alder	1/32	Dry	Mill run	75.00
Aspen	1/32	Dry	Mill run	75.00
Birch	1/32	Dry	Mill run	75.00

TABLE 21. Current (July 1992) hardwood plywood prices (FOB mill) (Source: R.J. Hyslop)

Species	Thickness (mm)	Grade	$Cdn/MSM
Aspen	6 (1/4")	S2S	368.00
Aspen	6	Carpet Strip	257.00
Poplar	19	Industrial	555.00
	11	Industrial	358.50

TABLE 22. Historic average selling price of OSB/waferboard (FOB Toronto, 7/16") (Source: Random Lengths Publications Inc., Eugene, Oregon)

Year	$Cdn/MSF
1984	196
1985	199
1986	206
1987	186
1988	172
1989	192
1990	147
1991	172
1992 (July)	228

Chip prices

The following measurements and conversion units are applied to chips:

BDU – Bone Dry Unit or 2400 pounds of oven-dry fibre.
BDT – Bone Dry Ton or 2000 pounds of oven-dry fibre.
SWE – Solid Wood Equivalent (m^3 green logs or bolts)

Species	SWE (m^3) per BDU	SWE (m^3) per BDT
Birch	2.2	1.8
Alder	2.8	2.3
Aspen	2.9	2.4
Cottonwood	3.2	2.7

Table 23 lists historic prices for red alder pulp chips (FOB vessel) in $US/BDU for 1982–July 1992. Table 24 lists prices for chips (alder, maple, and cottonwood) (FOB Tacoma) in $US/BDT for 1987–1991. As a point of comparison, Scott Paper's July 1992 purchase price for cottonwood chips ranged from $Cdn 50–55 per m^3, Solid Wood Equivalent.

Nawitka *et al.* (1990) indicated a provincial pulp chip price in 1989 at point of manufacture (coastal chipping plant) of 27.50–34.00 $Cdn per m^3 SWE for alder, and an estimated price stemming from overseas esquires of 27.50–30.00 $Cdn for aspen per m^3 SWE for the north-central Interior.

Pulp

Market pulp prices for aspen (short-fibre) pulp, (FOB B.C.) closely follow the market for short-fibre pulps from other producing regions. A current (July 1992) range of price is $US 540–555/tonne, CIF Northern Europe.

TABLE 23. Historic red alder pulp chip prices (FOB vessel)

Year		$US/BDU
1982	- 1[a]	87.50
	- 2[b]	91.00
1983	- 1	86.00
	- 2	86.00
1984	- 1	87.00
	- 2	88.00
1985	- 1	90.75
	- 2	89.25
1986	- 1	90.25
	- 2	91.75
1987	- 1	96.00
	- 2	96.00
1988	- 1	104.50
	- 2	111.00
1989	- 1	117.00
	- 2	124.50
1990	- 1	114.00
	- 2	113.00
1991	- 1	121.00
	- 2	120.00
1992	- 1	117.00

[a] Jan. - June
[b] July - Dec.

TABLE 24. Hardwood pulp chip prices (FOB Tacoma) (Source: Simpson Timber Company, reported by R.J. Hyslop)

Year	$US/BDT
1987	56.00
1988	71.00
1989	83.00
1990	77.00
1991	82.00

5.2.5 Specifications

For many deciduous-based products, existing published standards are either nonexistent or not applicable. In many instances (e.g., log sales), specific standards are developed and set by the buyer based on his product requirement, or are simply mutually agreed between buyer and seller. For other products, such as OSB, waferboard, and plywood, standards are published by government organizations such as the Canadian Standards Association (CSA), U.S. Product Standards (USPS), Japanese Agricultural Standards (JAS), and established industry organizations such as the National Hardwood Lumber Association (NHLA).

Simons (1991)[10] and Thomson (1992)[11] have clearly indicated the importance of the raw material requirements and specifications for hardwood products. These risks are not repeated in this section.

Specifications applicable to British Columbia are summarized in Appendix 8. Where published specifications exist, the applicable specification is cited. Specific buyer-seller specifications in use are given in summary form. Company developed detailed specifications are also provided.

[10] Simons Strategic Services Division. 1991. The hardwood processing sector in British Columbia.

[11] Thomson, T.M. and Associates. 1992. Kispiox Forest District hardwood management strategy.

5.3 Economic Benefits

5.3.1 Current employment and income

To estimate employment in the British Columbia forest sector, employment coefficients were compiled from recognized sources that indicate employment per 1000 m^3 of timber harvested. These coefficients were then adjusted to depict a hardwood rather than a conifer situation. Three types of utilization were considered:

- the manufacture of a mix of products,
- hardwood chip export, and
- hardwood log export.

These coefficients are shown in Table 25. In general, hardwood resource use should create as much, if not more, employment than conifers on a per unit volume basis, provided the industry is well developed, a variety of products is produced, and remanufacturing and secondary manufacturing occur. This is not the case in British Columbia, and during the development period less employment than in the more-developed coniferous situation will occur until the industry matures.

TABLE 25. Employment per 1000 m^3 of timber harvested in British Columbia

	Current mix (mainly coniferous timber)[a]	Estimated for deciduous timber		
Activity	All products	Mixed products	Chip export	Log export
Logging	0.25	0.18	0.18	0.20
Wood industries	0.49	0.41[b]	0.26	nil
Pulp and allied	0.22	0.19	n/a	nil
Forestry services	0.17	0.05	0.05	0.05
Transportation	0.12	0.12	0.06	0.06
Wholesale trade	0.01	nil	nil	0.01
Total	1.26	0.95	0.55	0.32

[a] Based on B.C. Ministry of Forests, Economics and Trade Branch (1991) unpublished estimates for 1984–88 updated with Statistics Canada data for 1989 and 1990. Forestry services, transportation, and wholesale trade coefficients estimated from Dobie (1992).

[b] Includes some remanufacture and secondary manufacture.

Income from employment was compiled on a similar basis (i.e., per 1000 m^3 of harvest) by the Forest Resources Commission (1992). These annual incomes are less than those reported by larger firms and firms with union employees. They include small firms as well as firms that may operate only seasonally. Table 26 shows the 1990 income by type of activity and the income per 1000 m^3 of harvest for each activity.

Tables 27 and 28 show the employment and income from the utilization of the hardwood resource. They were compiled using the previous two tables and the annual harvest reported by Simons (1991)[12] for 1989–90. The type of use was estimated to be 70% mixed products, 25% chips for export, and 5% log exports. Total employment was estimated using a multiplier of 3.4, which has been used in the province for planning purposes (Ministry of Finance and Corporate Relations 1991).[13] This multiplier is slightly less than the one estimated by Baack (1989) for the well-established Oregon hardwood industry (i.e., 3.6). Total income was estimated using a multiplier of 2.2. This is slightly higher than the 2.0 recommended by Marvin Shaffer and Associates (1992)[14] for the B.C. Integrated Resource Planning Committee, but less than the 2.3 estimated by Baack (1989) for the Oregon hardwood industry.

[12] Simons Strategic Services Division. 1991. The hardwood processing sector in British Columbia.

[13] Ministry of Finance and Corporate Relations. 1991. The structure of the B.C. economy: a land use perspective. Unpubl. rep. for B.C. Round Table on the Environment and the Economy.

[14] Marvin Schaffer and Assoc. Ltd. 1992. Social and economic impact assessments of forest land management options. Unpubl. rep. for The Province of B.C. Integrated Resource Planning Committee.

TABLE 26. Estimated employment income in the forest sector (1990) per 1000 m^3 of current deciduous timber harvest (Source: Forest Resources Commission [1992] and previous employment estimates)

Activity	Annual income (1990)	Estimated income: Current harvest	Estimated income for deciduous: Mixed products	Chip export	Log export
Logging	$37 660	$ 9 415	$ 6 780	$ 6 780	$7 530
Wood industries	38 550	18 890	15 805	10 025	nil
Pulp and allied	38 550	8 480	7 325	n/a	nil
Forestry services	37 660	6 400	1 885	1 885	1 885
Transportation	35 170	4 220	4 220	2 110	2 110
Wholesale trade	27 790	280	nil	n/a	280
Total direct income		47 685	36 015	20 800	11 805

TABLE 27. Employment attributable to the 1989–1990 level of hardwood use

Use	Volume[a] (000 m3)	Employment in person years: Direct	Indirect and induced	Total
Mixed products	990	940	2256	3196
Chip export	360	198	475	673
Log export	75	24	58	82
All hardwood use	1425	1162	2789	3951

[a] Compiled on the basis of Simons Strategic Services Division. 1991. The hardwood processing sector in British Columbia. Unpubl. rep. The new pulp mill recently completed near Chetwynd will add significant employment and income. The estimating procedure developed in this section can be used to estimate this additional employment and income.

Based on a harvest of 1.425 million m^3 of hardwoods in 1989–1990, direct employment was estimated to be just under 1200 jobs and total employment just under 4000 jobs. About 2800 jobs (indirect and induced employment) were created by the direct jobs. The same harvest created about $44 million in direct employment income and about $97 million in total employment income.

5.3.2 Current harvest comparison

Table 29 shows the employment and employment income based on the total timber harvest compared to the previous hardwood estimates. The hardwood component contributes just over 1% of the employment and employment income for the forest sector in British Columbia.

5.3.3 Potential employment and income

If hardwood use increased to the magnitude estimated in Table 12 and the type of use (mixed products, chip exports, log exports) remained in the same proportion, employment and employment income estimates can be made using the previously established coefficients and multipliers. These estimates are shown in Tables 30 and 31. A harvest of about 7 million m^3 would provide about 5700 direct jobs, as well as 13 700 indirect and induced jobs. Employment income for the direct jobs would total about $217 million and a further $260 million would accrue to indirect and induced employment. Both employment and income from employment would increase as the industry matured.

TABLE 28. Employment income attributable to the current level of hardwood use (1989–90)

		Employment income (million $)		
Use	Volume (000 m^3)	Direct	Indirect and induced	Total
Mixed products	990	35.7	42.8	78.5
Chip export	360	7.5	9.0	16.5
Log export	75	0.9	1.1	2.0
All hardwood use	1425	44.1	52.9	97.0

Table 29. Employment and employment income comparison, total timber harvest versus deciduous harvest, 1989–1990 (Source: Derived from previous tables and the B.C. Ministry of Forests' Annual Report)

		Employment (person-years)		Income (million $)	
Harvest	Volume (mil m^3)	Direct	Total	Direct	Total
Total harvest	86.935	109 538	372 430	4 145.5	9 120.1
Hardwood component	1.425	1 162	3 951	44.1	97.0
Softwood component	85.51	108 376	368 479	4 101.4	9 023.1

TABLE 30. Employment attributable to hardwood use if estimated 20-year annual harvest materializes

		Employment (person-years)		
Use	Volume (000 m^3)	Direct	Indirect and induced	Total
Mixed products	4 892.6	4 648	11 155	15 803
Chip export	1 747.3	961	2 306	3 267
Log export	349.5	112	269	381
All hardwood	6 989.4	5 721	13 730	19 451

TABLE 31. Employment income attributable to hardwood use if estimated 20-year annual harvest materializes

		Income from employment (million $)		
Use	Volume (000 m^3)	Direct	Indirect and induced	Total
Mixed products	4 892.6	176.2	211.4	387.6
Chip export	1 747.3	36.3	43.6	79.9
Log export	349.5	4.1	4.9	9.0
All hardwood use	6 989.4	216.6	259.9	476.5

6 IMPLICATIONS FOR HARDWOOD DEVELOPMENT, MANAGEMENT AND RESEARCH

6.1 New Utilization Policies

Development and utilization of hardwoods will not follow the same pattern as softwoods. Softwoods support a sawnwood economy in which the chips derived from lumber manufacture are the major pulp mill input. Some hardwood chips from sawing may be pulped, but unlike softwoods, most of the volume will be used at pulp mills or board plants. If, for economic reasons, a large volume use cannot be established, the export of pulp chips may have to be considered. On a small local scale, the manufacture of lower-grade lumber, such as pallet, may support harvesting in some stands.

The quality of hardwoods is as important, if not more important than with softwoods. Most hardwood uses are based on high-quality wood with the volume uses, such as pulp and oriented strand board, based on moderate quality. Few, if any, uses are available for poor-quality wood, except perhaps firewood. Small specialty plants that demand quality timber can only use 10–25% of the merchantable stand volume. Without the development of volume uses, these plants are unlikely to establish. In British Columbia, where many stands are mature and overmature, quality is going to be a major issue.

6.2 Excessive Mature and Overmature Stands

Hardwoods, unlike softwoods, do not improve in quality once they age beyond a certain point. Hardwood stands will need to be considered on a pathological rotation, depending on management, site, and species. This poses a serious problem of (1) how to handle initial short-term uses; and (2) how to plan for future use based on vigorously growing higher-quality younger stands.

Under condition (1) stand recycling will need serious consideration; under condition (2) close utilization will not be feasible initially, but may become so in the longer term.

Stands that have a small amount of usable volume may require a combination of salvage and recycling. Planning for defective mature and overmature stands will be more of a policy and management problem than a use problem.

6.3 Hardwood Manufacturing Equipment

Hardwood lumber and veneer, and specialty items (e.g., flooring) need to be cut with equipment designed and manufactured for hardwood use. Several milling enterprises were established but failed because of inadequate financing and poor-quality timber. However, this frequently given general reason is not really accurate. Many of the enterprises failed when softwood milling equipment (frequently second-hand) was used because new hardwood equipment was not available (i.e., was too expensive). Also, too high a volume of the stand was supposed to be, or estimated to be, merchantable. In essence, a severe product grade decrease occurred because fewer quality logs were delivered to the mill than was anticipated, and improper manufacturing equipment was used. These mills are highly dependent on grade-related revenues. If low volumes of high-grade product are produced, then revenue is drastically reduced and the enterprise generally fails.

The following conditions are vital if small, quality hardwood manufacturing firms, or small, quality milling units, in conjunction with a higher-volume use (i.e., pulp mill, pulp chips, board plant; pallet, dunnage, plank mill; hog fuel, firewood) are to be successful.

a) Do not attempt to support high-quality hardwood product manufacture with cheap access to low-quality hardwoods. The enterprise will usually incur a very serious waste or waste disposal problem. The key is to avoid low-quality stands, and use good- and moderate-quality stands with a minimal low-quality component. Some wood may be directed to volume uses but, in many cases, either waste disposal or recycling will be needed in stands that have a significant low-quality component. Both research and policy are required before industry location decisions are made.

b) Do not allocate moderate- or high-quality stands to supporting a manufacturing enterprise unless manufacturing equipment specifically designed for hardwoods is to be used. The following should be considered:

Sawn products: The mill will use hardwood sawing and handling equipment, and the system will be configured to cut logs or bolts of 16 feet *or less*. The mill will have or will have access to a hardwood dry kiln with a humidity control system for hardwood drying.

Veneer: The mill will be designed for hardwood manufacture and equipped with hardwood lathes or slicers. It will have hardwood drying capability if appropriate.

6.4 Tenure and Allocation

As hardwood use increases, policies for resource allocation and tenure will need to be revised. Further development of tenure agreements that deal specifically with hardwoods and mixedwoods may also be necessary. The replacement of mature and overmature stands with young high-quality hardwood stands, as well as mixedwood forest management, has implications for the levels of softwood harvest. This will have to be reconciled and recognized to support forest product manufacture. More attention should be directed toward the costs of producing the specific timber inputs for manufacture and the contributions of manufacturing to the provincial economy. It may be necessary to consider which species or mixes incur the least management costs or provide the better return, especially when it is biologically sound and when significant value-added opportunities exist.

6.5 New Forest Management

While hardwood management techniques and practices in North America are well known and well documented, their application in British Columbia may require some adaptation and revision. Foresters and other forestry professionals in the province will have to improve and develop their expertise in the area of hardwood management. With increasing public awareness and attention to integrated resource management, trial and error will not be acceptable. In addition to manuals and reference materials, workshops and continuing education will likely be required at a more specific level (e.g., working groups attacking specific problems as opposed to symposia).

Hardwood management will present a new and unique set of integrated resource management problems. One area of concern surrounds the imposition of hardwood management on a land base where the coniferous component was managed but the deciduous component was not. In general, if both hardwood and softwood lands are managed for forest production, will new integrated management concerns arise? If hardwood lands are managed, will there be any new effects or implications for adjacent areas managed for softwoods that are not being considered now? And, would integrated resource management improve if mixedwood management increases?

Intensive management of hardwoods may involve more attention to volume and shorter rotations. Piece size is a major concern in softwood intensive management. If piece size is of less concern, at least with some hardwoods, will cultivation, genetics, less diversity, and establishment of dense, fast-growing plantations on a smaller, more intensively managed land area increase land use conflicts?

To date, the word "plantation" in British Columbia has only meant "planted." In other jurisdictions it also implies the intense cultivation and management of a forest crop. Some lands in the province, managed by Scott Paper Company for cottonwood, have this connotation.

The costs and benefits of silviculture investments in hardwoods need to be estimated and compared to coniferous silviculture investments. While the costs involved are relatively easy to estimate, the benefits are not. Studies to determine the size and stability of long-term markets for a variety of species and products will be required. In some cases, more valuable coniferous products will justify high silviculture investment costs, but in others they may not. In parts of the province, growing more hardwoods and fewer conifers may not be a viable option. Hardwood products usually cannot be substituted for softwood products. The selection of appropriate management techniques will depend heavily on market analyses for species-related products.

6.6 Harvesting Systems and Policies

Harvesting of hardwoods will differ from softwoods in many situations. On the Coast, highlead and grapple yarding equipment designed for large conifer logs will generally not be appropriate for hardwoods. Also, whole-tree or long-log harvesting may or may not be used. In some cases short-log or pulpwood systems will be applicable. High-quality hardwood logs for sawing should be over 10 feet but need not necessarily be 16 feet long.

Hardwoods are usually skidded by track or rubber-tired vehicles and some species (e.g., birch) are frequently harvested in the winter. Soil compaction (particularly under spring conditions) should be avoided and skidtrails must be laid out to minimize residual stock damage when selection harvesting is used. Whole-tree harvesting may not be appropriate in some areas as nutrient removal can occur when tops are taken from the site. Other alternatives include limbing and winter harvesting.

In some regions or locations where large volumes of hardwoods are moved to a central manufacturing point, weight scaling is used. This procedure can improve efficiency and lower delivered wood costs; however, animosity may develop between buyer and sellers if good conversion factors are not available. In most cases, seasonal woods-run weight moisture content relationships can be developed and used. Applied research or testing may be necessary to support the above.

6.7 Additional Inventory Needs

Hardwood use and management will require new and revised inventory statistics. Three different areas need additional effort:

1. A summary reporting system that focuses on hardwoods and/or mixedwoods as opposed to, or in addition to, softwoods.

2. Revised definition and attribute verification are needed. In British Columbia, forest inventory defines a stand as mature at 80 years of age. This is too high for most hardwoods. The definition of maturity for hardwoods should consider pathological rotations of less than 80 years. Data are also needed to strengthen and verify age classes and height classes. Not satisfactorily restocked (NSR) land and non-commercial brush (NCBr) may require additional field updating where reversion to hardwoods has occurred. Decay, waste, and breakage factors need to be further developed, particularly for younger or near-mature stands. Site index definition needs to be further refined for hardwoods. Technically this would include more research and operational application of top heights in hardwood stand measurement. Also, more emphasis should be placed on

improved definition of the hardwood components in mixed stands.

3. Improved growth-and-yield data and information are necessary for the longer-term allocation, utilization, and management of hardwoods. Growth predictions for a variety of types or species and site conditions are needed for modelling and strategic planning.

6.8 Ecological Research Needs for Hardwoods

The four areas defined by the Hardwood and Vegetation Management Technical Advisory Committee are as follows, in decreasing order of priority:

1. **Integrated Resource Management**, to provide information on nontimber resources associated with hardwood forests, and the impacts of use and management of hardwood forests on nontimber resources;

2. **Forest Health**, including investigations into the nature, impacts, and control of organisms that damage hardwoods, and into the role of hardwoods in maintaining forest health;

3. **Hardwood Silviculture**, to provide information on the effectiveness and appropriateness of silvicultural treatments; and

4. **Ecology**, including site selection, stand dynamics, and site productivity studies to assist in operational decision-making.

Three of these priorities—forest health, hardwood silviculture, and ecology—provide a basis for research planners in the B.C. Ministry of Forests and Forestry Canada to group the research suggestions in Sections 3.4 and 3.5, as well as those suggested in Sections 6.8.1 to 6.8.4. The subsections that follow complement the research suggestions made in Sections 3.4 and 3.5 by focusing on linkages among use, management, and ecology; the role of hardwoods in more intensive stand-tending practices; and the influence of hardwoods upon insects and diseases that create diversity in forest landscapes. Subsection 6.8.4 provides a synopsis of hardwood-related research suggested by several other analysts. Subsection 6.8.5 is a summary of suggestions for the highest priority hardwood-related research.

6.8.1 Linkages among use, management, and ecological research needs

Research required to improve the existing knowledge of ecological characteristics of British Columbia's hardwood species should not be defined in isolation from trends in use and management practices. There are close linkages among research needs in ecology, management, and utilization. The ecological information required to encourage more uses of British Columbia's hardwoods will change as the uses of this resource change.

There are two possible approaches to determining information requirements. The traditional one is for the forest manager to say: "Here are the ecological realities of hardwood and mixedwood stands, now what can we do with these resources, within the limits of those realities, using today's utilization and manufacturing technologies?" This is favoured by research managers who prefer a proactive approach to studies into basic ecological processes. It is also the approach that provides the greatest possibility of available information when unexpected technological advances occur in forest use and management.

Another possible approach is for the forest manager to begin with the question: "Here are today's technological and utilization realities, now what ecological information do we need to make the best use of these realities for British Columbia's hardwood resource?" An advantage of this approach is that it encourages researchers to respond to unanticipated changes in industrial uses of forest resources. However, defensible data may take several years to obtain, often after a management or use change has started on an operational scale.

In practice, the two approaches should be considered complementary when defining and designing ecological research. Because the second approach is less traditional than the first, some examples are given below to suggest how it might be applied to hardwood-related research planning.

Examples of recent changes in hardwood use that will require different kinds of ecological information for Interior hardwoods include: increased use of panelboard and pulping facilities that can economically use small-stemmed raw material; increased use of whole-tree harvesting methods; increased use of chunkwood systems, and the use of forest residue and total tree woody biomass; increased use of chippers at harvest sites, and field drying of harvested material, with crown and foliage intact during the drying process, to improve the efficiency of field chipping and transport of chips.

These examples suggest that new standards, which involve the use of ever-smaller biomass pieces and an increase in the range of acceptable woody species, together with increased conversion directly at the harvest site, will create new kinds of post-harvest ecological conditions. Therefore, ecological studies should be designed to provide better information on the structural dimensions of forest stands and the dimensions of all woody components of all usable hardwood species. Slash, forest floor, and nutrition management are other recommended areas of research.

Ecological research priorities for hardwood species will be increasingly defined by what managers and users are doing with the trees. This will include, at one end of the spectrum, stands and forests that are mainly used as areas for watershed management, recreational use, or wildlife management. At the other end of the spectrum is the management for maximum biomass production with the highest level of use technologically possible. For the latter case, future ecological research will need to give more attention to fundamental **morphological features,** such as crown dimensions, relative proportions of various biomass components, branch sizes, and branch integrity during transport; and **physiological processes,** such as seasonal changes in water content, field drying of harvested material, and nutrient cycling phenomena (Peterson *et al.* 1989a).

These research trends will not replace the need for traditional autecological and synecological studies that define growth patterns for individual hardwood species and interspecific relations within hardwood-dominated ecosystems. For example, there is a need to more precisely quantify the overall abundance and significance of hardwoods in each of the province's biogeoclimatic zones and subzones, with the highest priority given to the relative importance of hardwoods in the most productive ecosystems of any given subzone.

6.8.2 The trend to increased stand-tending procedures

Stand tending is increasingly recognized as an essential component of sustainable forest development. As Mitchell (1992) and other analysts have concluded, this means that research on responses to stand tending must continue to be broadened, from studies of diameter and volume growth, to studies of crown development, leaf nutrition, and integration of below- and aboveground responses. Such information is required to develop more refined growth models.

The gradually increasing potential of hardwood species underlines the importance of Mitchell's conclusion that silviculture in established stands should minimize any limitations that decisions made today might place on future options. Utilization changes can give economic value to previously unwanted tree species. This will change the forest manager's challenges and opportunities. The marked differences that exist between hardwoods and softwoods of production structure (stem, branch, and crown dimensions), regeneration strategies, nutrient relations, longevity, and place in successional sequences mean that the addition of management responsibility for one hardwood species has a greater impact on the silviculturist's opportunities than would the addition of one coniferous species. Also, increasing interest in managing for biodiversity is expected to change how hardwoods are viewed when they occur in conifer stands.

Observations on competition between paper birch and planted Douglas-fir (Simard 1990) indicate the need for a more detailed documentation of the hypothesis that there are specific ecological competition thresholds where deciduous and coniferous species co-exist. As in other vegetation management research, this would require studies of both paper birch and Douglas-fir to obtain information on physiological responses to competition, and effects of that competition on site productivity, soil development, and ecosystem diversity. The competition concepts developed by Simard (1990) for paper birch–Douglas-fir also need to be investigated for other mixedwood combinations, such as aspen–lodgepole pine or aspen–white spruce.

6.8.3 Influence of hardwoods on diseases and insects that create diversity in forest landscapes

Forest managers have been slow to recognize that native forest pathogens are major agents of spatial and temporal diversity in forests, responsible for creation of special habitats, influencing the speed and direction of succession, as well as the structure of subsequent forest stands (van der Kamp 1991). Hardwoods have an ecological role in this context. For example, van der Kamp gave examples from interior British Columbia where early successional stands of conifers, especially Douglas-fir, dominate the landscape. Within these uniform stands are patches, often tens of hectares in size, of mixed conifer and hardwood cover. These patches of mixed forest serve as root disease centres for *Armillaria ostoyae* and *Phellinus weirii*. The centres are probably very old, possibly a thousand or more years. The result, in infected areas, is a mixed forest in which more disease-resistant hardwoods (birch, cottonwood, and aspen) assume a dominant position.

The mixed-forest communities created by these pathogens are regarded by van der Kamp as root disease climaxes, typically with a well-developed brush and herb layer. This understorey is often heavily browsed by ungulates, and the combination of cover in the surrounding conifer stands and browse available in the root disease centres may provide near optimum conditions for moose and deer. Also, these root disease centres create a constant supply of snags in all stages of deterioration, thus providing essential habitat for cavity-nesting birds. These cavity nesters, in turn, may play a role in insect population regulation in the disease centres and in the surrounding forests. Other forest features are also modified in root disease centres. More open stands might lead to deeper snow accumulation and possibly slower snowmelt. Root diseases create special habitats that may favour plant and animal species not well adapted to living in dense, even-aged coniferous stands.

The strategic roles of hardwoods for silviculturally manipulated disease control are not as well developed as they could be. For example, in the southern Interior no tree species shows resistance to *Armillaria ostoyae* before age 15, with the possible exception of paper birch. Early survival of conifers, such as western larch, might therefore be enhanced if planted in a mix with birch (Morrison *et al.* 1991). Hardwoods are also immune to the Douglas-fir variety of *Phellinus weirii.*

The strategic importance of mixed hardwood–softwood stands deserves to be quantified in more detail. The example above is based on root diseases, but the role of hardwood and mixedwood stands in insect control and insect influences over forest succession equally deserve more research attention, as suggested for alder by Massie (1990) and aspen–balsam poplar by Peterson and Peterson (1992).

6.8.4 Other recently suggested hardwood-related research needs

Although there has been a recent survey of forest research in British Columbia (Binkley and Watts 1992), the 10 forest research categories used were not specific to either softwoods or hardwoods, nor to mixed stands of softwoods and hardwoods. The most up-to-date information on hardwood-related research is being assembled by Marilyn Blache, Hardwood Management Program Administrator, Research Branch, B.C. Ministry of Forests. The summary identifies 29 research projects that deal with hardwoods. A simplified breakdown of research topics by species is provided in Table 32.

Several research priorities for paper birch and black cottonwood were recently suggested by Perala and Alm (1990a) and Simard and Vyse (1992). These include a better understanding of the semi-persistent birch seedbanks in the forest floor, and the exact nature and form of the organic-matter seedbeds necessary for germination and growth of healthy stands of birch (Perala and Alm 1990a).

TABLE 32. Summary of current British Columbia research related to hardwoods, 1993[a]

Species	Research topics under investigation in 1992–93
All hardwoods	Strategic assessment of the hardwood resource (the present study); impacts of hardwood management on wildlife; stand dynamics and growth models of mixed-species stands.
Red alder	Spacing studies; influences on conifer growth and whole-stand yield; stand-tending regimes in relation to growth and yield; influences of alder control on growth of conifers; use of alder to enhance Sitka spruce growth; geographic variation in germination rate, seedling growth, biomass production, phenology, and nitrogen fixation; wildlife diversity in alder stands; decay in harvested alder logs and identity of fungal organisms involved in decay; use of alder in managing *Phellinus* root disease.
Paper birch	Thinning trials; species interactions between birch and conifer seedlings; suitability for reforestation and effects on soil nutrient status; biomass study and estimates of birch contribution to site nutrient capital; effects of mixedwood forest management on bird species; *Armillaria* root disease study in pure and mixed birch stands.
Aspen and/or balsam poplar	Microenvironments under aspen canopies in relation to spruce seedling performance; stand-tending strategies to maximize productivity; suitability for reforestation and effects on soil nutrient status; effects of aspen density and stocking on conifer plantation performance; carbon budgets and sustainable production of aspen and mixedwood stands; changes in bird diversity and abundance after aspen clearcutting; diversity of bird assemblages at different seral stages of aspen; effects of mixedwood forest management on bird species; significance of site in predicting decay in aspen; diagnostic tools for diseases of native and hybrid poplars; database for growth modelling of aspen and aspen-conifer stands.
Black cottonwood	Suitability for reforestation and effects on soil nutrient status; poplar demonstration plantation and growth of irrigated versus nonirrigated plantations; analysis of cottonwood management problems and related research needs; diagnostic tools for diseases of native and hybrid poplars.

[a] Information provided by M. Blache, Hardwood Management Program Administrator, Research Branch, B.C. Ministry of Forests.

Research priorities recommended for paper birch and black cottonwood by Simard and Vyse (1992) include:

- classification of sites as good or excellent for growth of paper birch, black cottonwood, and mixedwood;
- refinement of existing ecosystem classification for paper birch and black cottonwood types to assist regeneration strategies;
- trials to determine appropriate densities, proportions, and spacings of hardwoods and conifers;
- development of target and free-growing stocking standards in relation to ecosystem, age, density, and species proportions; birch thinning trials to determine any increased growth and yield;
- identity of sites that have the best potential for birch lumber or veneer production;
- trials to determine the best age for release and greatest conifer growth, and methods of overstorey removal with minimal damage;
- studies to determine the effects of root rot on birch, and how birch affects the persistence and spread of root rot;
- competition studies to define the effect of neighbouring vegetation on birch growth; and
- long-term ecosystem studies of managed stand growth and yield and the effects of management practices on stand dynamics, including the nutrient capital lost from whole-tree harvesting.

McLennan and Mamias (1992) provide detailed, categorized research recommendations for black cottonwood according to research topic, forest region, management system, and extensive, intensive, or mixedwood management. Many topics parallel those suggested by Simard and Vyse (1992) for black cottonwood, but they also recommended research to determine the role of black cottonwood as a tool for enhancing wildlife and fish habitat, the use of cottonwood as a nurse species to regenerate shade-tolerant conifers, collection and evaluation of cottonwood genetic material, and further study of existing intensively managed cottonwood plantations.

The 16 research needs identified by Peterson and Peterson (1992) for boreal aspen and balsam poplar apply equally to northeastern British Columbia as they do to the mixedwood section in the prairie provinces. Those that pertained to ecological and silvicultural concerns dealt with:

- humus layer dynamics;
- root information for various age classes and in various proportions of mixedwood species composition, since regeneration silviculture for those species is mainly manipulation of clonal root systems;
- more detail on conifer-hardwood interspecific relations;
- more inventory detail on growth and yield for the hardwood component of boreal mixedwood stands;
- additional information on the epidemiology of *Armillaria* and other root rots in managed aspen stands;
- increased attention to insects and diseases in young aspen stands; and
- methods to better incorporate wildlife management criteria into hardwood and mixedwood silviculture.

A recent review by Massie (1990) emphasized the need for better information on growth and yield, age-class distributions, and stocking for red alder. Massie also pointed out that there has been relatively little work on insects and diseases associated with alder. Other research needs noted for alder include:

information on managed second-growth alder as a forest crop in both pure stands and in mixture with conifers; and the role of alder as a buffer zone along streams and small lakes, particularly in relation to land management for both habitat protection and timber production.

6.8.5 Summary of highest priority research needs

Research priorities for the areas of forest health, hardwood silviculture, and ecology are outlined below in descending order:

Forest health

1. Better definition of the ecological basis for the nurse crop concept for each of the main hardwood species.
2. Increased attention to disease and insect influences in young stands of the key hardwood species.
3. Continued documentation of the circumstances and ecosystems in which hardwoods may play a moderating role on diseases or insects of importance in coniferous or mixedwood stands.
4. More precise definition of site associations where a silvicultural choice between hardwood versus softwood species would aid forest health through long-term management of nitrogen supply, a major determinant of forest productivity.
5. Hydrologic comparisons of hardwood, softwood, and mixedwood stands in relation to snow and rainfall interception, snowmelt rates, subsurface and overland flow of water, and water quality.

Hardwood silviculture

1. Continued search for innovative ways to encourage and manage conifers and deciduous species in mixedwood stands.
2. Better definition of the circumstances where deciduous–conifer mixtures, including silvicultural underplanting of conifer seedlings, might enhance the wood supply of both hardwood and softwood components.
3. Improved background information on desirable stocking levels for hardwoods, particularly in relation to incremental silviculture.
4. Increased attention to silvicultural methods for maximizing the beneficial role of hardwoods in riparian zone management.
5. More precise information (except for black cottonwood where there is already a good information base) on the definitions of hardwood maturity in managed and unmanaged stands, and in relation to presence or absence of conifers.

Ecology

1. Better quantification of the hardwood-dominated land areas involved and the hardwood biomass production rates in the most productive ecosystems of the province's biogeoclimatic zones and subzones.
2. Long-term studies of managed stand growth in hardwood and mixedwood stands, and the effects of management practices on stand dynamics, including the nutrient capital lost from whole-tree harvesting.
3. Continued definition of competition thresholds in various conifer–deciduous mixtures that occur naturally in the province.
4. Increased attention to soil and humus factors that influence vegetative reproduction of the main hardwood species.
5. Increased attention to hardwood features that influence whole-tree use, including tree dimensions, production structure, and physiological characteristics.

6.9 Summary of Multiple Resource Use Concerns

The main deciduous stand management areas and the multiple resource use importance values for areas of the province with an abundant hardwood component can be further classified and condensed in Table 33.

6.10 Sources of Uncertainty and Management Concerns

6.10.1 Summary of the sources of uncertainty

The following data gaps or interpretive problems with the information base were identified:

1. Some inaccuracies of pure deciduous age class: Many of the current age classes for deciduous leading inventory type groups at the young and old ends of the age distribution may have been statistically derived from older data during inventory updating without factoring in the life history of deciduous species. Therefore, many of the age classes for deciduous and conifer inventory type groups are greater than 81 years. Sixty years has been identified as the age of maturity for aspen, so presumably stands may no longer be dominated by broken-up deciduous, although they may have a juvenile deciduous understorey with some veterans in the overstorey. Therefore areas of hardwoods may be underestimated for the younger stages in pure deciduous and overestimated for the older stages. Accurate age classes are required for interpretation of wildlife habitat suitability and capability, especially when managing seral or "overmature" using species with large territory sizes and specific habitat requirements.

2. Some inaccuracies exist for mixedwood age class: Because of the same concerns expressed in item 1, some of the coniferous-deciduous and deciduous-coniferous inventory type groups may no longer have deciduous components if they were first identified as old-aged (e.g., >50 years) during the last air photo interpretation. Those deciduous tree species still retained in the inventory statistics as leading species are now, through succession, either secondary or broken-up. It is not known how extensive these inaccuracies are, or are likely to be.

3. Multiple resource data are missing (Enns *et al.* 1992): Because of the recent shift from managing game fish, game animals, and only selected recreational activities to a broader mandate, the multiple resource management sector is lacking information to assess the potential conflicts between the hardwood industry and multiple resource use. A set of poorly known species and recreational opportunities now exist within the hardwood resource.

   - Baseline data requirements include: fish and wildlife species occurrence, habitat utilization patterns, critical habitats, identification of vulnerable periods of lifecycles, range sizes, and subsequent data on the impacts of management on those variables.

   - Little is known about the response of wildlife and fish to harvesting of hardwoods, and how that response changes over time and with various post-harvest management scenarios.

   - Linkage between primary and secondary cavity users in hardwoods targeted for harvesting need to be identified.

4. The age-related ecological characteristics of hardwoods and hardwood stands are poorly known. There is a lack of information about stand structural changes and plant community changes over time in deciduous stands. These unknowns have made it impossible to quantify (except in a rudimentary way) the characteristics of hardwoods as they relate to wildlife habitat use or habitat changes over time. This may cause problems in integrating wildlife and recreational needs with the hardwood rotation.

TABLE 33. Location of hardwood use and classification for multiple resource use discussions

Location	Leading species	Wildlife/fisheries recreation potential
South Coast; Vancouver	Alder, cottonwood, bigleaved maple exist in mostly pre-harvested stands of a mid- to late-seral stage, some overmature stages.	High small mammal and bird diversity; moderate (relative) recreation use of forests; important riparian fisheries habitat; native land claims an issue. Some concerns about whether areas should be conifer regenerated, and how to integrate wildlife habitat.
South-central Interior; Williams Lake, Quesnel, 100 Mile House, Kamloops	Aspen and birch stands in mostly fire-mediated stands, now mainly a mixedwood, with spruce or lodgepole pine co-dominant. Part of the "Interior Hardwood Band."	Cavity-nesting birds; a wide variety of wildlife needs, especially ungulates; occasionally adjacent to important inland streams and lakes for fish; high recreation use for nature viewing, fishing. Native land claims may be an issue. Some concerns about oriented strandboard plant and commercial use of hardwood becoming active; most management is still for vegetation control in coniferous plantation.
Northern Interior; Prince George	Aspen, birch, mixedwood, some relatively young stages.	Ungulate habitat, trapping and hunting are important, recreational use of forests is moderate, Native Land Claims an issue.
Central Coast; Kalum, Bulkley	Aspen, birch and mixedwood in late mature to overmature stages. Northern reach of "Interior Hardwood Band."	Birds, small and large furbearing mammals are important and under considerable scientific scrutiny. Passive recreational use is very high relative to the rest of the province. Hunting and fishing also important. Native land claims a defined issue in some areas.

TABLE 33. (continued)

Location	Leading species	Wildlife/fisheries recreation potential
Boreal and Taiga plain; Fort St. John, Dawson Creek, Fort Nelson	Aspen, and to a lesser extent balsam and cottonwood poplar species in mid- to overmature state, often as a pine mixedwood in upland or a spruce mixed wood in moist areas.	Many unknowns surround fish and wildlife population data, although some species uncommon in the rest of the province occur here. High abundance and diversity of aspen-using species. Compared to the rest of the province, fisheries are not heavily used, and populations are poorly understood. Recreational use is mainly hunting, moderate to low compared to the rest of the province. Considerable trapping activity. As in many areas of the province, native land claims will be an issue, but here hardwoods will be a large part of the negotiations.

5. There is a need for mapped data at scales that are useful to generalized land management. Hardwood leading inventory type groups, age sizes, and size classes should be mapped at 1:100 000 to 1:250 000 scale for planning purposes.

6. Fragmentation and old growth is poorly understood especially from a wildlife perspective: Data gaps exist in the assessment of response by wildlife to fragmentation of hardwood habitat. This is particularly important in the northeast where planning to prevent some of the more negative impacts of fragmentation may be possible. Data gaps exist in the description of the physical and biological elements of old-growth hardwoods and their importance to wildlife populations.

7. Identification of requirements for deciduous-dominated riparian leave-strips including: associated vegetation characteristics and sizes, how they influence habitat use, and whether or not they should be managed.

8. Hardwood forest understorey vegetation characteristics and response to harvesting, grazing, wildlife use, and other effects are poorly understood. These data are needed for adequate silvicultural planning of hardwoods and for wildlife and range management. This gap is a large one and is present for nondeciduous inventory as well. D. Campbell (pers. comm., 1992) has a system for classifying the understorey of inventory type groups, but he cautions that forest cover characteristics, on which the

Range Inventory Strata is based, can be a poor indicator of species composition, productivity, and other features important for range management.

9. Data gaps exist in the description of the physical and biological characteristics of high-use recreational areas, including such features as hardwood forests. The current movement toward using biophysical habitat analysis to describe parks could be applied to forest recreation areas for planning purposes.

10. Data gaps exist in the description of hardwood stand elements viewed by the public as most important to recreational use, and wildlife habitat. The potential they may have for enhancement of recreational/wildlife use is also poorly known.

11. B.C. Ministry of Forests district staff may require information about the potential hardwood components of stands based on a site series grid. It has been suggested that the identification of wildlife habitat requirements within a site series may also be useful but this type of classification may be too artificial.

The uncertainty surrounding the hardwood resource relates mainly to its economic future. There is also considerable uncertainty about the importance of hardwoods to wildlife and fish populations. This has received less attention than that paid to coniferous-wildlife and fisheries interactions.

The concerns about data viability are perhaps less widespread than the B.C. Ministry of Forest Inventory Branch suspects. Apart from the above concerns, the large and detailed database for volumes, ages, and species compositions is remarkable in its completeness and accuracy.

6.10.2 Future inventory needs

The incorporation of multiple resource use information into future forest inventory procedures is both possible and necessary. The obvious advantage is the enormous savings incurred by avoiding the duplication of effort that occurs when several separate (and occasionally the same) groups of highly trained individuals describe the same resource from slightly different perspectives. The basic forest inventory information needs are often the same as cultural, tourism, wildlife, and fisheries habitat needs. Such variables as overstorey characteristics, crown closure, stand age, and site class are some of the most useful background information for biophysical habitat mapping for wildlife, and often serve as a truthing check for overstorey species composition when field checking is not possible. Measures critical to the determination of habitat suitability and capability are not mysterious or undefinable, but they do require that field personnel are trained in interpretation of habitat suitability and potential. Inventory field crews can be trained to recognize and measure wildlife and fisheries variables, provided that these can be measured consistently and that the field crews are well versed in the habitat requirements of a variety of species groups, and of individual species. This can be done on a regional basis, and using the tables provided in Section 4 as a first approximation of existing species and habitats, a field inventory program based on the principals of biophysical habitat analysis can be designed (Demarchi and Lea 1989).

There are two basic approaches:

Option 1: Allow a pre-stratification of the Terrain Resource Inventory Mapping (TRIM) using a broad-scale classification such as Land Cover at 1:250 000 for most of the province and at 1:50 000 for areas of multiple resource management concern. (Land cover classification systems are being developed for the forest inventory for non-forested lands[15] [Enns 1993; Lea pers. comm., 1993])

[15] Enns, K.A. 1993. Achieving representativeness in protected areas strategy in B.C.: a problem analysis. Unpubl. rep. prep. for the Canadian Council on Ecological Areas, Toronto, Ont. 75 p.

Option 2: Train the inventory mapping teams to collect or observe at 1:15 000 all variables that are important to multiple resource use. This includes an understanding of basic wildlife habitat use patterns in forested landscapes, and recognition and accurate description of those landforms with high diversity or use patterns (e.g., shear versus bluffed cliffs).

The first option of pre-stratification will result in large polygons with land cover names, within which the inventory teams can apply the process of standard forest inventory as described in Iles (1992). The B.C. Ministry of Environment, Lands and Parks may want to provide this pre-classification, because it would give them land management information that they cannot get with large-scale forest cover mapping. Biophysical stratification of the TRIM will result in large polygons within which forest cover polygons can be nested. The raw data used in the forest inventory can then be revised from the old inventory within these polygons.

Use of remote sensing was discussed recently by Tomlins (unpublished correspondence, 1992). He recommends that because of costs, data sharing should be coordinated between agencies. By using remote-sensing data in a digital format and a PC-based geographic system such as ARC-View, a valuable image backdrop for viewing and editing map linework is provided. The user could then relate the map linework to an aerial view of the terrain. Further, Enns (pers. comm., 1992) and Tomlins (pers. comm., 1992) have discussed the feasibility of storing aerial photography digitally on a CD-ROM. Both formats are attractive because of the ability to draw polygons on a TRIM format without the air photo handling time.

There is a need (regardless of whether Options 1 or 2 are followed) for ground truthing to a greater degree than was done in the past. This may seem to be an expensive suggestion, but it is probably cheaper than expected using field-check teams. In a recent government mapping exercise, consultants were given 5 days to ground truth Landsat imagery for southern Vancouver Island (mapsheets 92B,C, F, G) and a high degree of accuracy was attained. It will be necessary to use ground plots because of the need for accurate age determinations and understorey descriptions. It is possible to classify the understorey vegetation in forested stands according to seral stage, although structural features of the stand should also be considered. This classification can draw upon pre-existing site associations in mature forests used in the BEC system. However, experience with seral stages indicates that considerable variation in species composition, rates of change, and biomass production occur in these associations after harvesting. Therefore, managers should be prepared for additions to the classification of understorey characteristics in post-harvest, established stands.

6.10.3 Future topics of concern and research needs

The following research topics relate to future hardwood-wildlife management. Research is needed to satisfy many of the concerns about hardwood use and stand management.

Fisheries Management

- Timing of harvest near stream channels
- Timing of in-stream work (i.e., machinery, culverting activity, timing of road building)
- Net downs or leave-strip quality (i.e., species composition), size, placement and distances between leave-strips in hardwood-dominated riparian areas.
- Age class utilization
- Baseline data on fish species use of streams in post-harvest stands
- Species diversity in small feeder streams in managed areas vs. nonmanaged areas

- Impacts of harvesting on water quality and quantity
- Training for hardwood forest managers in fish population and habitat inventory techniques
- Long-term riparian area management plans
- Vegetation succession in fish habitat
- Impacts of road maintenance over the long term

Aesthetics and Recreation

- Visual fragmentation
- Viewscape impacts
- Period of time for green-up of blocks
- Importance of human sentimental values for specific properties that may be harvested
- Active operations near recreational areas
- Potential conflicts between industrial traffic and recreational road use
- Species composition for fall coloration, visual softening effects
- Recreational use in hardwood seral stands
- Preservation of traditional native land use

Wildlife Management

- Database availability for wildlife species occurrence and use in managed stands
- Successional sequences and duration to be expected in managed stands
- Post-harvest management objectives (i.e., conversion to coniferous dominated stands, subsequent site preparation, planting, and stand maintenance)
- Rotation lengths
- How nonmerchantable, overmature stands will be managed
- Training for hardwood forest managers in wildlife population and habitat inventory techniques

Native, Cultural

- Hunter and trapper access management
- Preservation of traditional native land use
- Water quality
- Questions of safety in silvicultural techniques (e.g., uncertainty about the use of herbicides)
- Importance of human sentimental values for specific properties that may be harvested

Given these topics of concern, the following suggestions are made for baseline, operational, and ongoing academic research:

- Collection of baseline small-scale data on geographic location of hardwood inventory types that are primary targets for hardwood harvesting is required.
- The forest inventory needs to better reflect habitat suitability and capability.
- Baseline data on the wildlife species that use various inventory types is required. There are few examples of static use patterns that could be applied in a pan-provincial way. For example, it was assumed that Pileated Woodpecker used conifers (based on coastal work) and Demarchi (pers. comm., 1992)[16] records the use of primarily western larch in the

[16] Demarchi, R. 1992. B.C. Min. Environ., Lands, Parks, Victoria, B.C.

Kootenays, but Keisker (1987) found that they prefer to use birch and aspen in the interior of the province. Use patterns need further definition, on a regional basis.

- Monitoring efforts should be designed to track the effect of habitat fragmentation and temporal spacing of blocks in the larger landscape.
- An evaluation of how to increase diversity with changes to prescriptions and other enhancement activities is required.
- Determine the timber harvesting and longer term post-harvest impacts on wildlife populations.
- Determine if putting forest access roads "to bed" actually protect wildlife population status significantly, or do some other measures need to be implemented.
- Determine if habitat enhancement in harvested or nonharvested hardwood stands actually result in increased population recruitment.
- A baseline inventory of fish species diversity and habitats in merchantable hardwood dominated riparian areas is needed.
- The production of map overlays of fisheries habitat and fisheries population data on the stream atlas for the province is required.
- Determine the critical seasonal and longer-term periods in the lifecycle of key species in merchantable hardwood dominated riparian areas.
- Determine if watercourse low-flow problems coincide with critical periods in the lifecycle of fish species.
- Determine which deciduous forest types have recreational or cultural value.
- Determine if there is a method of incorporating hardwood characteristics into the Recreation Opportunity Spectrum mapping.

The following operational strategy is suggested as a high priority:

1. Compile baseline multiple resource data in selected TSAs with a high potential for hardwood utilization, at a 1:50 000 or 1:250 000 scale using land cover mapping.
2. Incorporate extensive, quick-plot ground truthing in selected inventory type groups and age class determinations to calibrate the inventory data.

On a TSA basis, the suggestions for research priorities are:

Kalum: fisheries baseline data, riparian wildlife habitat use studies.

Fort Nelson: forest fragmentation studies, more warbler work.

Fort St. John: large cavity-using species.

Quesnel, Williams Lake: vegetation understorey characteristics in deciduous–mixedwood used as rangeland; where possible use the existing ecosystem variants and associations but try to determine the within association variation.

Prince George: determine NSR lands that have the successional potential to support commercial deciduous crops.

Kamloops: determine the territory size for Pileated Woodpecker and other primary cavity-nesting birds.

Arrow: pland bird use of hardwood stands.

REFERENCES

Addison, P.A., S.S. Malhotra, and A.A. Khan. 1984. Effects of sulfur dioxide on woody boreal forest species grown on native soils and tailings. J. Environ. Qual. 13:333–336.

Ahrens, G.R., A. Dobkowski, and D.E. Hibbs. 1992. Red alder: guidelines for successful regeneration. Oreg. State Univ., For. Res. Lab., Corvallis, Oreg., Spec. Publ. No. 24.

Alban, D.H. and D.A. Perala. 1990. Impact of aspen timber harvesting on soils. *In* Sustained productivity of forest soils, 7th N. Am. For. Soils Conf., S.P. Gessel, D.S. Lacate, G.F. Weetman, and R.F. Powers (editors), Univ. B.C., Fac. For., Vancouver, B.C., pp. 377–391.

______. 1992. Carbon storage in Lake States aspen ecosystems. Can. J. For. Res. 22:1107–1110.

Aldous, S.E. 1938. Beaver food utilization studies. J. Wildl. Manage. 2:215-222.

Anonymous 1986. On location: housekeeping in Nelson. Real West Magazine. 2(3):21–24.

______. Impact of hardwood harvesting on natives of Fort Nelson–Fort St. John. Dept. of Indian and Northern Affairs, Ottawa, Ont.

Archibold, W.O. 1980. Seed input into a postfire forest site in northern Saskatchewan. Can. J. For. Res. 10:129–134.

Arlidge, J.W.C. 1967. The durability of scarified seedbeds for spruce regeneration. B.C. For. Serv., Victoria, B.C., Res. Note No. 42.

Atterbury, T. 1978. Alder characteristics as they affect utilization. *In* Utilization and management of alder. D.G. Briggs, D.S. DeBell, and W.A. Atkinson, (compilers). U.S. Dep. Agric. For. Serv., Pac. NW For. Range Exp. Sta., Portland, Oreg., Gen. Tech. Rep. PNW–70, pp. 71–81.

Bailey, A.W. and H.G. Anderson. 1979. Brush control on sandy rangelands in central Alberta. J. Range Manage. 32:29–32.

Bailey, A.W., B.D. Irving, and W.D. Willms. 1985. Effect of 2,4-D and fire on mortality of aspen. Univ. Alta. Agric. & For. Bull. Suppl. 8:81–82.

Baker, R.W. 1989. Site preparation and aspen control in the SBS. *In* Learning from the past: looking to the future. Proc. North. Silvic. Comm. 1988 Winter Workshop, Feb. 2–3, 1988, Prince George, B.C. B.A. Scrivener and J.A. MacKinnon (editors). For. Can. and B.C. Min. For., Victoria, B.C., FRDA Rep. No. 030, pp. 99–103.

Bancroft, B. 1989. Response of aspen suckering to pre-harvest stem treatments: a literature review. For. Can. and B.C. Min. For., Victoria, B.C., FRDA Rep. No. 087.

Bancroft, B., G. Butt, and J.D. Lousier. 1990. Red alder seed tree control in coastal British Columbia: a review. For. Can. and B.C. Min. For., Victoria, B.C. FRDA Rep. No. 159.

Barnes, B.V. 1966. The clonal growth habit of American aspens. Ecology 47:439–447.

Beaudry, P.G., D.L. Hogan, and J.W. Schwab. 1990. Hydrologic and geomorphic considerations for silvicultural investments on the Lower Skeena River floodplain. For. Can. and B.C. Min. For., Victoria, B.C., FRDA Rep. No. 122.

Behrend, D.F. and E.F. Patrick. 1969. Influence of site disturbance and removal of shade on regeneration of deer browse. J. Wildl. Manage. 33:394–398.

Benecke, P. 1976. Soil water relations and water exchange of forest ecosystems. Ecol. Stud. 19:101–131.

Benson, E.M., J.M. Peters, M.A. Edwards, and L.A. Hogan. 1973. Nutritive value of wild edible plants of the Pacific Northwest. J. Am. Dietetic Assoc. 62:142–147.

Benson, R.E., S.F. McCool, and J.A. Schileter. 1985. Attaining visual quality objectives in timber harvest areas: landscape architects evaluation. U.S. Dep. Agric. For. Serv., Intermtn. Res. Sta., Ogden, Utah. Res. Pap. INT–348.

Berry, A.B. and W.M. Stiell. 1978. Effect of rotation length on productivity of aspen sucker stands. For. Chron. 54:265–267.

Beschta, R.L., R.E. Bilby, G.W. Brown, L.B. Holby, and T.D. Hofstra. 1987. Stream temperature and aquatic habitat: fisheries and forestry interactions. In Streamside management: forestry and fisheries interactions. E.O. Salo and T.W. Cundy (editors). Univ. Wash., Inst. For. Resources, Seattle, Wash. pp. 191–232.

Bianci, V. 1989 A Fisher management strategy. B.C. Min. Environ., Bulletin 63. 127 p.

Bilby, R.E. 1988. Interactions between aquatic and terrestrial systems. *In* Streamside management: riparian wildlife and forestry interactions. K.J. Raedeke (editor). Univ. Wash., Inst. For. Resources, Seattle, Wash.

Binkley, C.S and S.B. Watts. 1992. The status of forestry research in British Columbia. For. Can. and B.C. Min. For., Victoria, B.C., B.C. For. Resources Advisory Council, Rep. No. 1.

Binkley, D. 1984. Douglas-fir stem growth per unit of leaf area increased by interplanted Sitka alder and red alder. For. Sci. 30:259–263.

Binkley, D. and P. Sollins. 1990. Factors determining differences in soil pH in adjacent conifer and alder-conifer stands. Soil Sci. Soc. Am. J. 54:1427–1433.

Binkley, D., R. Bell, and P. Sollins. 1992. Comparison of methods for estimating soil nitrogen transformations in adjacent conifer and alder–conifer forests. Can. J. For. Res. 22:858–863.

Birong, B. S., P. G. Comeau, and J. O. Boateng. [In press] Effectiveness of forest vegetation control methods in British Columbia. B.C. Min. For., Victoria, B.C.

Bisson, P.A. and J.R. Sedell. 1984. Salmonid populations in streams in clear-cut vs. old-growth forests of western Washington. *In* Fish and wildlife relationships in old-growth forests. T. Meehan, H. Merrell, and M. Hanley (editors). Am. Inst. Fish. Res. Biol. Juneau, Alaska, pp. 9–16.

Bisson, P.A., R.E. Bilby, and M.D. Bryant. 1987. Large woody debris in forested streams in the Pacific Northwest: past, present and future. *In* Streamside management: forestry and fishery interactions. E.O. Salo and T.W. Cundy (editors). Univ. Wash. Inst. For. Resources, Seattle, Wash. pp. 143–189.

Bjorkbom, J.C., D.A. Marquis, and F.E. Cunningham. 1965. The variability of paper birch seed production, dispersal, and germination. U.S. Dep. Agric. For. Serv., NE For. Exp. Sta., Broomall, Pa., Res. Pap. NE–41.

Blood, D. Undated. Management guidelines in British Columbia: muskrat; marten. B.C. Min. Environ. Victoria, B.C.

Boateng, J.O. 1984. Estimates of forest brush problems in British Columbia. B.C. Min. For., Silv. Br., Victoria, B.C.

Boateng, J.O. and G. Ackerman. 1988. Manual and chemical control treatments of bigleaf maple coppices. Expert Committee on Weeds. West. Can. Section Meet., Nov. 29–Dec. 1, 1988. Winnipeg, Man.

Bowes, G.G. 1991. Long-term control of aspen poplar and western snowberry with dicamba and 2,4-D. Can. J. Plant Sci. 71:1121–1131.

Brand, D.G. [1984] Assessment of the growth of Douglas-fir plantations. IV. Characteristics and dynamics of competing vegetation. Univ. B.C., Vancouver, B.C. Unpubl. rep.

Brayshaw, T.C. 1978. Catkin bearing plants of British Columbia. B.C. Prov. Museum, Prov. Mus. Occas. Pap. Series No. 18.

Brissette, J.C. and B.V. Barnes. 1984. Comparisons of phenology and growth of Michigan and western North American sources of *Populus tremuloides*. Can. J. For. Res. 14:789–793.

British Columbia Ministry of Environment. Undated. Management guidelines for British Columbia: beaver; mink; wolverine; lynx.

______. 1991. Managing wildlife to 2001: a discussion paper. Victoria, B.C.

______. 1992. Hunter records. MOE data files, c/o J. Thornton, Victoria, B.C.

British Columbia Ministry of Environment, Lands and Parks, Surveys and Resource Mapping Branch. 1992. Baseline thematic mapping of southern Vancouver Island. 1:250 000 scale. Portions of mapsheets 92B, C, F, G. Based on 1990 inventory, Victoria, B.C.

British Columbia Ministry of Forests. Undated. Recreation guide. Resource Manage. Br., Victoria, B.C.

______. 1981. Forest Landscape Handbook. Recreation Manage. Br., Victoria, B.C.

______. 1987. Application for a pulpwood agreement. Louisiana-Pacific Panel Products, Ltd.

______. 1988. BEC map. 1:2 000 000, Research Br., Victoria, B.C.

______. 1989a. A discussion paper on natural areas and wilderness-type recreation policy. Victoria, B.C.

______. 1989b. Managing wilderness in provincial forests: A policy framework. Integrated Resources Br., Victoria, B.C.

______. 1989c. Primitive and semiprimitive areas of B.C.

______. 1990a. Established licensees and apportionment within TSAs, Vancouver Region, Vancouver, B.C..

______. 1990b. Summary of backlog not satisfactorily restocked forest land. Victoria, B.C.

______. 1992a. March data output using PSR. Inventory Br., Victoria, B.C.

______. 1992b. Towards an old growth strategy: public review draft. B.C. Min. For., Old Growth Strategy Project, Victoria, B.C.

______. 1992c. British Columbia Coastal Fisheries/Forestry Guidelines. 3rd ed. Victoria, B.C. 25 p.

Brown, J.K. 1985. Fire effects and application of prescribed fire in aspen. *In* Rangeland fire effects: a symposium. K. Sanders and J. Durham, (editors). U.S. Dep. Int., Bur. Land Manage. and Univ. Idaho, Boise, Idaho, pp. 38–47.

Brown, J. and J. Nisbet. 1894. The forester. Blackwood, Edinburgh, U.K.

Brown, T.C. 1987. Production and cost of scenic beauty: examples for a ponderosa pine forest. For. Sci. 33(2):394–410.

Brown, T.C. and T.C. Daniel. 1985. Modelling forest scenic beauty. U.S. Dep. Agric. For. Serv., Rocky Mtn. For. Range Exp. Sta., Fort Collins, Col. Res. Pap. RM–256.

______. 1986. Predicting scenic beauty of timber stands. For. Sci. 32(2):471–487.

Brozek, S. 1990. Effect of soil changes caused by red alder (*Alnus rubra*) on biomass and nutrient status of Douglas-fir (*Pseudotsuga menziesii*) seedlings. Can. J. For. Res. 20:1320–1325.

Bryant, M.D. 1983. The role and management of woody debris in west coast salmonid nursery streams. N. Am. J. Fish. Manage. 3:322–330.

Buckman, R.E. and L.H. Blankenship. 1965. Abundance and vigor of aspen root suckering. J. For. 63:23–25.

Bull, E.L. and J.M. Skovlin. 1985. Relationships between avifauna and streamside vegetation. Proc. 47th N. Am. Wildl. Conf., pp. 496–506.

Bunnell, F.L. 1990. Ecology of black-tailed deer. *In* Deer and elk habitats in coastal forests of southern British Columbia. J.B. Nyberg and D.W. Janz (editors). 1990. B.C. Min. For. and B.C. Min. Environ. Special Rep. Series No. 5, pp. 31–63.

Bunnell, P., S. Rautio, C. Fletcher, and A. Van Woudenberg. [In press] Problem analysis for integrated resource management of riparian ecosystems. Prep. for B.C. Min. For. and B.C. Min. Environ., Victoria, B.C. by ESSA Environmental and Social Systems Analysts Ltd., Vancouver, B.C.

Burns, R.M. (compiler) 1983. Silvicultural systems for the major forest types of the United States. U.S. Dep. Agric. For. Serv., Washington, D.C., Agric. Handb. No. 445.

Burton, P.J., A.C. Balisky, L.P. Coward, S.G. Cumming, and D.D. Kneeshaw. 1992. The value of managing for biodiversity. For. Chron. 68:225–237.

Calder, J.A. and R.L. Taylor. 1968. Flora of the Queen Charlotte Islands (I). Dep. Agric., Ottawa, Ont. Monogr. No. 4(1).

Campbell, R.W., N.K. Dawe, I. McTaggart-Cowan, J.M. Cooper, G.W. Kaiser, and C.E. McNall. 1990. The birds of British Columbia. Vols. 1 and 2. Environ. Can. and Can. Wildl. Serv., Ottawa, Ont.

Campbell, R.W., K.H. Morgan, and C. Palmateer. 1988. Species notes for selected birds. Vol. 2. *In* Wildlife habitat handbooks for the southern Interior ecoprovince. A.P. Hardcombe (technical editor). Min. Environ. and Min. For., Victoria, B.C., 135 p.

Canada Department of Fisheries and Oceans. 1989. Coastal/ estuarine fish habitat description and assessment manual. Environ. Can., Vancouver, B.C.

Canadian Forest Industries Directory. 1992. Southam Business Communications, St. Laurent, Quebec.

Cannell, M.G.R., D.C. Malcolm, and P.A. Robertson (editors). 1992. The ecology of mixed-species stands of trees. Blackwell Sci. Publ., Oxford, U.K.

Cannings, R.A., R.J. Cannings, and S.G. Cannings. 1987. Birds of the Okanagan Valley, British Columbia. Royal British Columbia Museum. Victoria, B.C.

Carl, G.C., W.A. Clemens, and C.C. Lindsey. 1977. The fresh-water fishes of British Columbia. B.C. Provincial Museum, Victoria, B.C., Handb. No. 5.

Carlson, M. 1992. Municipal effluent irrigation of fast-growing hybrid poplar plantations near Vernon, British Columbia. For. Chron. 68:206–208.

Carlton, G.C. 1988. The structure and dynamics of red alder communities in the central Coast Range of western Oregon. M.Sc. thesis. Oreg. State Univ., Corvallis, Oreg.

Carlyle, J.C. 1986. Nitrogen cycling in forested ecosystems. For. Abstracts 47(5):306–336.

Casteel, J. 1989. Foliar herbicide treatments for aspen: an operational viewpoint from John Casteel, Lakeland Mills Ltd., Prince George, B.C. *In* UBC INFORMS Newsl. 3(1). S. Watts (editor). For. Can, Victoria, B.C., FRDA Rep. No. 088, pp. 7–8.

Chamberlain, T.W. (editor). 1988. Applying 15 years of Carnation Creek results: Proc. Workshop. Environ. Can. Dep. Fish. Oceans, Pac. Biol. Sta., Nanaimo, B.C.

Chester, R.A. 1988. Management and use of red alder in the Vancouver Forest Region. M.Sc. thesis. Simon Fraser Univ., Burnaby, B.C.

Cline, S.P. and C.A. Phillips. 1983. Coarse woody debris and debris-dependent wildlife in logged and natural riparian zone forests—a western Oregon example. *In* Proc. symp. Snag habitat management, U.S. Dep. Agric. For. Serv., Rocky Mtn. For. Range Exp. Sta., Fort Collins, Col., Gen. Tech. Rep. No. 99, pp. 33–39.

Coates, D. and S. Haeussler. 1986. A preliminary guide to the response of major species of competing vegetation to silvicultural treatments. B.C. Min. For., Victoria, B.C., Land Manage. Handb. No. 9.

Coates, D., S. Haeussler, and J. Mather. 1990. A guide to the response of common plants in British Columbia to management treatments. For. Can. and B.C. Min. For., Victoria, B.C., FRDA Handb. No. 008.

Cole, D.W., J. Compton, H. Van Miegroet, and P. Homann. 1990/91. Changes in soil properties and site productivity caused by red alder. Water Air Soil Poll. 54:231–246.

Cole, E.C. and M. Newton. 1990. Efficacy of different herbicides on bigleaf maple sprout clumps. Proc. West. Soc. Weed Sci. 43:37–44.

______. 1991a. Efficacy of cut stump treatment for controlling bigleaf maple. Proc. West. Soc. Weed Sci. 44:50–53.

______. 1991b. Herbicide stem injection treatments for controlling paper birch in high latitude forests. *In* Res. Prog. Rep. West. Soc. Weed Sci., Mar. 12–14, 1991, Seattle, Wash. The West. Soc. Weed Sci., Reno, Nev., pp. 56–59.

Comeau, P. and D. Sachs. 1992. Simulation of the consequences of red alder management on the growth of Douglas-fir using FORCYTE-11. For. Can. and B.C. Min. For., Victoria, B.C., FRDA Rep. No. 187.

Coordinated Research on Alternative Forestry Treatments and Systems (CRAFTS). [1987.] Annual report. For. Res. Lab., Oreg. State Univ., Corvallis, Oreg. Unpubl. rep.

______. [1988.] Annual report. For. Res. Lab., Oreg. State Univ., Corvallis, Oreg. Unpubl. rep.

COPE (Coastal Oregon Productivity Enhancement Program). [1989.] Silvicultural management of riparian areas for multiple resources, a COPE Workshop, Dec. 12–13, 1989, Gleneden Beach, Oreg. U.S. Dep. Agric., Pac. NW. For. Exp. Sta., Portland, Oreg. and Oreg. State Univ, Coll. For., Corvallis, Oreg. Unpubl. docs.

Culp, J.M. 1987. The effects of streambank clearcutting on the benthic invertebrates of Carnation Creek, British Columbia. *In* Applying 15 years of Carnation Creek results: Proc.Works. T.W. Chamberlain (editor). Environ. Can., Dep. Fish. Oceans, Pac. Biol. Sta., Nanaimo, B.C., pp. 87–92.

Culp, J.M. and R.W. Davies. 1985. Responses of benthic invertebrate species to manipulation of interstitial detritus in Carnation Creek, British Columbia. Can. J. Fish. Aquat. Sci. 43:139–146.

Culp, J.M., S.J. Walde, and R.W. Davies. 1983. Relative importance of substrate particle size and detritus to stream benthic macroinvertebrate microdistribution. Can. J. Fish. Aquat. Sci. 40:1568–1574.

D'Anjou B. 1990. Growth response of several vegetation species to herbicides and manual cutting treatment in the Vancouver Forest Region. For. Can. and B.C. Min. For., Victoria, B.C., FRDA Rep. No. 135.

Davidson, E.A., D.D. Myrold, and P.M. Groffman. 1990. Denitrification in temperate forest ecosystems. *In* Sustained productivity of forest soils, Proc. 7th N. Am. For. Soils Conf., S.P. Gessel, D.S. Lacate, G.F. Weetman, and R.F. Powers (editors). Univ. B.C., Fac. For., Vancouver, B.C., pp. 196–220.

Davison, R.W., R.C. Atkins, R.D. Fry, G.D. Racey, and D.H. Weingartner. 1988. A silvicultural guide for the Poplar Working Group in Ontario. Ont. Min. Nat. Resources, Toronto, Ont. Sci. and Tech. Series, Vol. 5.

DeBell, D.S. 1990. *Populus trichocarpa* Torr. & Gray. Black cottonwood. Salicaceae: willow family. *In* Silvics of North America. Vol. 2, Hardwoods. R.M. Burns and B.H. Honkala, (technical coordinators). U.S. Dep. Agric. For. Serv., Washington, D.C., Agric. Handb. No. 654, pp. 570–576.

DeBell, D.S. and T.C. Turpin. 1989. Control of red alder by cutting. U.S. Dep. Agric. For. Serv., Pac. NW For. Range Exp. Sta., Portland, Oreg., Res. Pap. PNW–414.

DeBell, D.S., M.A. Radwan, C.A. Harrington, and D.L. Reukema. 1984. Culture of red alder (*Alnus rubra)* in biomass plantations. *In* Energy from biomass and wastes VIII. D.L. Klass (chairman). Jan. 30–Feb. 3, Lake Buena Vista, Florida. Inst. Gas Technol., Chicago, Ill.

DeByle, N.V. 1985a. Animal impacts. *In* Aspen: ecology and management in the western United States. N.V. DeByle and R.P. Winokur (editors). U.S. Dep. Agric. For. Serv., Rocky Mtn. For. Range Exp. Sta., Gen. Tech. Rep. RM-119, pp. 115–123.

______. 1985b. Wildlife. *In* Aspen: ecology and management in the western United States. N.V. DeByle and R.P. Winokur (editors). U.S. Dep. Agric. For. Serv., Rocky Mtn. For. Range Exp. Sta., Gen. Tech. Rep. RM-119, pp. 135–152.

______. 1990. Aspen ecology and management in the western United States. *In* Aspen Symposium '89, Proc. symp., July 25–27, 1989, Duluth, Minn. R.D. Adams (editor). U.S Dep. Agric. For. Serv., North Cent. For. Exp. Sta., St. Paul, Minn. Gen. Tech. Rep. NC-140, pp. 11–20.

DeByle, N.V. and R.P. Winokur (editors) 1985. Aspen: ecology and management in the western United States. U.S. Dep. Agric. For. Serv., Rocky Mtn. For. Range Exp. Sta., Fort Collins, Col. Gen. Tech. Rep. RM–119.

DeLong, C. 1988. A field guide for identification and interpretation of seral aspen ecosystems of the BWBSc1, Prince George Forest Region. B.C. Min. For. and Lands, Victoria, B.C., Land Manage. Handb. No. 16.

Demarchi, D.A. and E.C. Lea. 1989. An example of biophysical habitat mapping in British Columbia. *In* Proc. Land classifications based on vegetation: applications for resource management. U.S. Dep. Agric. For. Serv., Intermtn. Res. Sta., Odgen, Utah, Gen. Tech. Rep. INT–257, pp. 271–276.

Densmore, R.V. and J.C. Page. 1992. Paper birch regeneration on scarified logged areas in south-central Alaska. North. J. Appl. For. 9(2):63–66.

Dobie, J. 1992. Estimating forest sector employment in British Columbia. For. Can. and B.C. Min. For., Victoria, B.C., FRDA Rep. No. 179.

Dobson, M.C. 1991. De-icing salt damage to trees and shrubs and its amelioration. *In* Research for practical arboriculture. S.J. Hodge (editor). For. Comm., H.M.S.O., London, U.K., For. Comm. Bull. No. 97, pp. 141–151.

Doffield, J.W. 1970. Silviculture need not be ugly. J. For. Sci. 68:464–467.

Drouin, J.A. 1989. Herbicide efficacy trials in Alberta and Manitoba 1980–85. For. Can., North. For. Cent., Edmonton, Alta., Inf. Rep. NOR-X-306.

Dryburgh, J.G. 1982. Carnation Creek logging and silvicultural treatment program. *In* Proc. Carnation Creek workshop: a ten-year review, Feb. 24–26, 1982, Nanaimo, B.C. G.F. Hartman (editor). Dep. Fish. Oceans, Pac. Biol. Sta., Nanaimo, B.C. 36–43.

Dugle, J.R. 1966. A taxonomic study of western Canada species in the genus *Betula*. Can. J. Bot. 4:929–1007.

Dunlap, J.M., P.E. Heilman, and R.F. Stettler. 1992. Genetic variation and productivity of *Populus trichocarpa* and its hybrids. V. The influence of ramet position on 3-year growth variables. Can. J. For. Res. 22:849–857.

Ebata, T. 1989. Pest concerns during backlog reforestation. *In* Learning from the past: looking to the future. Proc. North. Silv. Committee's 1988 Winter Workshop, Feb. 2-3, 1988, Prince George, B.C. B.A. Scrivener and J.A. MacKinnon (editors). For. Can. and B.C. Min. For., Victoria, B.C., FRDA Rep. No. 030, pp. 134–135.

Ehrlick, P.R. and G.C. Daily. 1988. Red-napped sapsuckers feeding at willows: possible keystone herbivores. Am. Birds 42(3):357–365.

Emmingham, W.H., M. Bondi, and D.E. Hibbs. 1989. Underplanting western hemlock in a red alder thinning: early survival, growth, and damage. New For. 3:31–43.

Enns, K.A., E.B. Peterson, and D. McLennan 1993. Impacts of hardwood management on B.C. wildlife: problem analysis. For. Can. and B.C. Min. For., Victoria, B.C. FRDA Rep. No. 208.

Enns, K.A. and C. Siddle. [1992.] The distribution, abundance and habitat requirements of rare warblers of northeastern B.C.: a first approximation. Prepared for B.C. Min of Environ., Lands and Parks. Victoria, B.C., Unpubl. draft.

Entry, J.A. and W.H. Emmingham. 1991. Hybrid poplar and red alder in coastal riparian zones for control of nonpoint-source pollution, fish and wildlife habitat, and wood fiber. COPE Rep. 4(4):5–7.

Ethos Consulting, Land Sense Ltd., and Youds Planning Consultants. 1988. Wildlife viewing in British Columbia: the tourism potential. Funded under the Canada-British Columbia Tourism Industry Development Subsidiary Agreement.

Ethos Consulting, Tourism Research Group, BioQuest International, and Henderson Associates. 1991. The commercial wildlife viewing product: a discussion of market and development potential. Report to the B.C. Min. of Tourism, Victoria, B.C.

Farnden, C. 1992. Cost and efficacy variation of forest vegetation management treatments in British Columbia. B.C. Min. Environ., Pesticide Manage. Prog., Nanaimo, B.C.

Fenger, M. 1990. The need for wildlife/forestry guidelines in British Columbia. *In* Proc. Wildl. For. Symp.: a workshop on resource integration for wildlife and forest managers, Mar. 7–8, 1990, Prince George, B.C. A. Chambers (editor). For. Can., B.C. Min. For., and B.C. Min. Environ., Victoria, B.C. FRDA Rep. 160, pp. 125–135.

Figueroa, P.F. 1991. Ground-applied herbicide methods for red alder control: herbicide efficacy, labor costs, and treatment method efficiency. Proc. West. Soc. Weed Sci. 44:53–59.

Figueroa, P.F. and T.E. Nishimura. 1992. Big-leaf maple control: basal thin-line applications using imazapyr liquids and ground applications of imazapyr granules. Proc. West. Soc. Weed Sci. 45:65–72.

Filion, F.L., S.W. Jones, J. Ducharme, W. Pepper, R. Reid, P. Boxall, and D. Teillet. 1983. The importance of wildlife to Canadians: highlights of the 1981 National Survey. Environ. Can., Can. Wildl. Serv., Ottawa, Ont.

Foote, M.J. 1983. Classification, description, and dynamics of plant communities after fire in the taiga of interior Alaska. U.S. Dep. Agric. For. Serv., Pac. NW For. Exp. Sta., Portland, Oreg. Res. Pap. PNW-307.

Forest Resources Commission. 1991. The future of our forests. Victoria, B.C.

______. 1992. British Columbia community employment dependencies. Background paper prepared by B.C. Min. of Fin. Corp. Relations, Planning and Statistics Div., Victoria, B.C.

Foster, D.R. and G.A. King. 1986. Vegetation pattern and diversity in S.E. Labrador, Canada: *Betula papyrifera* (birch) forest development in relation to fire history and physiography. J. Ecol. 74:465–483.

Fowells, H.A. (compiler). 1965. Silvics of forest trees of the United States. U.S. Dep. Agric. For. Serv., Washington, D.C., Agric. Handb. No. 271.

Franklin, J.F. 1992. Scientific basis for new perspectives in forests and streams. *In* Watershed management: balancing sustainability and environmental change. R.J. Naiman, (editor). Springer-Verlag, New York, N.Y., pp. 25–72.

Fried, J.S., J.C. Tappeiner II, and D.E. Hibbs. 1988. Bigleaf maple seedling establishment and early growth in Douglas-fir forests. Can. J. For. Res. 18:1226–1233.

Fried, J.S., J.R. Boyle, J.C. Tappeiner II, and K. Cromack, Jr. 1990. Effects of bigleaf maple on soil of Douglas-fir forests. Can. J. For. Res. 20:259–266.

Frivold, L.H. and K. Mielikäinen. 1990. The effects of hardwoods on softwood growth in mixed stands in Fennoscandia. *In* The silvics and ecology of boreal spruces. 1989 IUFRO Symp. Proc., St. John's, Nfld. B.D. Titus, M.B. Lavigne, P.F. Newton, and W.J. Meades (editors). For. Can., St. John's, Nfld., Inf. Rep. N-X-271, pp. 75–82.

Gedney, D.R. 1990. Red alder harvesting opportunities in western Oregon. U.S. Dep. Agric. For. Serv., Pac. NW Res. Sta., Portland, Oreg., Res. Bull. PNW-RB-173.

Gifford, G.F., W. Humphries, and R.A. Jaynes. 1984. A preliminary quantification of the impacts of aspen to conifer succession on water yield. II. Modeling results. Water Resources Bull. 20:181–186.

Good, J.E.G. 1991. Air pollution and tree health in relation to arboriculture. *In* Research for practical arboriculture. S.J. Hodge (editor). For. Comm., H.M.S.O., London, U.K., For. Comm. Bull. 97. pp. 107–119.

Grace, J.B. and D. Tilman. 1990. Perspectives on plant competition: some introductory remarks. Perspectives on plant competition. J.B. Grace and D. Tilman (editors). Academic Press, New York, N.Y., pp. 3–7.

Grant, W.F. and B.K. Thompson. 1975. Observations on Canadian birches, *Betula cordifolia, B. neoalaskana, B. populifolia, B. papyrifera* and *B.* x *caerulea*. Can. J. Bot. 53:1478–1490.

Gregory, S. [1989.] The effects of riparian vegetation on light, nutrient cycling and food production in streams. *In* Silviculture management on riparian areas for multiple resources: Proc. COPE workshop, Dec. 12–13 , Gleneden Beach, Oreg., Unpubl.

Gregory, S., B. Beschta, F. Swanson, J. Sedell, G. Reeves, and F. Everest. 1990. Abundance of conifers in Oregon's riparian forests. COPE Rep. 3(2):5–6.

Grime, J.P. 1979. Plant strategies and vegetation processes. John Wiley and Sons, Chichester, U.K.

Groot, C. and L. Margolis (editors). 1991. Pacific salmon life histories. Univ. B.C. Press, Vancouver, B.C.

Haeussler, S. 1992. Prescribed fire for forest management. For. Can. and B.C. Min. For., Victoria, B.C., FRDA Memo No. 198.

Haeussler, S., D. Coates, and J. Mather. 1990. Autecology of common plants in British Columbia: a literature review. For. Can. and B.C. Min. For., Victoria, B.C., FRDA Rep. No. 158.

Hagglund, B. and G. Peterson (editors). 1985. Broadleaves in boreal silviculture: an obstacle or an asset? Swedish Univ. Agric. Sci., Dep. Silv., Umea, Sweden. Rep. No. 14.

Hamilton, A.N., C.A. Bryden, and C.J. Clement. 1991. Impacts of glyphosate application on grizzly bear forage production in the Coastal Western Hemlock zone. For. Can. and B.C. Min. For., Victoria, B.C., FRDA Rep. No. 165.

Hamilton, E.H. 1988. Impacts of prescribed burning on soil-vegetation relationships in the Sub-Boreal Spruce zone. Wildlife and range prescribed burning workshop proc., Oct. 27-28, 1988. M.C. Feller and S.M. Thompson, (editors). Univ. B.C., Fac. For., Vancouver, B.C. pp. 171–184.

Hamilton, E.H. and K.H Yearsley. 1988. Vegetation development after clearcutting and site preparation in the SBS zone. Can. For. Serv. and B.C. Min. For., Victoria, B.C., FRDA Rep. No. 018.

Hansen, A., J. Peterson, and E. Horvath. 1990. Do wildlife species respond to stand and edge type in managed forests of the Oregon Coast Range? COPE Rep. 3(2):3–4.

Harrington, C.A. 1984. Factors influencing initial sprouting of red alder. Can. J. For. Res. 14:357–361.

______. 1990. *Alnus rubra* Bong. Red alder. Betulaceae: birch family. Silvics of North America. Vol. 2, Hardwoods. R.M. Burns and B.H. Honkala (technical coordinators). U.S. Dep. Agric. For. Serv., Washington, D.C., Agric. Handb. No. 654, pp. 116–123.

Hart, D. and P.G. Comeau. 1992. Manual brushing for forest vegetation management in British Columbia: a review of current knowledge and information needs. B.C. Min. For., Victoria, B.C., Land Manage. Rep. No. 77.

Hart, J.A. 1979. The ethnobotany of the Flathead Indians of western Montana. Botanical Museum Leaflets, Harvard Univ. 17(10):261–307.

Hartman, G.F. 1987. Carnation Creek, 15 years of fisheries–forestry work, bridges from research to management. *In* Applying 15 years of Carnation Creek results: Proc. workshop. T.W. Chamberlain (editor). Environ. Can., Dep. Fish. Oceans, Pac. Biol. Sta., Nanaimo, B.C., pp. 189–204.

Hartman, G.F. (editor) 1982. Proc. Carnation Creek Workshop: a ten-year review, Feb. 24-26, 1982, Nanaimo, B.C., Environ. Can., Dep. Fish. Oceans, Pac. Biol. Sta., Nanaimo, B.C.

Hartman, G.F., L.B. Holtby, and J.C. Scrivener. 1984. Some effects of natural and logging-related winter stream temperature changes on the early life history of coho salmon (*Oncorhynchus kisutch*) in Carnation Creek. *In* Fish and wildlife relationships in old-growth forests. T. Meehan, H. Merrell, and M. Hanley (editors). Am. Inst. Fish. Res. Biol., Juneau, Alaska, pp. 141–149.

Hatler, D.F. 1988. A lynx management strategy for British Columbia. B.C. Min. of Environ., Wildl. Bull. No. B-61.

Hawkes, B.C., M.C. Feller, and D. Meehan. 1990. Site preparation: fire. *In* Regenerating British Columbia's forests. D.P. Lavender, R. Parish, C.M. Johnson, G. Montgomery, A. Vyse, R.A. Willis, and D. Winston (editors). Univ. B.C. Press, Vancouver, B.C., pp. 131–137.

Hawkins, C.P., M.L. Murphy, and N.H. Anderson. 1982. Effects of canopy, substrate composition, and gradient on the structure of macroinvertebrate communities in Cascade Range streams of Oregon. Ecology 63:1840–1856.

Hawkins, C.P., M.L. Murphy, N.H. Anderson, and M.A. Wilzbach. 1983. Density of fish and salamanders in relation to riparian canopy and physical habitat in streams of the northwest United States. Can. J. Fish. Aquat. Sci. 40:1173–1185.

Helgerson, O.T., J.C. Gordon, and D.A. Perry. 1984. N_2 fixation by red alder (*Alnus rubra*) and scotch broom (*Cytisus scoparius*) planted under precommercially thinned Douglas-fir (*Pseudotsuga menziesii*). Plant Soil 78:221–233.

Herring, L.J. and R.G. McMinn. 1980. Natural and advance regeneration of Engelmann spruce and sub-alpine fir compared 21 years after site treatment. For. Chron. 56:55–57.

Hibbs, D.E. 1982. Gap dynamics in a hemlock–hardwood forest. Can. J. For. Res. 12:522–527.

______. 1987. The self-thinning rule and alder management. For. Ecol. Manage. 18:273–281.

Hibbs, D.E., P. Giordano, and S. Chan. 1991. Vegetation dynamics in managed coastal riparian areas. COPE Rep. 4(4):3–5. Oreg. State Univ., Newport, Oreg.

Hicks, B.J., R.L. Beschta, and R.D. Harr. 1991. Long-term changes in streamflow following logging in western Oregon and associated fisheries implications. Water Resources Bull. 27(2):217–226.

Higler, L.W.G. 1975. Reaction of some caddis larvae (*Trichoptera*) to different types of substrate in an experimental stream. Freshwater Biol. 5:151–157.

Hinckley, T.M., R.O. Teskey, F. Duhme, and H. Richter. 1981. Temperate hardwood forests. *In* Water deficits and growth. Vol. VI. Woody plant communities. T.T. Kozlowski, (editor). Academic Press, New York, N.Y., pp. 154–208.

Hiratsuka, Y. and A.A. Loman. 1984. Decay of aspen and balsam poplar in Alberta. Environ. Can., Can. For. Serv., Edmonton, Alta., Inf. Rep. NOR-X-262.

Holmsen, S.D. 1990. Comparison of four single-stem methods for controlling trembling aspen. For. Can. and B.C. Min. For., Victoria, B.C., FRDA Rep. No. 129.

Holtby, L.B. 1987. The effects of logging on stream temperatures at Carnation Creek. *In* Applying 15 years of Carnation Creek results: Proc. workshop. T.W. Chamberlain (editor). Environ. Can., Pac. Biol. Sta., Nanaimo, B.C., pp. 118–122.

Hosie, R.C. 1973. Native trees of Canada. 7th ed. Can. For. Serv. and the Can. Publ. Cent., Don Mills, Ont.

Hull, R.B. and G.J. Buyoff. 1988. The scenic beauty temporal distribution method: an attempt to make scenic beauty assessments compatible with forest planning efforts. For. Sci. 32(2): 271–286.

Hull, R.B., G.J. Buyoff, and T.C. Daniel. 1984. Measurement of scenic beauty: the law of comparative judgement and scenic beauty estimation procedures. For. Sci. 30(4):1084–1096.

Hultén, E. 1974. Flora of Alaska and neighboring territories: a manual of the vascular plants. Stanford Univ. Press, Stanford, Cal.

Hyvarinen, M.J. 1968. Paper birch: its characteristics, properties, and uses: a review of recent literature. U.S. Dep. Agric., For. Serv., North Cent. For. Range Exp. Sta., St. Paul, Minn., Res. Pap. NC-22.

Iles, K. 1992. Some characteristics of a good inventory. A discussion paper prepared for the Timber Inventory Task Force, Nanaimo, B.C.

Johnson, D.W. 1983. The effects of harvesting intensity on nutrient depletion in forests. *In* IUFRO Symp. of forest site and continuous productivity. R. Ballard and S.P. Gessel, (editors). U.S. Dep. Agric. For. Serv., Pac. NW For. Range Exp. Sta., Portland, Oreg., Gen. Tech. Rep. PNW-163, pp. 157–166.

______. 1992. Effects of forest management on soil carbon storage. Water Air Soil Poll. 64:83–120.

Johnson, R.R., C.D. Ziebell, D.R. Patton, P.F. Folliott, and R.H. Hamre (editors). 1985. Riparian ecosystems and their management: reconciling conflict uses, 5th N. Am. Riparian Conf., April 16–18, 1985, Tucson, Ariz. U.S. Dep. Agric. For. Serv., Rocky Mtn. For. Range Exp. Sta., Fort Collins, Col., Gen. Tech. Rep. RM-120.

Jones, J.R. 1974. Silviculture of southwestern mixed conifers and aspen: the status of our knowledge. U.S. Dep. Agric. For. Serv., Rocky Mtn. For. Range Exp. Sta., Fort Collins, Col., Res. Rep. RM-122.

Jones, J.R. and N.V. DeByle. 1985. Fire. *In* Aspen: ecology and management in the western United States. N.V. DeByle and R.P. Winokur (editors). U.S. Dep. Agric. For. Serv., Rocky Mtn. For. Exp. Sta., Fort Collins, Col., Gen. Tech. Rep. RM-119, pp. 77–81.

Kabzems, R. and J.D. Lousier. 1992. Regeneration, growth and development of *Picea glauca* under *Populus* spp. canopy in the Boreal White and Black Spruce zone. For. Can. and B.C. Min. For., Victoria, B.C., FRDA Rep. No. 176.

Kaufman, M.R. 1984. A canopy model (RM-CWU) for determining transpiration of sub-alpine forests. I. Model development. Can. J. For. Res. 14:218–226.

Keisker, D.G. 1987. Nest-tree selection by primary cavity-nesting birds in south-central British Columbia. Wildl. Rep. No. R-13. B.C. Wildl. Br., Victoria, B.C.

Kelpsas, B.R. 1978. Comparative effects of chemical, fire, and machine site preparation in an Oregon coastal brushfield. M.Sc. thesis. Oreg. State Univ., Corvallis, Oreg.

Kenady, R.M. 1978. Regeneration of red alder. *In* Utilization and management of alder. D.G. Briggs, D.S. DeBell, and W.A. Atkinson (compilers). U.S. Dep. Agric. For. Serv., Pac. NW For. Range Exp. Sta., Portland, Oreg., Gen. Tech. Rep. PNW-70, pp. 183–192.

Kerbes, E.L. 1968. Broadleaf maple in British Columbia. Can. For. Serv., For. Prod. Lab., Vancouver, B.C., Inf. Rep. VP-X-38.

Kimmins, J.P., D. Binkley, L. Chatarpaul, and J. de Catanzaro. 1985. Biogeochemistry of temperate forests ecosystems: literature on inventories and dynamics of biomass and nutrients. Environ. Can., Can. For. Serv., Petawawa Nat. For. Inst., Chalk River, Ont., Inf. Rep. PI-X-47.

Klinka, K. and A.M. Scagel. 1984. Selected ecological characteristics of some tree and shrub species in British Columbia: genera *Juniperus, Taxus, Populus, Alnus, Betula, Quercus, Prunus, Rhamnus, Acer, Cornus,* and *Arbutus*. Can. Cartographics Ltd., Coquitlam, B.C.

Klinka, K., M.C. Feller, R.N. Green, D.V. Neidinger, J. Pojar, and J. Worrall. 1990. Ecological principles: applications. *In* Regenerating British Columbia's forests. D.P. Lavender, R. Parish, C.M. Johnson, G. Montgomery, A. Vyse, R.A. Willis, and D. Winston (editors). Univ. B.C. Press, Vancouver, B.C., pp. 55–72.

Kochanski, M.L. 1987. Northern bushcraft. Lone Pine Publishing, Edmonton, Alta.

Kowall, R. and D. Eastman. 1992. Wildlife research projects active in British Columbia, April 1991 to March 1992, Min. Environ., Victoria, B.C.

Krajina, V.J., K. Klinka, and J. Worrall. 1982. Distribution and ecological characteristics of trees and shrubs of British Columbia. Univ. B.C. Press, Vancouver, B.C.

Kreutzweiser, D.P., P.D. Kingsbury, and J.C. Feng. 1989. Drift response of stream invertebrates to aerial application of glyphosate. Bull. Environ. Contam. Toxicol. 42:331–338.

Kunzli, N. 1985. Effects of a red alder overstory on growth of Sitka spruce and incidence of spruce weevil damage. B.S.F. thesis. Univ. B.C., Vancouver, B.C.

Larsen, J.A. 1980. The boreal ecosystem. Academic Press, New York, N.Y.

Lassoie, J.P., T.M. Hinckley, and C.C. Grier. 1985. Coniferous forests of the Pacific Northwest. *In* Physiological ecology of North American plant communities. B.F. Chabot and H.A. Mooney (editors). Chapman and Hall, New York, N.Y., pp. 134–161.

Lauterbach, P. and L.E. Warren. 1982. Control of resprouting hardwood clumps with applications of triclopyrester by hovering helicopter. Proc. West. Soc. Weed Sci. 35:36–38.

Leary, R.A. 1985. Interaction theory in forest ecology and management. Martinus Nijhoff / Dr. W. Funk Publ., Dordrecht, Netherlands.

Lees, J.C. 1966. Release of white spruce from aspen competition in Alberta's spruce–aspen forest. Can. Dep. For., Ottawa, Ont., Publ. No. 1163.

Levine, R.L. and E.E. Langenau. 1979. Attitudes toward clearcutting and their relationship to the patterning and diversity of forest recreation activities. For. Sci. 25:317–327.

Licht, L.A. 1992. *Salicaceae* family trees in sustainable agroecosystems. For. Chron. 68:214–217.

Lousier, J.D. and B. Bancroft. 1990. Guidelines for alder seed control. For. Can. and B.C. Min. For., Victoria, B.C., FRDA Memo No. 132.

Lutz, H.J. 1955. Ecological effects of forest fires in the interior of Alaska. U.S. Dep. Agric., Tech. Bull. No. 1133.

McCaughey, W.W. and D.E. Ferguson. 1988. Response of advance regeneration to release in the Inland Mountain West: a summary. *In* Future forests of the mountain west: a stand culture symp. W.C. Schmidt (editor). U.S. Dep. Agric. For. Serv., Intermtn. For. Exp. Sta., Ogden, Utah, Gen. Tech. Rep. INT-243, pp. 255–266.

McClellan, M.H. 1987. Denitrification potential in forest riparian soils of the western Oregon Cascades: spatial and temporal variation. M.Sc. thesis, Oreg. State Univ., Corvallis Oreg.

MacKinnon, A. 1992. Letters: old-growth memo misleads. B.C. Prof. For. 1992(6):8.

McLennan, D.S. 1990a. Management of black cottonwood, red alder, bigleaf maple and paper birch in coastal British Columbia. For. Can. and B.C. Min. For., Victoria, B.C., FRDA Memo No. 133.

______. 1990b. Vegetation management planning exercise: coastal alluvial ecosystems. *In* Vegetation management: an integrated approach, Proc. 4th Annual Vegetation Management Workshop, Nov. 14–16, 1989, Vancouver, B.C. E. Hamilton (compiler). For. Can. and B.C. Min. For., Victoria, B.C., FRDA Rep. No. 109, pp. 124–127.

McLennan, D.S. and K. Klinka. 1990. Black cottonwood: a nurse species for regenerating western redcedar on brushy sites. For. Can. and B.C. Min. For., Victoria, B.C., FRDA Rep. 114.

McLennan, D.S. and A.-M. Mamias. 1992. Cottonwoods in British Columbia. Vol. 1. Problem analysis. For. Can. and B.C. Min. For., Victoria, B.C., FRDA Rep. No. 195.

McMahon, T.E. and G.F. Hartman. 1989. Influence of cover complexity and current velocity on winter habitat use by juvenile coho salmon (*Oncorhynchus kisutch*). Can. J. Fish. Aquat. Sci. 46:1551–1557.

McTaggart-Cowan, I. and C.J. Guiguet. 1965, 1973. The mammals of British Columbia. 3rd ed. B.C. Provincial Museum, Victoria, B.C., Handb. No. 11.

Madison. 1991. Madison's 1991 Canadian Lumber Directory, Publ. by Madison's Canadian Lumber Reporter, Vancouver, B.C.

Maier, G.B. and D. Darrah. 1988. Decay levels in mature aspen stands, Whitecourt, Alberta. For. Can. and Alta. For. Serv., North. For. Centre, Edmonton, Alta., Alberta Project 1467–72.

Maini, J.S. 1972. Silvics and ecology in Canada. *In* Aspen: Symp. Proc. U.S. Dep. Agric. For. Serv., N. Cent. For. Exp. Sta., St. Paul, Minn., Gen. Tech. Rep. NC-1, pp. 67–73.

Marchant, C. and J. Sherlock. 1984. A guide to selection and propagation of some native woody species for land rehabilitation in British Columbia. B.C. Min. For., Victoria, B.C., Res. Rep. RR84007-HQ.

Marion, G.K. 1979. Biomass and nutrient removal in long-rotation stands. *In* Impact of intensive harvesting on forest nutrient cycling. A.L. Leaf (editor). State Univ. N. Y., Syracuse, N.Y., pp. 98–110.

Marquis, D.A. 1966. Germination and growth of paper birch and yellow birch in simulated strip cuttings. U.S. Dep. Agric. For. Serv., NE For. Exp. Sta., Broomall, Pa., Res. Pap. NE-54.

Mason, C.F. and S.M. MacDonald. 1982. The input of terrestrial invertebrates from tree canopies to a stream. Freshwater Biol. 12:305–311.

Massie, M.R.C. 1990. Current biomass status of red alder in coastal British Columbia. For. Can. and B.C. Min. For., Victoria, B.C., FRDA Rep. No. 115.

Massie, M.R.C., E.B. Peterson, and R.D. Kabzems. 1990. An economic strategy for managing aspen on private lands in northeast British Columbia. For. Can. and B.C. Min. For., Victoria, B.C., FRDA Rep. No. 124.

Mather, J. [1988.] Assessment of silvicultural practices used in the Interior Cedar–Hemlock Zone of the southern Interior: ICHm2, b and v subzones: Salmon Arm, Vernon, and Revelstoke Districts. B.C. Min. For., Kamloops, B.C., FRDA Project 3.47. Unpubl. rep.

Meehan, W.R., F.J. Swanson, and J.R. Sedell. 1977. Influences of riparian vegetation on aquatic ecosystems with particular reference to salmonid fishes and their food supply. *In* Importance, preservation and management of riparian habitat: a symposium. R.R. Johnson and D.A. Jones (editors). U.S. Dep. Agric. For. Serv., Rocky Mtn. For. Range Exp. Sta., Fort Collins, Col., Gen. Tech. Rep. RM-43, pp. 137–145.

Meidinger, D. and J. Pojar. 1991. Ecosystems of British Columbia. B.C. Min. For., Victoria, B.C., Special Rep. No. 6.

Merrit, R.W. and K.W. Cummins (editors). 1978. An introduction to the aquatic insects of North America. Kendall Hunt Publishing, Dubuque, Iowa.

Minore, D. 1979. Comparative autecological characteristics of northwestern tree species: a literature review. U.S. Dep. Agric. For. Serv., Pac. NW For. Range Exp. Sta., Portland, Oreg., Gen. Tech. Rep. PNW-87.

Minore, D. and J.C. Zasada. 1990. *Acer macrophyllum* Pursh. Bigleaf maple. *Aceraceae*: maple family. *In* Silvics of North America. Vol. 2, Hardwoods. R.M. Burns and B.H. Honkala (technical coordinators). U.S. Dep. Agric. For. Serv., Washington, D.C. Agric. Handb. No. 654, pp. 33–40.

Mitchell, A.K. 1992. Research solutions to problems in the management of established stands. For. Ecol. Manage. 49:119–132.

Montieth, J.L. (editor). 1975. Vegetation and the atmosphere. Vol. 1. Academic Press, New York, N.Y.

Morgan, K and B. Freedman. 1986. Breeding bird communities in a hardwood forest succession in Nova Scotia. Can. Field Nat. 100(4):506–519.

Morrison, D., H. Merler, and D. Norris. 1991. Detection, recognition and management of Armillaria and Phellinus root diseases in the southern interior of British Columbia. For. Can. and B.C. Min. For., Victoria, B.C., FRDA Rep. 179.

Murphy, M.L., C.P. Hawkins, and N.H. Anderson. 1981. Effects of canopy modifications and accumulated sediment on stream communities. Trans. Am. Fish. Soc. 110:469–478.

Nadkarni, N.M. 1984. Biomass and mineral capital of epiphytes in an *Acer macrophyllum* community of a temperate moist coniferous forest, Olympic Peninsula, Washington State. Can. J. Bot. 62:2223–2238.

National Forest Products Association. 1980. America grows on trees: the promise of private, non-industrial woodlands. Private Woodlands Committee, NFPA, Washington, D.C.

Navratil, S., K. Branter, and J. Zasada. 1991. Regeneration in the mixedwoods. *In* Northern mixedwood '89, Proc. symp., Sept. 12–14, 1989, Fort St. John, B.C. A. Shortreid, (editor). For. Can. and B.C. Min. For., Victoria, B.C., FRDA Rep. No. 164, pp. 32–48.

Navratil, S. and P.B. Chapman (editors). 1991. Aspen management in the 21st century, Proc. symp. Nov. 20–21, 1990, Edmonton, Alta. For. Can. and Poplar Council Can., Edmonton, Alta.

Navratil, S., P. Phillips, and R. Morton. 1990. Aspen competition and lodgepole pine growth in mixed regeneration in western Alberta. *In* Vegetation management: an integrated approach, Proc. 4th Annual Vegetation Management Workshop, Nov. 14–16, 1989, Vancouver, B.C. E. Hamilton (compiler). For. Can. and B.C. Min. For., Victoria, B.C., FRDA Rep. No. 109, pp. 43–44.

Nawitka Resource Consultants, R.J. Hyslop and Associates, and Phillip Musgrave. 1990. Increasing the utilization level of British Columbia's timber harvest. For. Can. and B.C. Min. For., Victoria, B.C., FRDA Rep. No. 121.

Neil, R. [In press.] Evaluation of riparian management on wildlife diversity. Silvicultural Systems Working Group Project. Cranbrook. B.C.

Newton, M. [1989.] Community response of riparian vegetation to forest management. *In* COPE (Coastal Oregon Productivity Enhancement Program). Silvicultural management of riparian areas for multiple resources, a COPE Workshop, Dec. 12–13, 1989, Gleneden Beach, Oreg. U.S. Dep. Agric. For. Serv. Pac. NW For. Exp. Sta., Portland, Oreg. and Oreg. State Univ., Coll. For., Corvallis, Oreg. pp. 1–3, Session II. Unpubl.

Newton, M. and E.C. Cole. 1991. Combinations of glyphosate and imazapyr for control of deciduous woody species in western Oregon and Alaska. Proc. West. Soc. Weed Sci. 44:69–72.

Newton, M. and P.G. Comeau. 1990. Control of competing vegetation. *In* Regenerating British Columbia's forests. D.P. Lavender, R. Parish, C.M. Johnson, G. Montgomery, A. Vyse, R.A. Willis, and D. Winston (editors). Univ. B.C. Press, Vancouver, B.C., pp. 256–265.

Noble-Hearle, G. [1989.] Treatment effectiveness checks: brushing and weeding program. B.C. Min. For., Penticton District, Kamloops Forest Region. Unpubl. rep.

North, M.E.A., M.W. Dunn, and J.M. Teversham. 1979. Vegetation of the southwestern Fraser Lowland, 1858–1880. Environ. Can., Lands Direc., Vancouver, B.C.

Northern Lights College. 1988. Forestry or agriculture: a case for diversification. For. Can and B.C. Min. For., Victoria, B.C., FRDA Rep. No. 042.

Orca Consulting Group Inc. 1991. Provincial summary reporting system. Version 1.0. Operations manual.

Orchard, S.A. 1988a. Species notes for reptiles. Vol. 3. *In* Wildlife habitat handbooks for the southern Interior ecoprovince. A.P. Harcombe (technical editor). Min. Environ. and Min. For., Victoria, B.C.

______. 1988b. Species notes for amphibians. Vol. 4. *In* Wildlife habitat handbooks for the southern Interior ecoprovince. A.P. Harcombe (technical editor). Min. Environ. and Min. For., Victoria, B.C.

Orchard, S.A. and A.P. Harcombe. 1988. Species habitat relationship models for amphibians. Vol. 8. *In* Wildlife habitat handbooks for the southern Interior Ecoprovince. A.P. Harcombe (technical editor). Min. Environ. and Min. For., Victoria, B.C.

Otchere-Boateng, J. 1990. Herbicide field handbook. For. Can. and B.C. Min. For., Victoria, B.C., FRDA Handb. No. 6.

Ovington, J.D. 1958a. Studies of the development of woodland conditions under different trees. 6. Soil sodium, potassium and phosphorus. J. Ecol. 46:127–141.

______. 1958b. Studies of the development of woodland conditions under different trees. 7. Soil calcium and magnesium. J. Ecol. 46:391–405.

Packee, E.C. 1976. An ecological approach toward yield optimization through species allocation. Ph.D. thesis. Univ. Minn., St. Paul, Minn.

Paine, R.T. 1966. Food web complexity and species diversity. Am. Nat. 100:65–75.

Palmer, G. 1975. Shuswap Indian ethnobotany. Syesis 8:29–81.

Pendl, F. and B. D'Anjou. [1984.] Operational trial of the herbicide "Roundup" at Pender Harbour. Establishment Rep. B.C. Min. For., Vancouver, B.C. Unpubl. rep.

______. 1990. Effect of manual treatment timing on red alder regrowth and conifer response. For. Can. and B.C. Min. For., Victoria, B.C., FRDA Rep. No. 112.

Perala, D.A. 1979. Regeneration and productivity of aspen grown on repeated short rotations. U.S. Dep. Agric. For. Serv., N. Cent. For. Exp. Sta., St. Paul, Minn., Res. Pap. NC-241.

______. 1990. *Populus tremuloides* Michx. Quaking aspen. *Salicaceae*: willow family. *In* Silvics of North America. Vol. 2, Hardwoods. R.M. Burns and B.H. Honkala (technical coordinators). U.S. Dep. Agric. For. Serv., Washington, D.C. Agric. Handb. 654, pp. 555–569.

Perala, D.A. and A.A. Alm. 1989. Regenerating paper birch in the Lake States with the shelterwood method. North. J. Appl. For. 6(4):151–153.

______. 1990a. Reproductive ecology of birch: a review. For. Ecol. Manage. 32:1–38.

______. 1990b. Regeneration silviculture of birch: a review. For. Ecol. Manage. 32:39–77.

Perala, D.A. and J. Russell. 1983. Aspen. *In* Silvicultural systems for the major forest types of the United States. R.M. Burns (compiler). U.S. Dep. Agric. For. Serv., Washington, D.C., Agric. Handb. No. 445, pp. 113–115.

Perry, J. 1983. Hardwood invasion on cutblocks in the Cariboo Forest Region. B.C. Min. For., Williams Lake, B.C. Unpubl. rep.

Peterson, E.B. and N.M. Peterson. 1992. Ecology, management and use of aspen and balsam poplar in the prairie provinces, Can. For. Can., North. For. Cent., Edmonton, Alta. Special Rep. 1.

Peterson, E.B., A. Kabzems, R.D. Kabzems, and N.M. Peterson. 1989a. Boreal mixedwood forest management challenges: a synopsis of opinions from 1988 interviews. For. Can., North. For. Res. Cent., Edmonton, Alta., ENFOR Project P-353.

Peterson, E.B., R.D. Kabzems, and N.M. Peterson. 1989b. Hardwood management problems in northeastern British Columbia: an information review. For. Can. and B.C. Min. For., Victoria, B.C., FRDA Rep. No. 066.

Peterson, E.B., V.M. Levson, and R.D. Kabzems. 1982. Upper limits of standing crop density for woody species in the prairie provinces. Can. For. Serv., North. For. Res. Cent., Edmonton, Alta., Inf. Rep. NOR-X-243.

Plank, M.E., T.A. Snellgrove, and S. Willits. 1990. Product values dispel "weed species" myth of red alder. For. Prod. J. 40(2):23–28.

Pollack, J. and P. LePage. 1990. Relative costs of red alder-to-conifer site conversion. For. Can. and B.C. Min. For., Victoria, B.C., FRDA Memo No. 145.

Pollard, D.F.W. 1985. A forestry perspective on the carbon dioxide issue. For. Chron. 61:312–318.

Presslee, D.J. 1989. Use of herbicides for site preparation and brushing and weeding in the Sub-Boreal Spruce Zone: a northwood perspective. *In* Learning from the past, looking to the future. Proc. North. Silvic. Committee's 1988 Winter Workshop, Feb. 2–3, 1988, Prince George, B.C. B.A. Scrivener and J.A. MacKinnon (editors). For. Can. and B.C. Min. For., Victoria, B.C., FRDA Rep. No. 030, pp. 103–107.

Province of British Columbia. Revised Statutes of British Columbia. 1979. Chapter 272, Section 4, Subsection C: Ministry of Forests Act. Looseleaf revision dated 1987.

______. 1991. A summary of public comments. Commercial backcountry recreation on Crown land in B.C. B.C. Min. Lands and Parks.

Pukkala, T., S. Kellomaki, and E. Mustonen. 1988. Prediction of the amenity of a tree stand. Scand. J. For. Res. 3:533–544.

Quintilio, D., M.E. Alexander, and R.L. Ponto. 1991. Spring fires in a semimature trembling aspen stand in central Alberta. For. Can., North. For. Res. Cent., Edmonton, Alta., Inf. Rep. NOR-X-323.

Rauscher, H.M., D.A. Perala, and G.E. Host. 1990. An aspen forest management advisory system. *In* Aspen symposium '89, Proc. symp., July 25–27, 1989, Duluth, Minn. R.D. Adams (editor). U.S. Dep. Agric. For. Serv., N. Cent. For. Exp. Sta., St. Paul, Minn. Gen. Tech. Rep. NC-140, pp. 185–194.

Rautio, S.L. and P. Bunnell. [In press.] Problem analysis of integrated resource management in riparian areas: Executive summary. B.C. Min. For. and B.C. Min. Environ., Victoria, B.C.

Registrar General of Canada. 1899. Treaty No. 8. pp. 290–293.

Revel, J. 1983. The impact of some hardwoods on silviculture in the Prince George Forest Region. B.C. Min. For., Prince George, B.C. Unpubl. pap.

Reynolds, H.G. 1969. Use of openings in spruce-fir forests of Arizona by elk, deer, and cattle. U.S. Dep. Agric. For. Serv., Rocky Mtn. For. Range Exp. Sta., Fort Collins, Col., Res. Note RM-138.

Ribe, R.G. 1991. The aesthetics of forestry: what has empirical preference research taught us? Environ. Manage. 13(1):55–74.

Roberts, P.L. 1983. Landowner perceptions of scenic beauty for eastern hardwood stands under different management regimes. M.A. thesis. Va. Polytech. Inst. and State Univ., Blacksburg, Va.

Rodin, L.E. and N.I. Bazilevich. 1967. Production and mineral cycling in terrestrial vegetation. Oliver and Boyd, Edinburgh, U.K. Eng. transl. by Scripta Technica Ltd.

Roe, A.L. 1958. Silvics of black cottonwood. U.S. Dep. Agric. For. Serv., Washington, D.C., Misc. Publ. 17.

Rood, S.B. and J.M. Mahoney (editors). 1991. The biology and management of southern Alberta's cottonwoods. Proc. Univ. Lethbridge Conf., May 4–6, 1990. Univ. Lethbridge, Lethbridge, Alta.

Rose, C.L. [1991.] Preliminary analysis of birch growth and yield in the central Interior of British Columbia. Prep. for B.C. Min. For., Victoria, B.C. Unpubl. draft.

Rutter, A.J. 1975. The hydrological cycle in vegetation. *In* Vegetation and the atmosphere. J.L. Montieth (editor). Academic Press, New York, N.Y., pp. 111–154.

Ryan, B. 1992. Poplar wars in northern Manitoba. Logging & Sawmilling J. 23(1):5–7.

Safford, L.O., J.C. Bjorkbom, and J.C. Zasada. 1990. *Betula payrifera* Marsh. Paper birch Betulaceae: birch family. *In* Silvics of North America. Vol. 2, Hardwoods. R.M. Burns and B.H. Honkala (technical coordinators). U.S. Dep. Agric. For. Serv., Washington, D.C., Agric. Handb. 654, pp. 158–171.

Salo, E.O. and T.W. Cundy (editors). 1987. Streamside management: forestry and fishery interactions. Univ. Wash., Inst. For. Resources, Seattle, Wash. Contrib. No. 57.

Schier, G.A. 1981. Physiological research on adventitious shoot development in aspen roots. U.S. Dep. Agric. For. Serv., Intermtn.. For. Range Exp. Sta., Ogden, Utah, Gen. Tech. Rep. INT-107.

Schier, G.A. and R.B. Campbell. 1978. Aspen sucker regeneration following burning and clearcutting on two sites in the Rocky Mountains. For. Sci. 24(2):303–308.

Schier, G.A., J.R. Jones, and R.P. Winokur. 1985. Vegetative regeneration. *In* Aspen: ecology and management in the western United States. N.V. DeByle and R.P. Winokur, (editors). U.S. Dep. Agric. For. Serv., Rocky Mtn For. Range Exp. Sta., Fort Collins, Col., Gen. Tech. Rep. RM-119, pp. 29–33.

Schopmeyer, C.S. 1974. Seeds of woody plants in the United States. U.S. Dep. Agric. For. Serv., Washington, D.C., Agric. Handb. No. 450.

Scrivner, J.C. 1987. Changes in composition of the streambed between 1973 and 1985 and impacts on salmonids in Carnation Creek. *In* Applying 15 years of Carnation Creek results: Proc. workshop. T.W. Chamberain (editor). Pac. Biol. Sta., Nanaimo, B.C., pp. 59–65.

Shainsky, L.J., M. Newton, and S.R. Radosevich. 1992. Effects of intra- and inter-specific competition on root and shoot biomass of young Douglas-fir and red alder. Can. J. For. Res. 22:101–110.

Shainsky, L.J. and S.R. Radosevich. 1992. Mechanisms of competition between Douglas-fir and red alder seedlings. Ecology 73:30–45.

Shepperd, W.D. and J.R. Jones. 1985. Nurse crop. *In* Aspen: ecology and management in the western United States. N.V. DeByle and R.P. Winokur (editors). U.S. Dep. Agric. For. Serv., Rocky Mtn. For. Range Exp. Sta., Fort Collins, Col., Gen. Tech. Rep. RM-119, pp. 181–184.

Simard, S. 1990. A retrospective study of competition between paper birch and planted Douglas-fir. For. Can. and B.C. Min. For., Victoria, B.C., FRDA Rep. No. 147.

Simard, S. and A. Vyse. 1992. Ecology and management of paper birch and black cottonwood in southern British Columbia. B.C. Min. For., Victoria, B.C., Land Manage. Rep. No. 75.

Smith, D.M. 1986. The practice of silviculture. 8th ed. John Wiley & Sons, Toronto, Ont.

Stebbins, G.L. 1972. Evolution and diversity of arid-land shrubs. *In* Wildland shrubs: their biology and utilization. C.M. McKell, J.P. Blaisdell, and J.R. Goodin, (editors). U.S. Dep. Agric. For. Serv., Intermtn. For. Range Exp. Sta., Ogden, Utah. Gen. Tech. Rep. INT-1, pp. 111–120.

Steneker, G.A. 1976. Guide to the silvicultural management of trembling aspen in the Prairie Provinces. Can. For. Serv., North. For. Res. Cent., Edmonton, Alta., Inf. Rep. NOR-X-164.

Steneker, G.A. and R.E. Wall. 1970. Aspen clones: their significance and recognition. Can. For. Serv., For. Res. Lab., Winnipeg, Man., Liaison and Serv. Note MS-L-8.

Stiell, W.M. and A.B. Berry. 1986. Productivity of short rotation aspen stands. For. Chron. 62:10–15.

Stubblefield, G. and C.D. Oliver. 1978. Silvicultural implications of the reconstruction of mixed alder/conifer stands. *In* Utilization and management of alder. D.G. Briggs, D.S. DeBell, and W.A. Atkinson (compilers). U.S. Dep. Agric. For. Serv., Pac. NW For. Range Exp. Sta., Portland, Oreg., Gen. Tech. Rep. PNW-70, pp. 307–320.

Sullivan, K, T.E. Lisle, C.A. Dolloff, G.E. Grant, and L.M. Reid. 1987. Stream channels: the link between forests and fishes. *In* Streamside management: forestry and fishery interactions. E.O. Salo and T.W. Cundy (editors). Univ. Wash., Inst. For. Resources, Seattle, Wash., pp. 39–97.

Surveys and Resource Mapping Branch. 1992. Baseline thematic mapping of southern Vancouver Island. 1:250 000 scale. Portions of mapsheets 92B, C, F, G. Based on 1990 inventory, Victoria, B.C.

Swank, G.W. 1990. Streamside management units in the Pacific Northwest. For. Ecol. Manage. 33/34: 419–424.

Swanson, F.J., L.E. Benda, S.H. Duncan, G.E. Grant, W.F. Megahan, L.M. Reid, and R.R. Ziemer. 1987. Mass failures and other processes of sediment production in Pacific Northwest forest landscapes. *In* Streamside management: forestry and fishery interactions. E.O. Salo and T.W. Cundy (editors). Univ. Wash., Inst. For. Resources, Seattle, Wash. pp. 9–39.

Tang, Z.C. and T.T. Kozlowski. 1982. Some physiological and growth responses of *Betula papyrifera* seedlings to flooding. Physiol. Plant. 55:415–420.

Taylor, R.L. and B. MacBryde. 1977. Vascular plants of British Columbia: a descriptive resource inventory. Univ. B.C., Bot. Garden, Vancouver, B.C., Tech. Bull. No. 4.

Tevershan, J.M. and J. Slaymaker. 1976. Vegetation composition in relation to flood frequency in Lillooet River Valley, B.C. Catena 3:191–129.

Thomas, G.P. and D.B. Podmore. 1953. Studies in forestry pathology. XI. Decay in black cottonwood in the middle Fraser region, British Columbia. Can. J. Bot. 31:672–692.

Thompson, C.F. 1989. Developing herbicide efficacy tables for the southern interior. For. Can. and B.C. Min. For., Victoria, B.C., FRDA Rep. 096.

Thomson, B. 1991. Annotated bibliography of large organic debris (LOD) with regards to stream channels and fish habitat. B.C. Min. Environ., Victoria, B.C., Tech. Rep. 32.

Tripp, D. 1986. Using large organic debris to restore fish habitat in debris-torrented streams. B.C. Min. of For. and Lands, Victoria, B.C., Land Manage. Rep. No. 47.

Turner, N.J. 1975. Food plants of British Columbia Indians. Part 1: Coastal peoples. B.C. Prov. Museum, Victoria, B.C., Handb. No. 34.

______. 1978 Food plants of British Columbia Indians: Part 2: Interior peoples. B.C. Prov. Museum, Victoria, B.C., Handb. No. 36.

______. 1979. Plants in British Columbia Indian technology. B.C. Prov. Museum, Victoria, B.C., Handb. No. 38.

______. [1992.] Plants for all reasons: culturally important plants of aboriginal peoples of southern Vancouver Island. Univ. Victoria, Victoria, B.C., Environ. Studies Program. Unpubl. manuscript.

Turner, N.J. and R.J. Hebda. 1990. Contemporary use of bark for medicine by two Salishan native elders of southeast Vancouver Island, Canada. J. Ethnopharm. 29:59–72.

Turner, N.J., L.C. Thompson, and M.T. Thompson. 1990. Thompson ethnobotany: knowledge and usage of plants by the Thompson Indians of British Columbia. Royal B.C. Museum, Victoria, B.C., Memoir No. 3.

University of British Columbia Forest Club. 1959. Forestry handbook for British Columbia. 2nd ed., Vancouver, B.C.

van der Kamp, B.J. 1991. Pathogens as agents of diversity in forested landscapes. For. Chron. 67(4):353–354.

Van Miegroet, H. and D.W. Cole. 1988. Influence of nitrogen-fixing alder on acidification and cation leaching in a forest soil. *In* Forest site evaluation and long-term productivity. D.W. Cole and S.P. Gessel (editors). Univ. Wash. Press, Seattle, Wash., Contrib. Inst. For. Resources No. 63, pp. 113–124.

Van Miegroet, H., D.W. Cole, and P.S. Homann. 1990. The effect of alder forest cover and alder forest conversion on site fertility and productivity. *In* Sustained productivity of forest soils, Proc. 7th N. Am. For. Soils Conf., S.P. Gessel, D.S. Lacate, G.F. Weetman, and R.F. Powers (editors). Univ. B.C., Fac. For., Vancouver, B.C., pp. 333–354.

Vermes, J.-F. and D.D. Myrold. 1992. Denitrification in forest soils of Oregon. Can. J. For. Res. 22:504–512.

Viereck, L.A. and E.L. Little. 1972. Alaska trees and shrubs. U.S. Dep. Agric. For. Serv., Washington, D.C., Agric. Handb. No. 410.

Vodak, M.C., P.L. Roberts, J.D. Wellman, and G.J. Buyoff. 1985. Scenic impacts of eastern hardwood management. For. Sci. 31:289–302.

Wagner, R.G. and J.C. Zasada. 1991. Integrating plant autecology and silvicultural activities to prevent forest vegetation management problems. For. Chron. 67(5):506–513.

Walker, L.R. and F.S. Chapin III. 1986. Physiological controls over seedling growth in primary succession on an Alaska floodplain. Ecology 67:1508–1523.

Wall, R.E. 1990. The fungus *Chondrostereum purpureum* as a silvicide to control stump sprouting in hardwoods. North. J. Appl. For. 7:17–19.

Walsh, R.G., J.B. Loomis, and R.A. Giman. 1984. Valuing option, existence and bequest demands for wilderness. Land Econ. 60(1):14–29.

Walstad, J.D., M. Newton, and R.J. Boyd, Jr. 1987. Forest vegetation problems in the Northwest. *In* Forest vegetation management for conifer production J.D. Walstad and P.J. Kuch (editors). John Wiley & Sons, New York, N.Y., pp. 15–53.

Walters, M.A., R.O. Teskey, and T.M. Hinckley. 1980. Impact of water level changes on woody riparian and wetland communities. Vol. VIII. Pacific Northwest and Rocky Mountain Regions. U.S. Dep. Interior, Fish Wildl. Serv., Off. Biol. Serv., Nat. Water Resources Analysis Group, Kearneysville, W. Va., FWS/OBS-78/94.

Watson, L.E., R.W. Parker, and D.F. Polster. 1980. Manual of species suitability for reclamation in Alberta. 2 Vols. Alta. Land Conserv. Reclamation Council, Edmonton, Alta., Rep. No. RRTAC 80-5.

Weetman, G.F., E. Panozzo, M. Jull, and K. Marek. 1990. An assessment of the opportunities for alternative silvicultural systems in the SBS, ICH and ESSF biogeoclimatic zones of the Prince Rupert Forest region. Contract rep. prep. for B.C. Min. For., Prince Rupert Forest Region, Smithers, B.C.

Weetman, G.F. and A. Vyse. 1990. Natural regeneration. *In* Regenerating British Columbia's forests. D.P. Lavender, R. Parish, C.M. Johnson, G. Montgomery, A. Vyse, R.A. Willis, and D. Winston (editors). Univ. B.C. Press, Vancouver, B.C., pp. 118–130.

Westell, C.J. Jr. 1954. Available browse following aspen logging in lower Michigan. J. Wildl. Manage. 18(2):266–271.

Westworth, D.A. and Associates Ltd. 1984. Impact on wildlife of short-rotation management of boreal aspen stands. E.S. Telfer (editor). Can. For. Serv.

Whitney, R.D. and K.M. McClain (editors). 1981. Boreal mixedwood symp. proc. Sept. 16–18, 1989, Thunder Bay, Ont. Dep. Environ., Can. For. Serv., Great Lakes For. Res. Cent., Sault Ste. Marie, Ont. COJFRC Symp. Proc. 0-P-9.

Worthington, N.P. 1957. Silvical characteristics of red alder. U.S. Dep. Agric. For. Serv., Pac. NW For. Exp. Sta., Portland, Oreg., Silv. Ser. 1.

Worthington, N.P., R.H. Ruth, and E.E. Matson. 1962. Red alder: its management and utilization. U.S. Dep. Agric. For. Serv., Washington, D.C., Misc. Publ. No. 881.

Young, W. 1990. Integrated resource management in British Columbia: an historical perspective. *In* Wildlife Forestry Symp. Proc., For. Can., B.C. Min. For., B.C. Min. Environ. and Can. Inst. For., Victoria, B.C., FRDA Rep. No. 160.

Zahner, R. and Crawford, N.A. 1965. The clonal concept in aspen site relations. *In* Forest-soil relationships in North America. Proc. 2nd N. Am. For. Soils Conf., August, 1963, Corvallis, Oreg. C.T. Youngberg (editor). Oreg. State Univ. Press, Corvallis, Oreg., pp. 229–243.

Zasada, J.C. 1971. Natural regeneration of interior Alaska forest-seed, seedbed and vegetative reproduction considerations. *In* Fire in the northern environment, a symposium. C.W. Slaughter, R.J. Barney, and G.M. Hansen (editors). U.S. Dep. Agric. For. Serv., Fairbanks, Alaska, pp. 231–246.

Zasada, J.C. and H.M. Phipps. 1990. *Populus balsamifera* L. Balsam poplar. Salicaceae: willow family. *In* Silvics of North America. Vol. 2, Hardwoods. R.M. Burns and B.H. Honkala (technical coordinators). U.S. Dep. Agric. For. Serv., Washington, D.C., Agric. Handb. No. 654, pp. 515–529.

Zasada, J.C. and J. Tappeiner. 1989. Reproductive ecology of riparian vegetation. *In* Silvicultural management of riparian areas for multiple resources, a COPE Workshop, Dec. 12–13, 1989, Gleneden Beach, Oreg. U.S. Dep. Agric. For. Serv., Pac. NW For. Exp. Sta., Portland, Oreg. and Oreg. State Univ, Coll. For., Corvallis, Oreg., pp. 1–4.

Zasada, J.C., J.C. Tappeiner II, and T.A. Max. 1990. Viability of bigleaf maple seeds after storage. West. J. Appl. For. 5(2):52–55.

Zasada, J.C., L.A. Viereck, M.J. Foote, R.H. Parkenson, J.O. Wolff, and L.A. Lankford, Jr. 1981. Natural regeneration of balsam poplar following harvesting in the Susitna Valley, Alaska. For. Chron. 57:57–65.

Zasada, J.C., R.A. Norum, R.M. van Veldhuizen, and C.E. Teutsch. 1983. Artificial regeneration of trees and tall shrubs in experimentally burned upland black spruce/feather moss stands in Alaska. Can. J. For. Res. 13:903–913.

Zavitkovski, J. and R.D. Stevens. 1972. Primary productivity of red alder ecosystems. Ecology 53:235–242.

Zsuffa, L. 1979. The features and prospects of poplar breeding in Ontario. *In* Poplar research, management and utilization in Canada. D.C.F. Fayle, L. Zsuffa, and H.W. Anderson (editors). Ont. Min. Nat. Resources, Toronto, Ont., For. Res. Inf. Pap. No. 102, pp. 1–6.

______. Northern mixedwood research—implications of genetic improvement. *In* Northern mixedwood '89, Proc. symp. Sept. 12–14, 1989, Fort St. John, B.C. A. Shortreid (editor). For. Can. and B.C. Min. For., Victoria, B.C., FRDA Rep. No. 164, pp. 111–115.

PERSONAL COMMUNICATIONS

Darryl Barron, B.C. Min. For., Williams Lake For. Dist., Williams Lake, B.C.
Marilyn Blache, B.C. Min. For., Res. Br., Victoria, B.C.
Mike Brownlee, B.C. Min. For., Integrated Resources Br., Victoria, B.C.
Anthony Britneff, B.C. Min. For., Inventory Br., Victoria, B.C.
Gary Bull, Lakehead University, Thunder Bay, Ont.
Dave Campbell, B.C. Min. For., Range Br., Victoria, B.C.
Bill Chalk, B.C. Min. For., Inventory Br., Victoria, B.C.
Steve Chatwin, B.C. Min. For., Res. Br., Victoria, B.C.
Dave Clark, B.C. Min. Environ., Lands, Parks, Wildl. Br., Victoria, B.C.
Ray Coupé, B.C. Min. For., Cariboo For. Region, Williams Lake, B.C.
Garry Darychuck, B.C. Min. For., Nelson For. Region, Nelson, B.C.
Ray Demarchi, B.C. Min. Environ., Lands, Parks, Victoria, B.C.
Hans Dyck, B.C. Min. Aboriginal Affairs, Victoria, B.C.
Bruce Enns, Computer Consultant, Victoria, B.C.
Malcom Grey, B.C. Min. Environ., Lands, Parks, Victoria, B.C.
Alex Grzybowski, B.C. Min. Tourism, Tourism Div., Victoria, B.C.
S. Hawthorn, B.C. Min. Environ., Lands, Parks, Victoria, B.C.
Bruce Hillaby, Dep. Fish. Oceans, Pac. Biol. Cent., Nanaimo, B.C.
Kim Iles, Consulting Forester, Nanaimo, B.C.
Dave Jones, B.C. Min. Environ., Lands, Parks, Southern Interior Sub-Regional Office, Penticton, B.C.
Harold McEachern, B.C. Min. For., For. Dist. Fort St. John, B.C.
Al Martin, B.C. Min. Environ., Lands, Parks, Wildl. Br., Fish. Br., Victoria, B.C.
Bill Munro, B.C. Min. Environ., Lands, Parks, Wildl. Br., Victoria, B.C.
Ted Murray, B.C. Min. For., Rec. Branch, Victoria, B.C.
Teresa Newsome, Research Silviculturist, Cariboo Region, B.C. Min. For. Williams Lake, B.C.
Ken Raedeke, Univ. Wash., Inst. For. Resources, Seattle, Wash.
Al Rodine, B.C. Min. For., Dawson Creek For. Dist., Dawson Creek, B.C.
Charles Scrivner, Dep. Fish. Oceans, Pac. Biol. Sta., Nanaimo, B.C.
Suzanne Simard, B.C. Min. For., Kamloops For. Region, Kamloops, B.C.
Victoria Stevens, Wildlife Biologist, Victoria, B.C.
Geoff Tomlins, Binary Image Corp., White Rock, B.C.
Peter Tschaplinski, B.C. Min. For., Res. Br., Victoria, B.C.
Terje Vold, B.C. Min. For., Rec. Br., Victoria, B.C.
Carla Warth, Univ. Wash., Cent. Streamside Studies, Seattle, Wash.
Reg Whiten, Treaty 8 Association, Fort St. John, B.C.
Guy Woods, B.C. Min. Environ., Lands, Parks, Kootenay Regional Headquarters, Nelson, B.C.

APPENDIX 1. Reference maps [a1]

Provincial transportation network

British Columbia forest regions and forest districts

British Columbia forest regions and timber supply areas

Delineation of Coast and Interior TSAs

Lead species analysis: white birch

Lead species analysis: interior cottonwood

Lead species analysis: coast alder

Lead species analysis: coast maple

Lead species analysis: coast cottonwood

Lead species analysis: aspen

Prince Rupert Forest Region TSAs

Prince George Forest Region TSAs

Cariboo Forest Region TSAs

Kamloops Forest Region TSAs

Nelson Forest Region TSAs

Vancouver Forest Region TSAs - northerly portion

Vancouver Forest region TSAs - southerly portion

[a1] Sources: Inventory Branch and Timber Supply Reports

Provincial transportation network

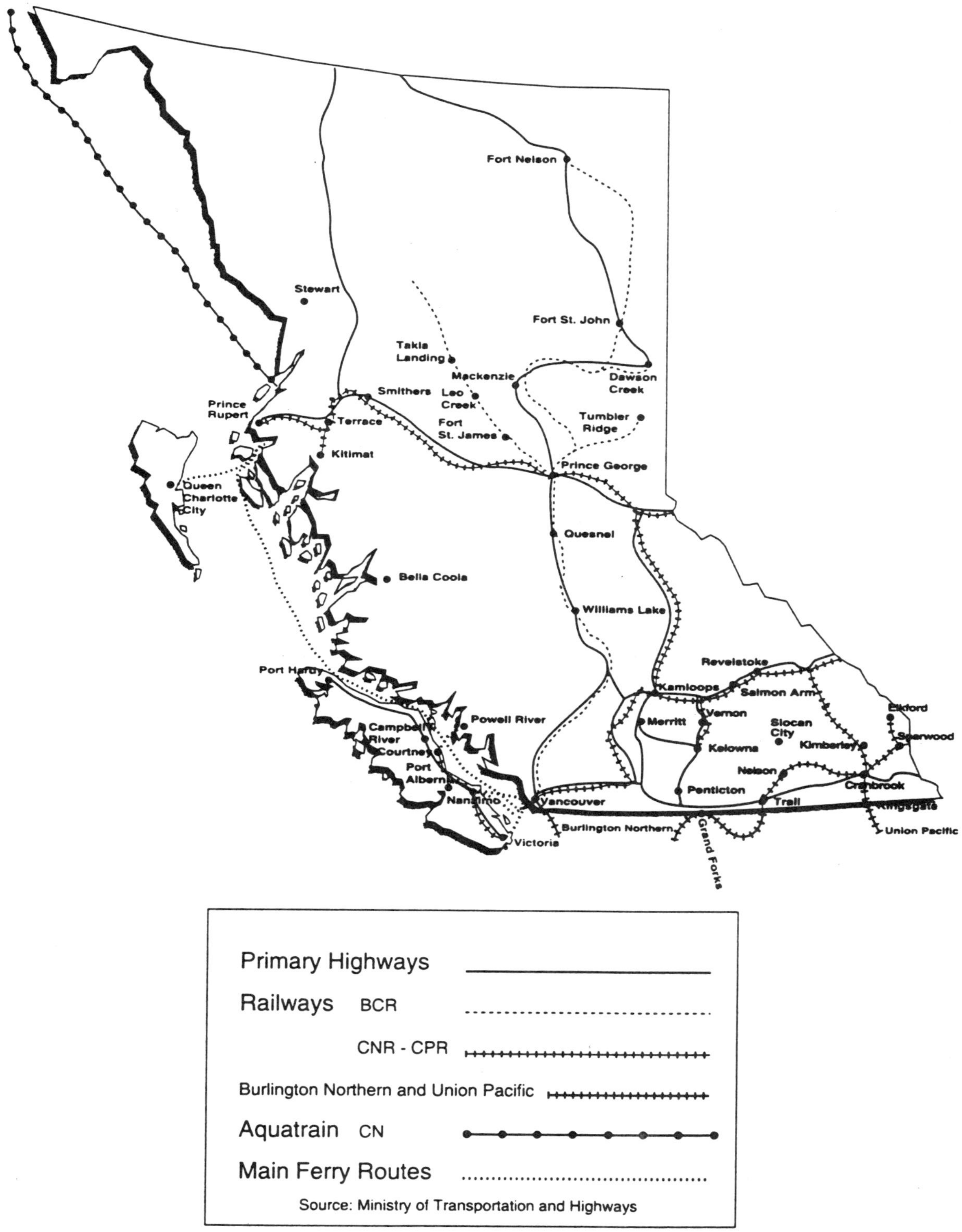

British Columbia forest regions and forest districts

VANCOUVER

11 Chilliwack
13 Squamish
15 Sunshine Coast
16 Duncan
17 Port Alberni
18 Campbell River
19 Port McNeill
1A Mid-Coast
1B Queen Charlotte

PRINCE RUPERT

21 Lakes
22 Morice
23 Bulkley
24 Kispiox
25 Kalum
28 North Coast
29 Cassiar

KAMLOOPS

31 Clearwater
32 Kamloops
33 Salmon Arm
34 Vernon
35 Penticton
36 Merritt
37 Lillooet

PRINCE GEORGE

41 Prince George
43 Robson Valley
44 Vanderhoof
45 Fort St James
46 Mackenzie
47 Dawson Creek
48 Fort St John
49 Fort Nelson

NELSON

51 Cranbrook
52 Invermere
53 Golden
54 Revelstoke
55 Arrow
56 Boundary
57 Kootenay Lake

CARIBOO

61 Quesnel
62 Williams Lake
63 Horsefly
64 100 Mile House
65 Chilcotin

94/01/01 E:\Misc\Overview\

British Columbia forest regions and timber supply areas

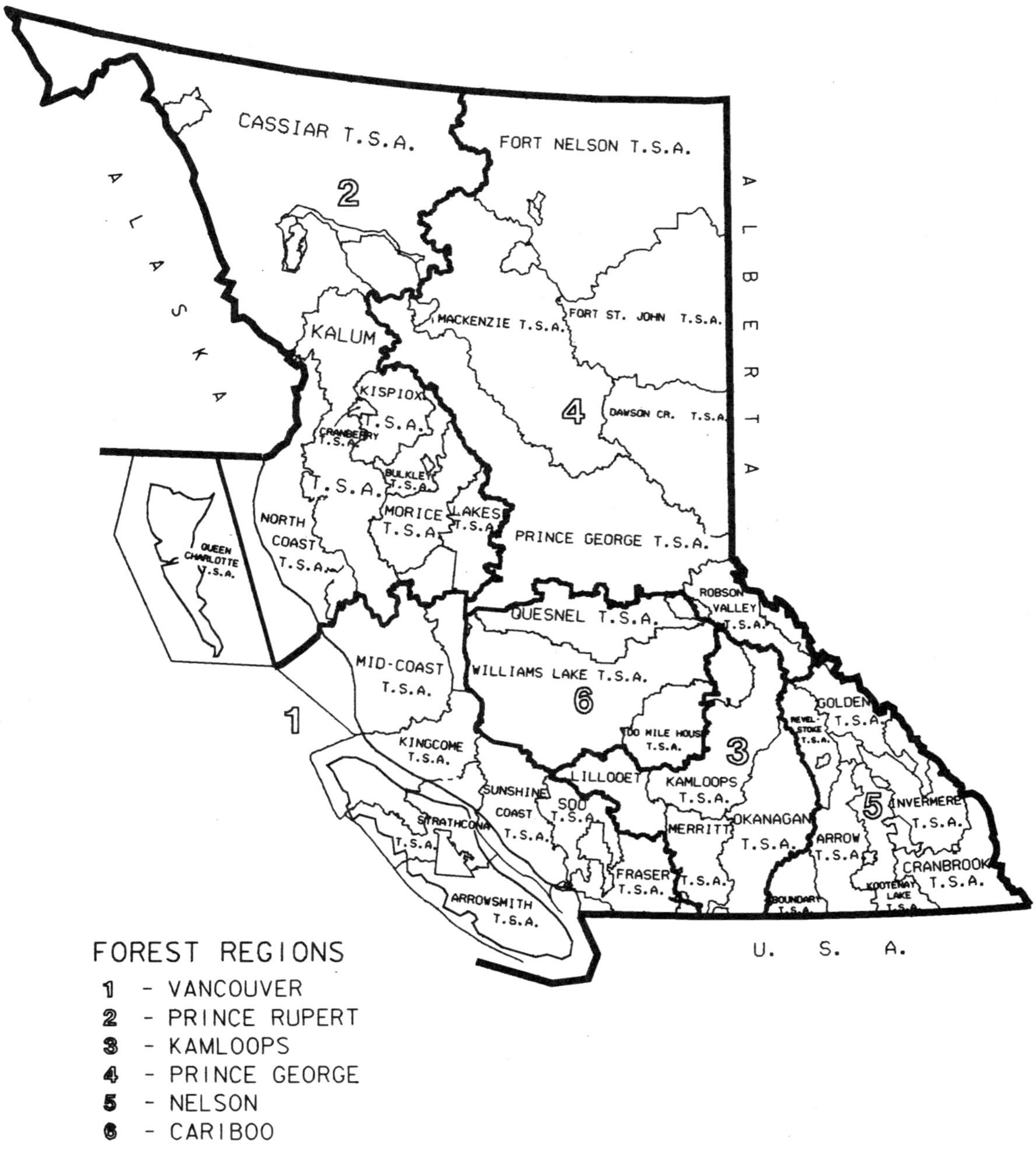

94/01/01 E:\Misc\Overview\

Delineation of Coast and Interior TSAs

94/01/01 E:\Misc\Overview\

Lead species analysis: white birch

Hectares (in 000's) in the Timber Supply Area where harvesting is permitted, not including poor site

Fort Nelson	103.0
Fort St. John	34.0
Okanagan	23.9
Prince George	15.7
Kamloops	14.2
Kispiox	9.8
Williams Lake	8.7

Lead species analysis: interior cottonwood

Hectares (in 000's) in the Timber Supply Area where harvesting is permitted, not including poor site

Dawson Creek	75.3
Fort Nelson	67.2
Fort St. John	17.8
Prince George	9.6
Kalum	7.7
Kispiox	7.7
Okanagan	4.0

Lead species analysis: coast alder

Hectares (in 000's) in the Timber Supply Area where harvesting is permitted, not including poor site

Sunshine Coast	38.2
Fraser	33.6
Strathcona	22.2
Kingcome	17.1
Arrowsmith	14.2

Lead species analysis: coast maple

Hectares (in 000's) in the Timber Supply Area where harvesting is permitted, not including poor site

Fraser	11.6
Sunshine Coast	2.0

Lead species analysis: coast cottonwood

Hectares (in 000's) in the Timber Supply Area where harvesting is permitted, not including poor site

Sunshine Coast	5.1
Fraser	4.6
Soo	3.9
Kingcome	3.7

Lead species analysis: aspen

Hectares (in 000's) in the Timber Supply Area where harvesting is permitted, not including poor site

Fort Nelson	1 050.0
Fort St. John	660.0
Dawson Creek	473.8
Prince George	364.4
Mackenzie	205.0
Williams Lake	93.0
Lakes	73.0
Quesnel	62.2

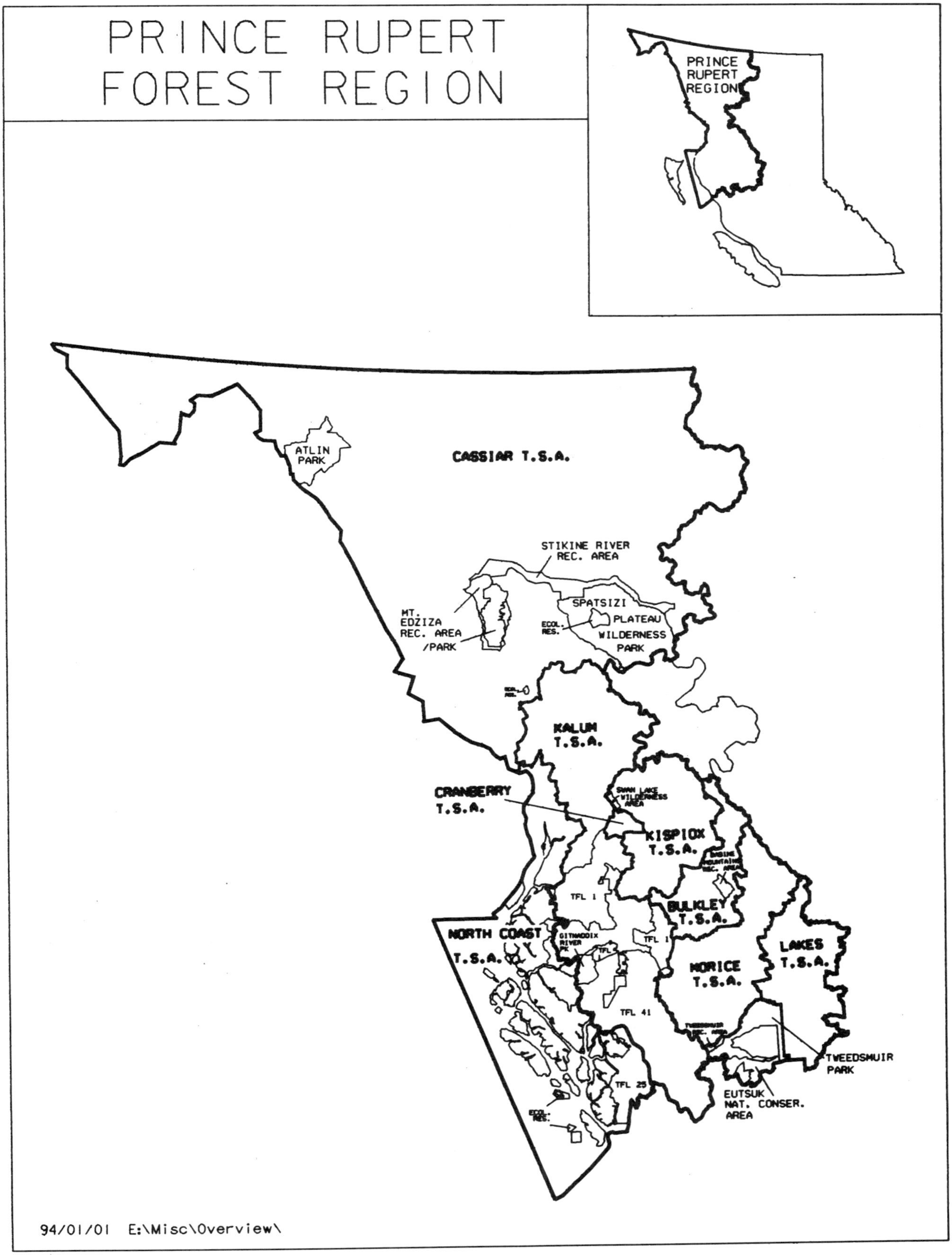
PRINCE RUPERT
FOREST REGION
PRINCE RUPERT REGION
CASSIAR T.S.A.
ATLIN PARK
STIKINE RIVER REC. AREA
MT. EDZIZA REC. AREA /PARK
SPATSIZI PLATEAU WILDERNESS PARK
ECOL. RES.
KALUM T.S.A.
CRANBERRY T.S.A.
SWAN LAKE WILDERNESS AREA
KISPIOX T.S.A.
TFL 1
BULKLEY T.S.A.
NORTH COAST T.S.A.
GITNADOIX RIVER PK
TFL 1
MORICE T.S.A.
LAKES T.S.A.
TFL 41
TFL 25
ECOL. RES.
TWEEDSMUIR PARK
EUTSUK NAT. CONSER. AREA
94/01/01 E:\Misc\Overview\

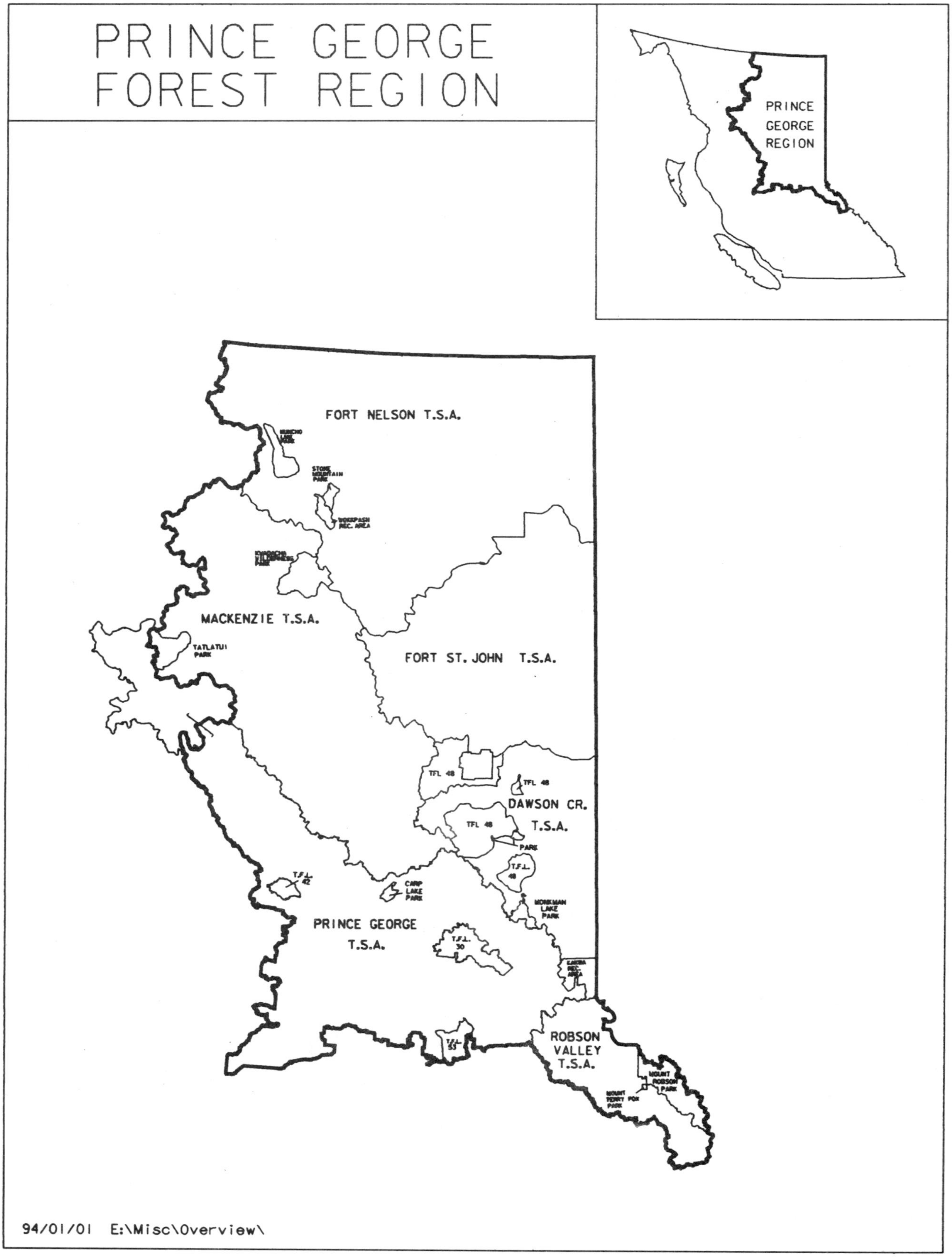
PRINCE GEORGE
FOREST REGION
PRINCE
GEORGE
REGION
FORT NELSON T.S.A.
STONE
PARK
REC. AREA
MACKENZIE T.S.A.
FORT ST. JOHN T.S.A.
TFL 48
TFL 48
DAWSON CR.
T.S.A.
TFL 48
PARK
T.F.L.
48
LAKE
PARK
T.F.L.
42
CARP
LAKE
PARK
PRINCE GEORGE
T.S.A.
T.F.L.
30
REC.
ROBSON
VALLEY
T.S.A.
T.F.L.
53
MOUNT
ROBSON
PARK
MOUNT
FOX
PARK
94/01/01 E:\Misc\Overview\

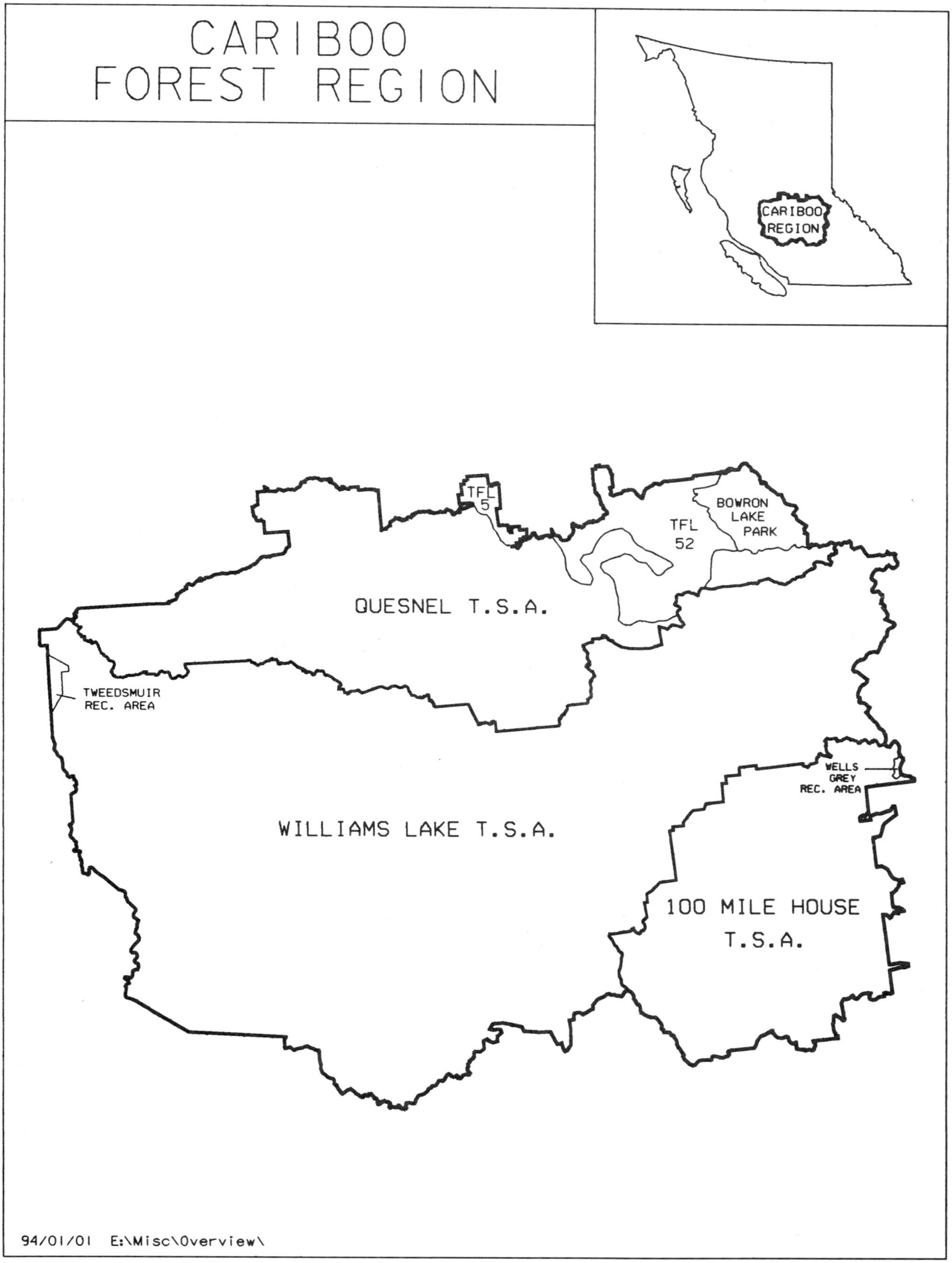
CARIBOO
FOREST REGION
CARIBOO
REGION
TFL
5
TFL
52
BOWRON
LAKE
PARK
QUESNEL T.S.A.
TWEEDSMUIR
REC. AREA
WILLIAMS LAKE T.S.A.
WELLS
GREY
REC. AREA
100 MILE HOUSE
T.S.A.
94/01/01 E:\Misc\Overview\

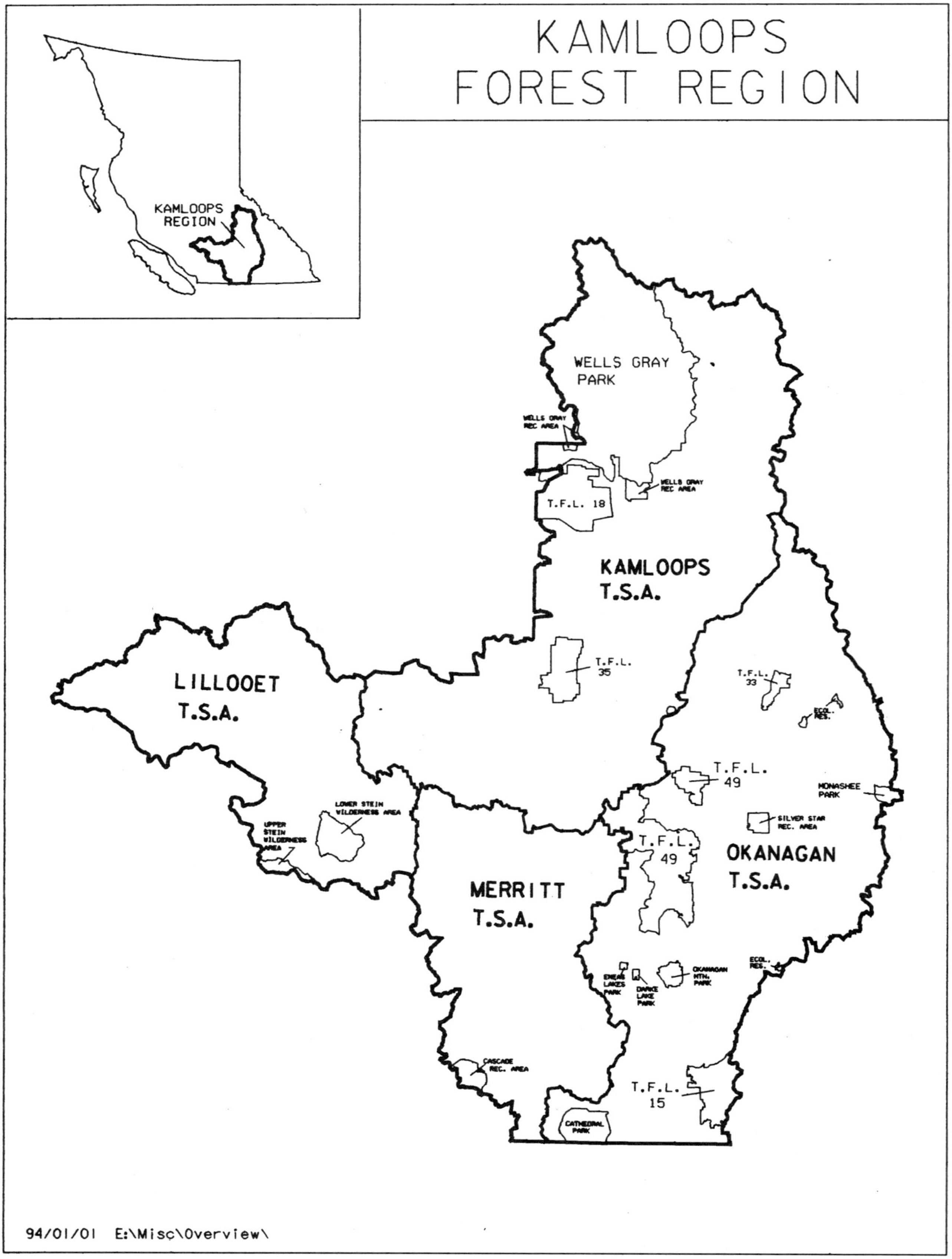

KAMLOOPS
FOREST REGION
KAMLOOPS
REGION
WELLS GRAY
PARK
WELLS GRAY
REC AREA
WELLS GRAY
REC AREA
T.F.L. 18
KAMLOOPS
T.S.A.
T.F.L.
35
LILLOOET
T.S.A.
T.F.L.
33
ECOL.
RES.
T.F.L.
49
MONASHEE
PARK
SILVER STAR
REC. AREA
LOWER STEIN
WILDERNESS AREA
UPPER
STEIN
WILDERNESS
AREA
T.F.L.
49
OKANAGAN
T.S.A.
MERRITT
T.S.A.
ECOL.
RES.
OKANAGAN
MTN.
PARK
ENEAS
LAKES
PARK
DARKE
LAKE
PARK
CASCADE
REC. AREA
T.F.L.
15
CATHEDRAL
PARK
94/01/01 E:\Misc\Overview\

NELSON FOREST REGION

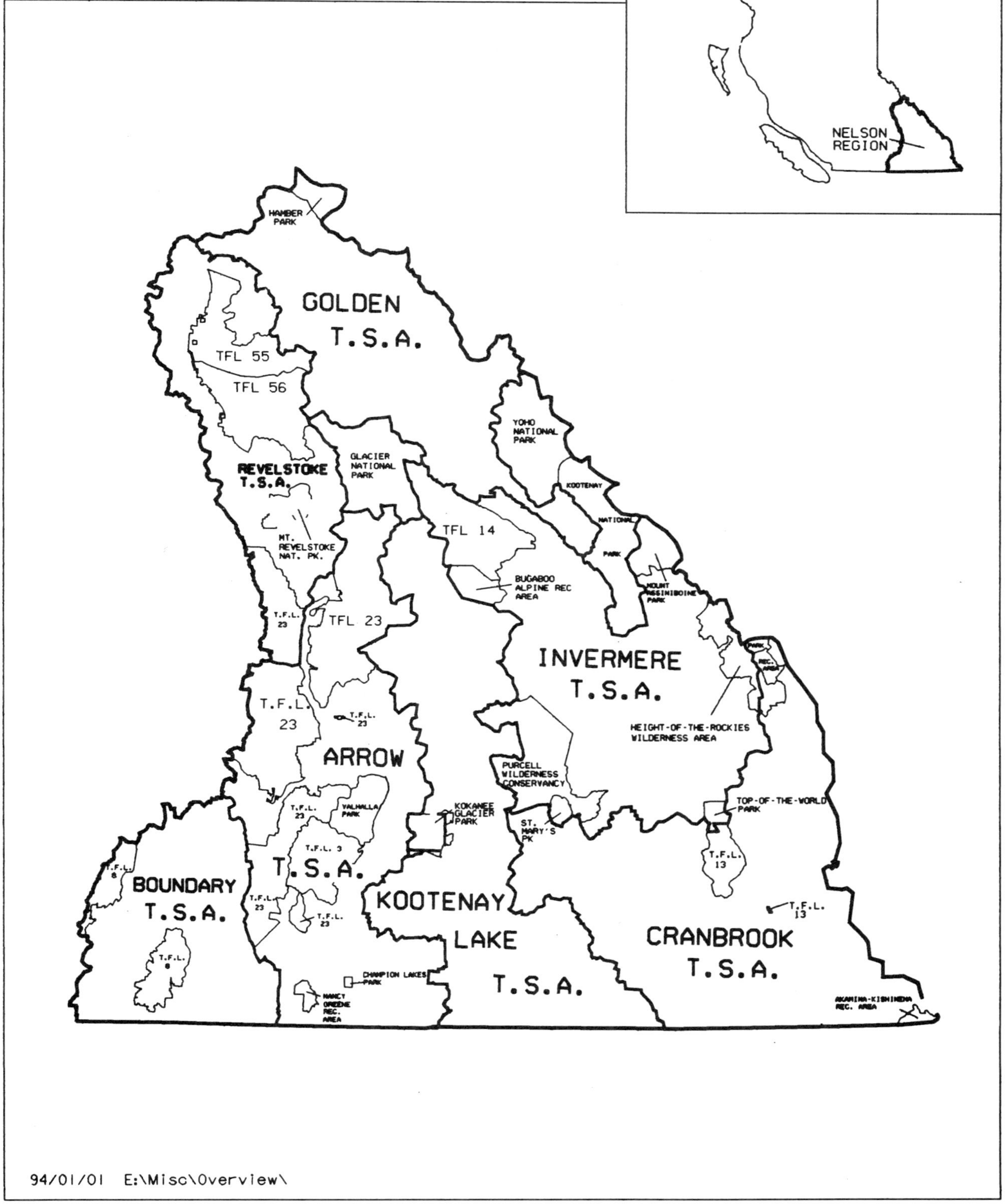

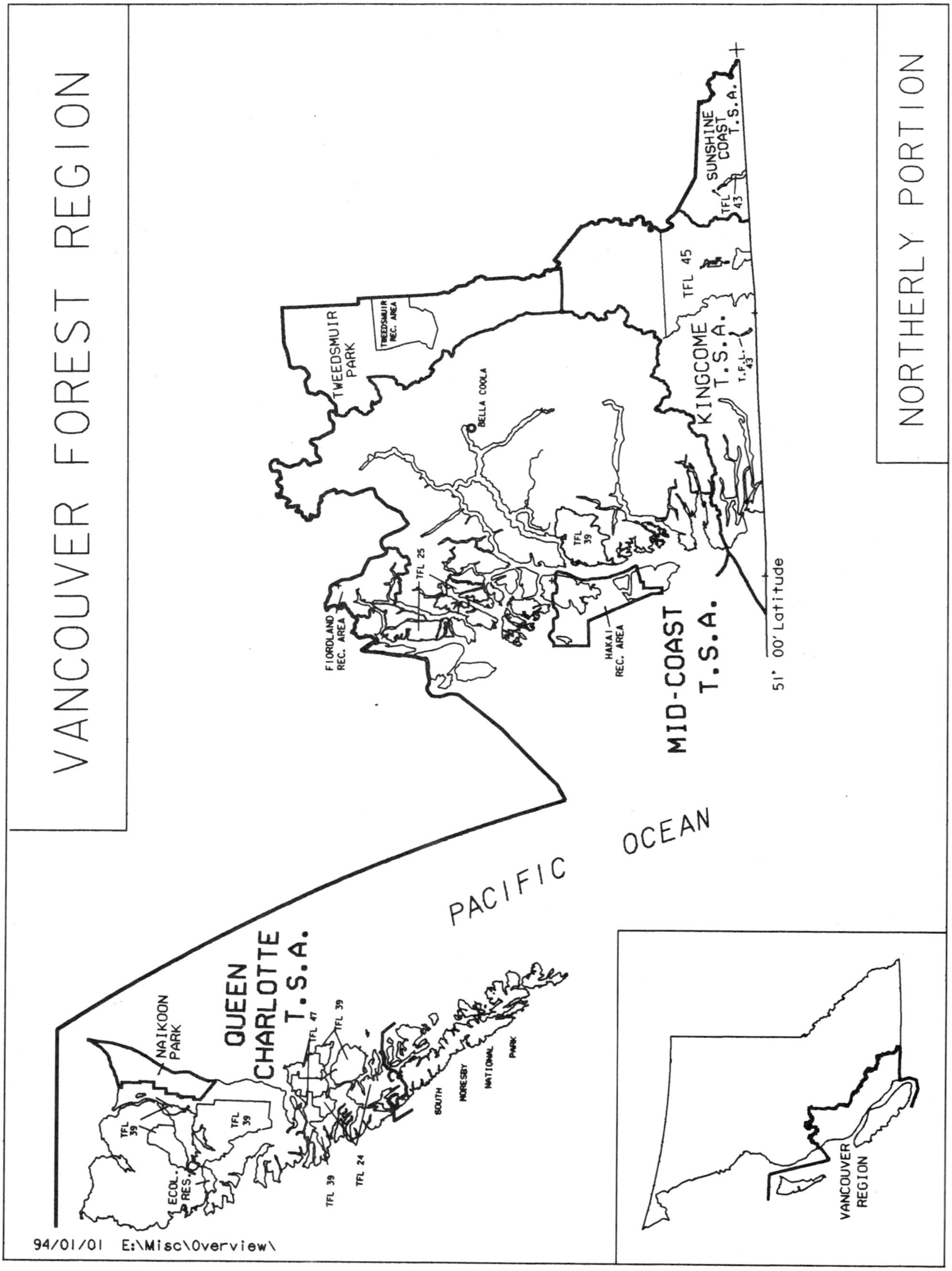

VANCOUVER FOREST REGION
NORTHERLY PORTION
TWEEDSMUIR PARK
TWEEDSMUIR REC. AREA
BELLA COOLA
SUNSHINE COAST T.S.A.
TFL 43
TFL 45
KINGCOME T.S.A.
T.F.L. 43
TFL 39
TFL 25
FIORDLAND REC. AREA
HAKAI REC. AREA
MID-COAST T.S.A.
51° 00' Latitude
PACIFIC OCEAN
QUEEN CHARLOTTE T.S.A.
NAIKOON PARK
TFL 47
TFL 39
TFL 24
ECOL. RES.
SOUTH MORESBY NATIONAL PARK
VANCOUVER REGION
94/01/01 E:\Misc\Overview\

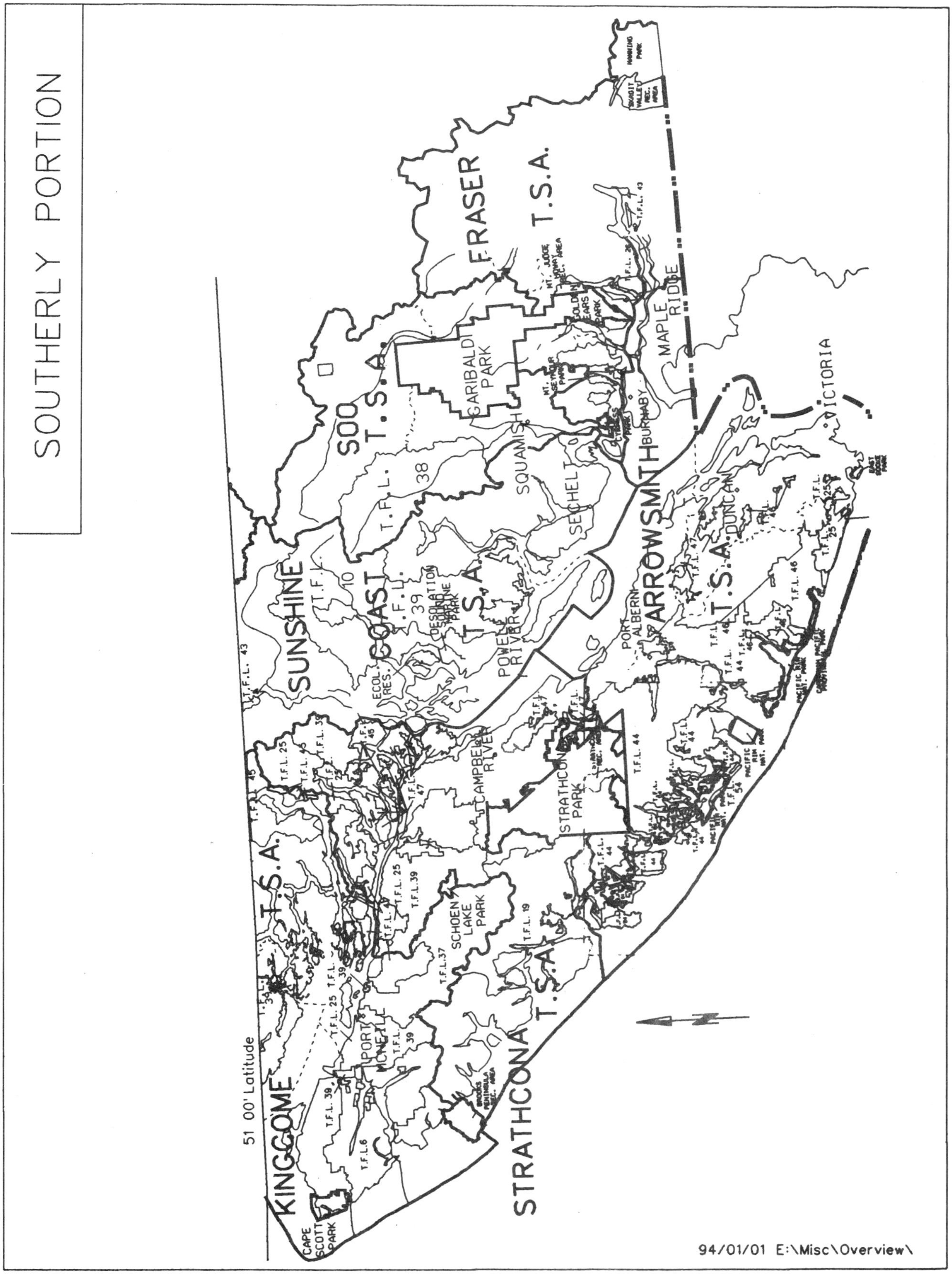
SOUTHERLY PORTION
51 00' Latitude
KINGCOME
T.S.A.
SUNSHINE
COAST
T.S.A.
SOO
T.S.A.
FRASER
T.S.A.
STRATHCONA
T.S.A.
ARROWSMITH
T.S.A.
CAPE SCOTT PARK
PORT MCNEILL
SCHOEN LAKE PARK
STRATHCONA PARK
CAMPBELL RIVER
POWELL RIVER
GARIBALDI PARK
SQUAMISH
SECHELT
PORT ALBERNI
DUNCAN
VICTORIA
BURNABY
MAPLE RIDGE
ECOL. RES.
T.F.L. 38
T.F.L. 39
T.F.L. 10
T.F.L. 43
T.F.L. 44
T.F.L. 46
T.F.L. 19
T.F.L. 37
T.F.L. 25
T.F.L. 6
94/01/01 E:\Misc\Overview\

APPENDIX 2a. Example of the Provincial Summary Reporting System summary data page used to derive figures in Appendix 2b

[PSR12APJ] 2 March 1992

MINISTRY OF FORESTS
INVENTORY BRANCH

PROVINCIAL SUMMARY REPORTlNG SYSTEM

ARROWSMITH TSA NO. 38

AREA (HECTARES) BY INVENTORY TYPE GROUP BY AGE RANGE
All Ownerships - Timber Supply Areas - All Sites

INVENTORY TYPE GROUP	AGE RANGE (Years) 1-20	21-40	41-60	61-80	81-100	101-120	121-140	141-250	251+	Total
1	1,316	5,810	16,033	6,935	2,038	1,634	196	434	307	34,704
2	45	144	708	96	78	86	36	34	111	1,320
3	964	1,182	2,924	805	496	362	105	161	213	7,212
4	23	0	13	0	18	0	0	0	0	54
5	12	23	377	103	217	2	0	0	0	734
8	11	258	1,050	832	50	127	0	0	0	2,128
9	157	19	71	26	46	34	0	3,127	4,752	8,232
10	19	0	26	0	14	0	0	26	2	86
11	718	622	49	129	220	239	13	12,477	18,671	33,138
12	413	1,542	320	227	265	122	120	387	393	3,788
13	915	253	366	85	363	24	7	441	169	2,644
14	921	697	203	87	138	34	76	4,853	6,093	13,101
15	256	289	15	25	34	85	263	3,358	6,316	10,641
16	131	14	11	0	0	73	34	125	22	410
17	22	269	143	96	27	5	41	0	0	603
18	383	18	13	0	2	11	4	100	0	532
19	603	36	0	0	0	0	7	1,078	818	2,543
21	83	2	0	0	0	19	86	383	278	851
23	256	0	0	0	0	15	0	216	360	846
27	16	0	0	0	0	0	0	0	0	16
28	0	0	204	106	13	6	0	0	0	331
29	0	38	53	23	209	40	11	0	0	374
30	0	0	0	24	0	0	0	0	0	24
31	0	0	0	3	0	0	0	0	0	3
32	10	0	0	0	0	0	0	0	0	10
35	0	0	7	0	0	0	0	6	0	13
36	0	0	10	10	0	0	0	0	0	20
37	158	171	2,205	323	66	20	10	2	0	2,956
33	36	500	3,822	319	2	14	0	0	0	4,693
33	8	4	157	117	29	15	6	0	0	338
TOTAL	7,476	11,892	28,782	10,172	4,346	2,947	1,016	27,209	38,505	132,356

APPENDIX 2b. Areas of deciduous inventory type group age classes for selected TSAs (all ownerships)

The following inventory type groups were included in this analysis:

8	FDecid
17	HDecid
26	SDecid
31	PlDecid
35	CotConif
36	CotDecid
37	DConif
38	DDecid
39	Mb
40	Bi
41	AConif
42	ADecid

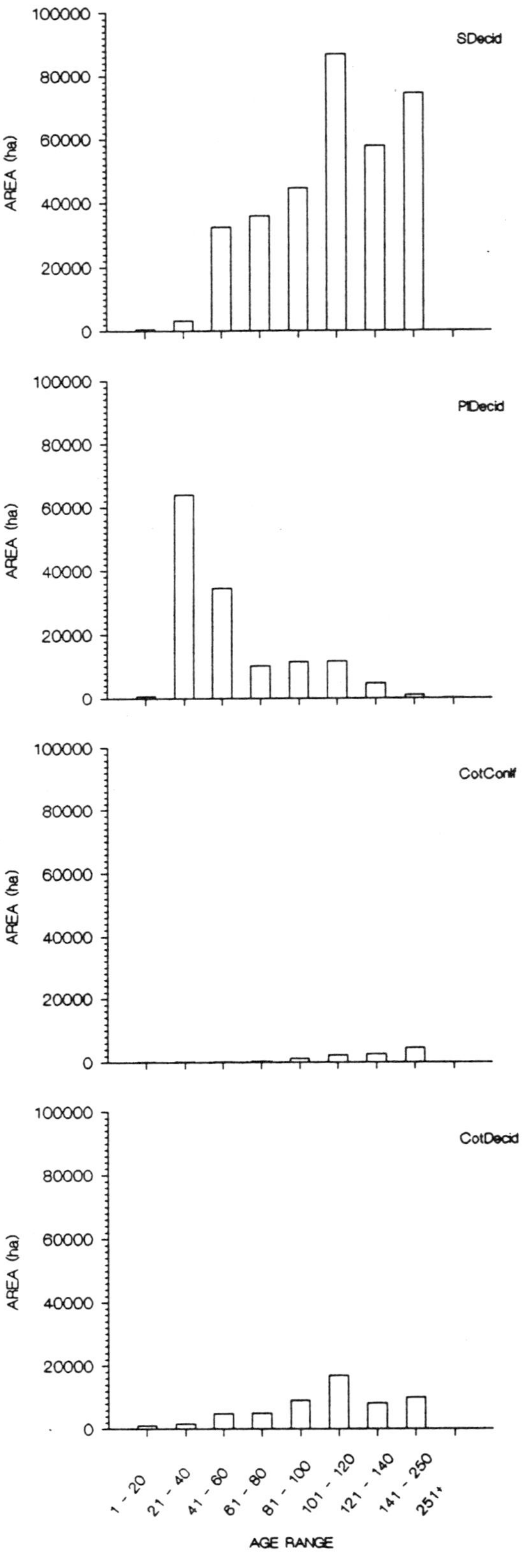

TSA 8 Fort Nelson – Area by age range for inventory type groups SDecid, PlDecid, CotConif, and CotDecid.

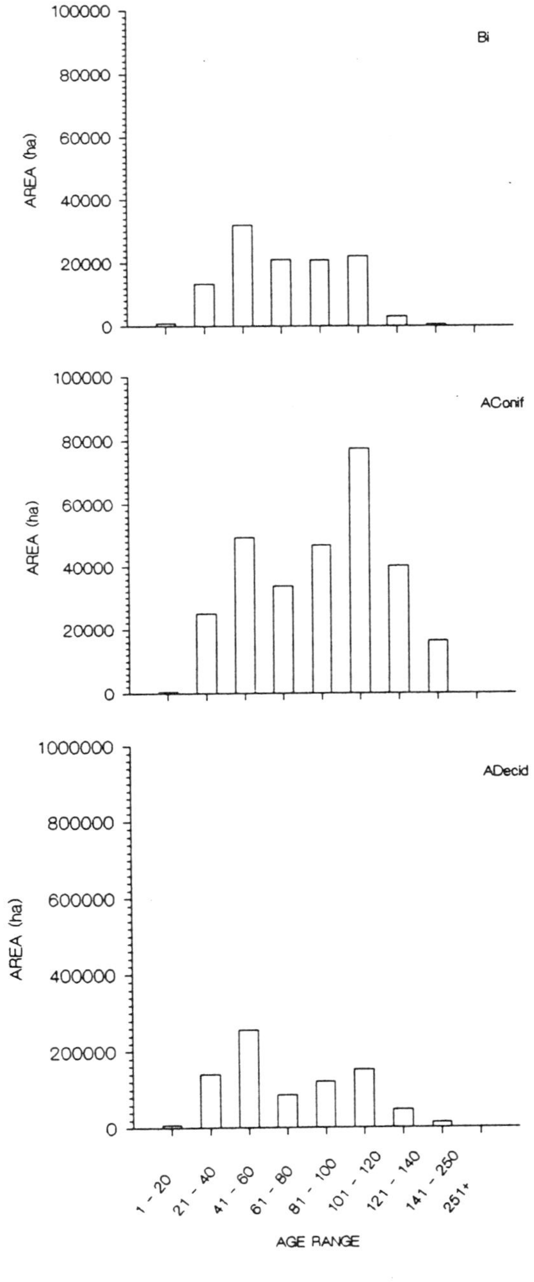

TSA 8 Fort Nelson – Area by age range for inventory type groups Bi, AConif, and ADecid.

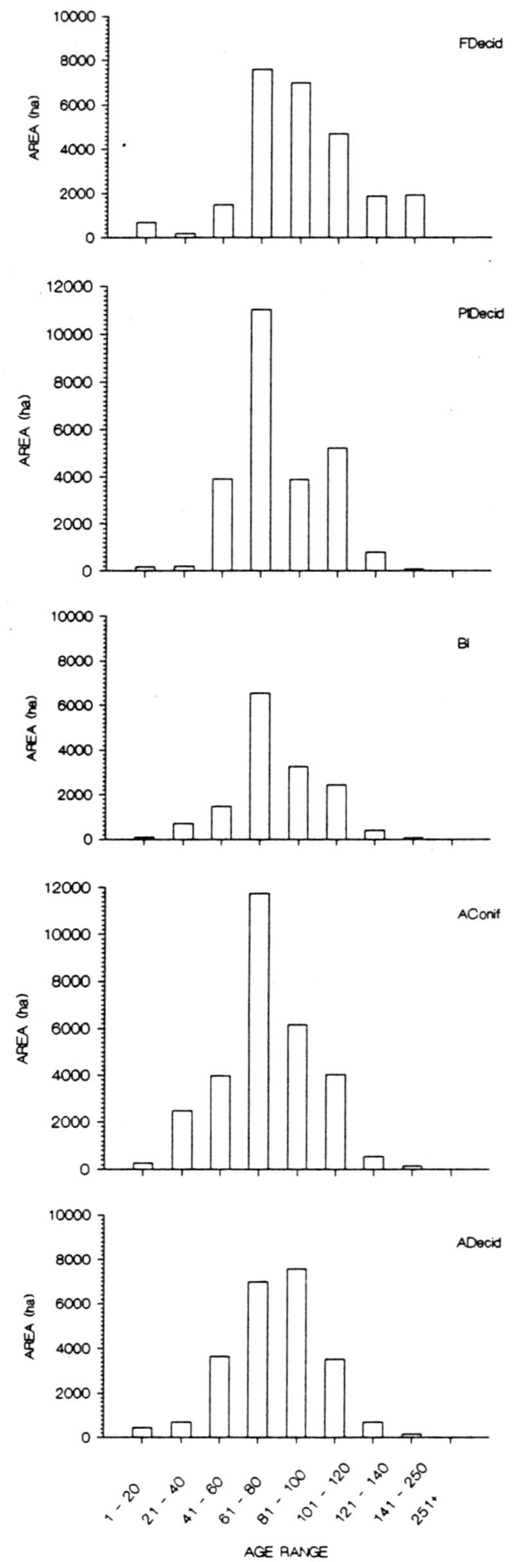

TSA 11 Kamloops – Area by age range for inventory type groups FDecid, PlDecid, Bi, AConif, and ADecid.

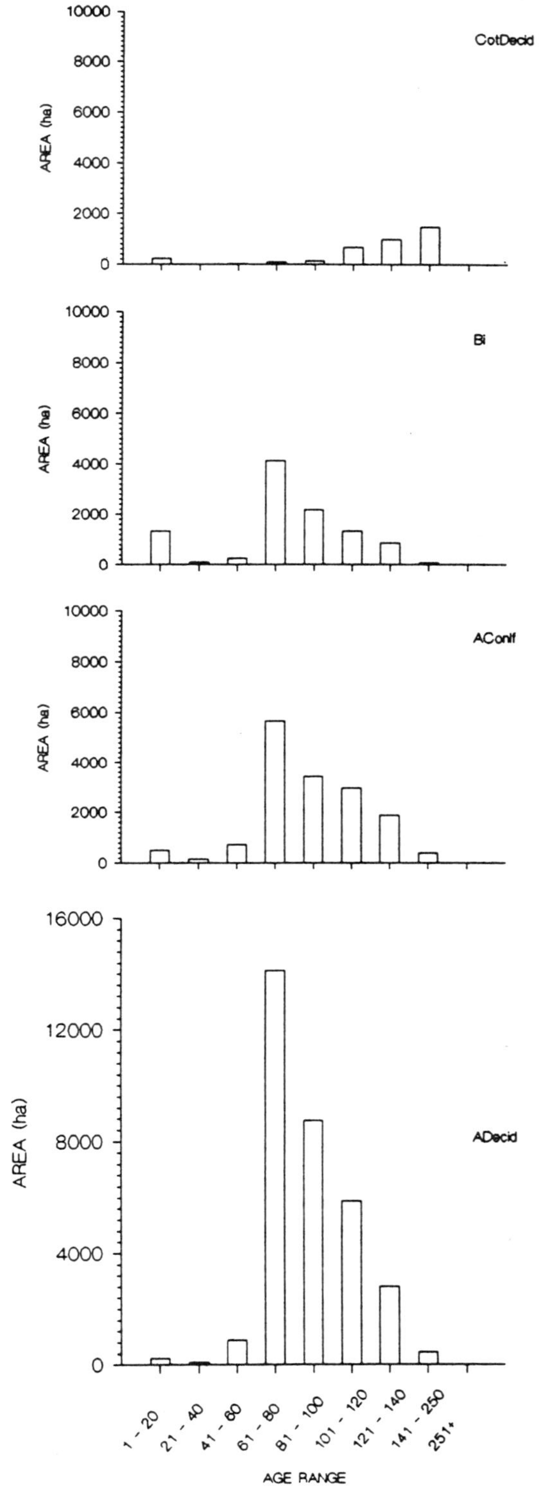

TSA 12 Kispiox – Area by age range for inventory type groups CotDecid, Bi, AConif, and ADecid.

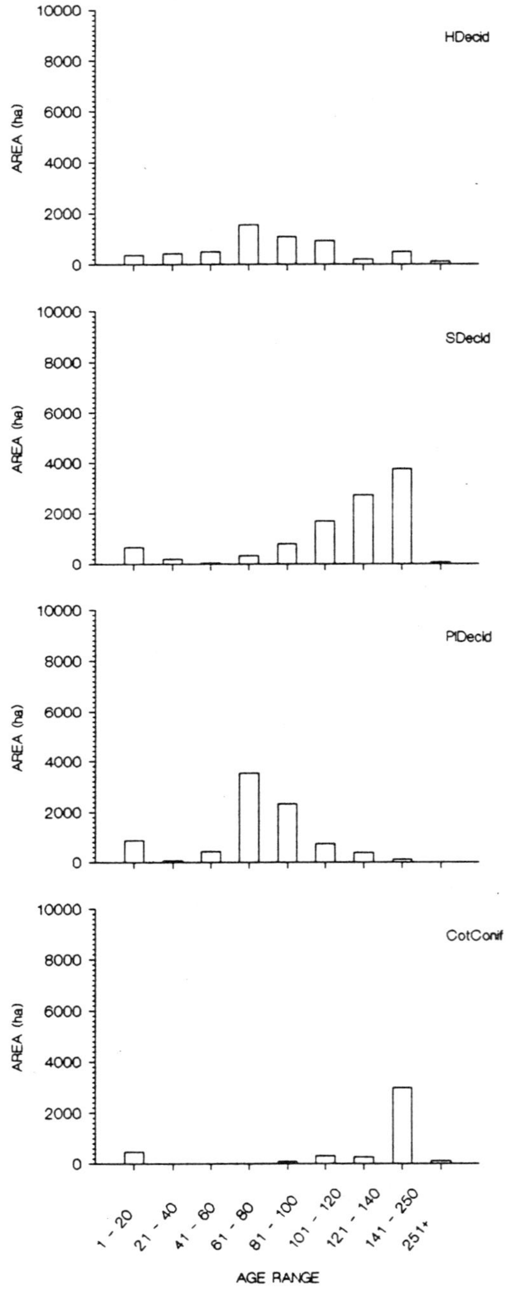

TSA 12 Kispiox – Area by age range for inventory type groups HDecid, SDecid, PlDecid, and CotConif.

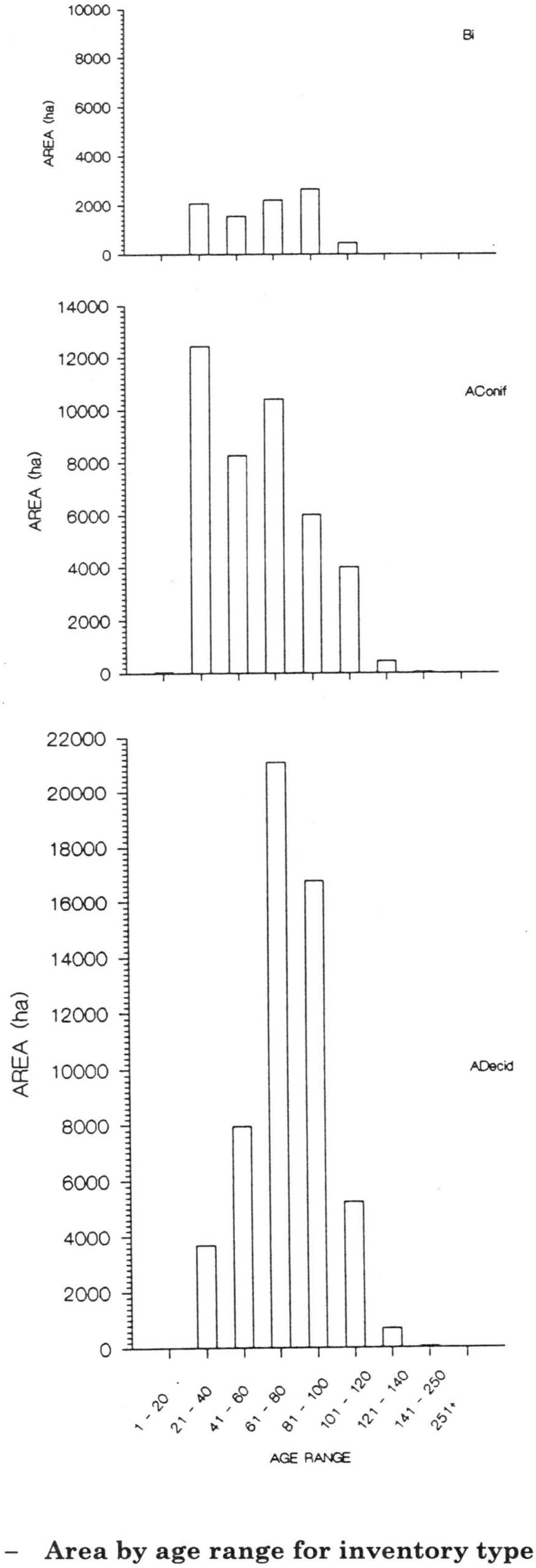

TSA 29 Williams Lake – Area by age range for inventory type groups Bi, AConif, and ADecid.

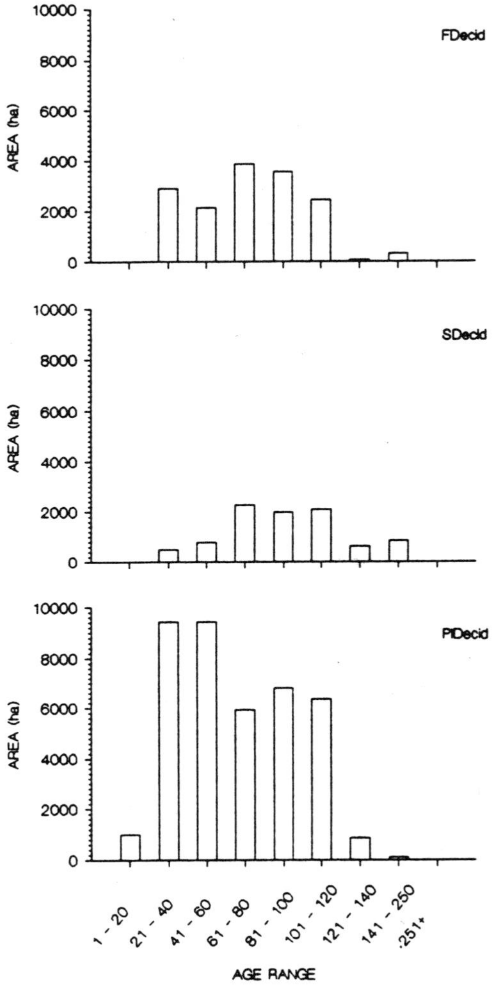

TSA 29 Williams Lake – Area by age range for inventory type groups FDecid, SDecid, and PlDecid.

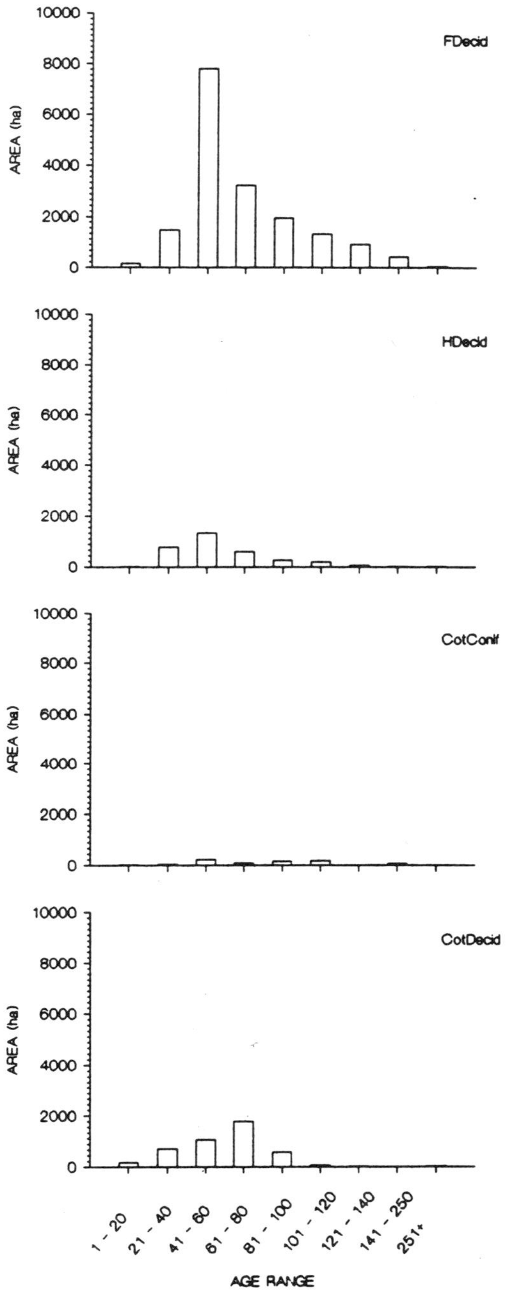

TSA 30 Fraser – Area by age range for inventory type groups FDecid, HDecid, CotConif, and CotDecid.

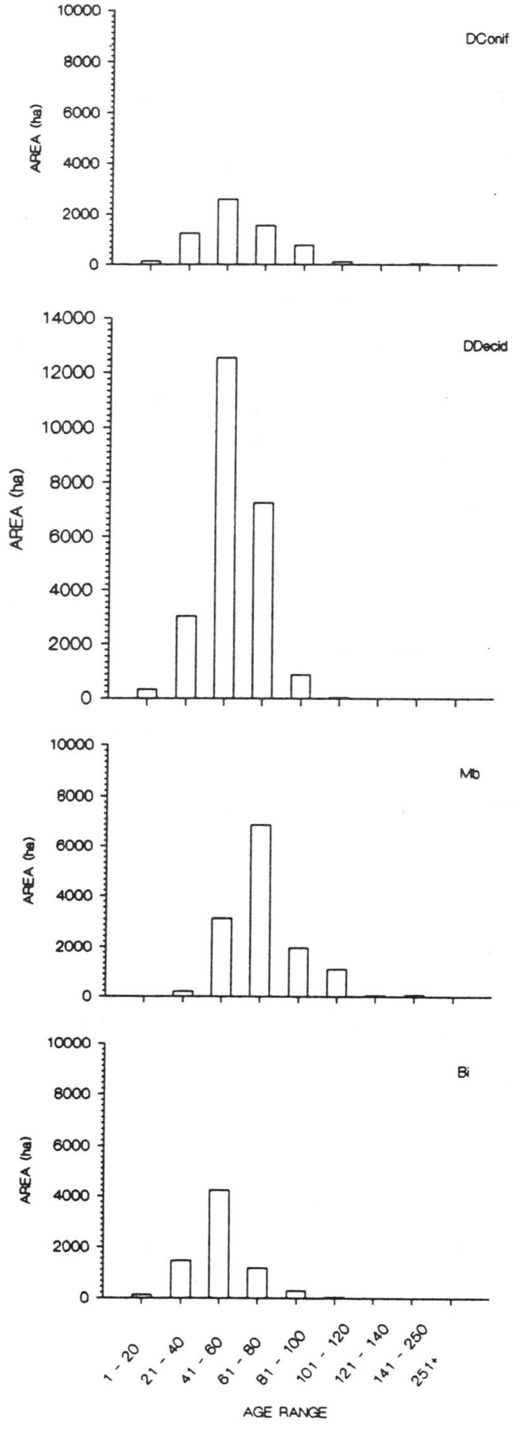

TSA 30 Fraser – Area by age range for inventory type groups DConif, DDecid, Mb, and Bi.

APPENDIX 2c. Not satisfactorily restocked forestlands

Backlog NSR – NSR lands resulting from land denuded before January 1, 1982

Net NSR – NSR remaining after deductions are made for areas that are noneconomic, inaccessible, inoperable, of poor and low site classes, or likely to naturally regenerate

Provincial summary of the net backlog of not satisfactorily restocked land for good and medium site class land (area in hectares)

Forest Region	1984 resource analysis	1988 summary	1990 summary	% difference in summaries 1984 and 1990
Cariboo	43 400	30 747	26 346	-38%
Kamloops	51 400	74 241	57 869	15%
Nelson	93 700	60 787	44 273	-53%
Prince George	488 700	271 747	244 205	-54%
Prince Rupert	40 500	106 396	78 130	93%
Vancouver	20 300	9 227	5 868	-71%

Regional summary of net backlog not satisfactorily restocked land (in TSAs) (area in hectares)

	Site Class				
Forest region	Good	Medium	Poor	Low	Total
Cariboo	10 449	15 549	6 891	77	32 966
Kamloops	9 137	40 418	15 583	39	65 177
Nelson	5 742	27 685	13 749	282	47 458
Prince George	46 760	144 371	111 556	16 368	319 055
Prince Rupert	6 905	68 486	30 815	398	106 604
Vancouver	433	4 688	2 197	27	7 345
Province	79 426	301 197	180 791	17 191	578 605

Cariboo Forest Region

TSA	Good	Site class Medium	Poor	Low	Total
26 Quesnel	6 487	8 527	771	0	15 785
29 Williams	3 265	4 659	4 851	77	12 852
23 100 Mile	697	2 363	1 269	0	4 329

Kamloops Forest Region

TSA	Good	Site class Medium	Poor	Low	Total
11 Kamloops	3 669	17 621	4 422	8	25 720
15 Lillooet	583	2 027	3 618	31	6 259
18 Merrit	1 523	4 336	3 559	0	9 418
22 Okanagan	3 362	16 434	3 984	0	23 780

Nelson Forest Region

TSA	Good	Site class Medium	Poor	Low	Total
1 Arrow	776	3 306	1 675	0	5 757
2 Boundary	108	828	252	0	1 188
5 Cranbrook	878	4 669	2 238	260	8 045
7 Golden	2 669	8 696	5 663	0	17 028
9 Invermere	486	2 651	1 581	22	4 740
13 Kootenay Lake	342	4 215	1 987	0	6 544
27 Revelstoke	483	3 320	353	0	4 156

Prince George Forest Region

TSA	Good	Site class Medium	Poor	Low	Total
8 Fort Nelson	8 555	11 662	18 905	15 352	54 474
16 Mackenzie	4 403	17 785	62 345	57	84 590
17 Robson Valley	1 000	5 433	1 672	642	8 747
24 Prince George	30 031	76 295	24 035	317	130 678
40 Fort St John	2 069	16 231	637	0	18 937
41 Dawson Creek	702	16 965	3 962	0	21 629

Prince Rupert Forest Region

TSA	Good	Site Class Medium	Poor	Low	Total
3 Bulkley	584	4 255	1 710	0	6 549
4 Cassiar	257	39 570	1 683	0	41 510
10 Kalum	2 007	1 984	9 862	0	13 853
12 Kispiox	1 261	2 029	3 067	0	6 357
14 Lakes	965	10 714	4 274	268	16 221
20 Morice	1 302	8 713	219	66	10 300
21 N Coast	529	1 221	10 000	64	11 814

Vancouver Forest Region

TSA	Good	Site Class Medium	Poor	Low	Total
19 Mid-coast	32	128	91	6	257
25 Queen C	23	10	0	0	33
30 Fraser	4	953	802	0	1 759
31 Soo	61	561	705	0	1 327
33 Kingcome	121	430	44	0	595
37 Strathcona	17	323	196	0	536
38 Arrowsmith	0	453	45	0	498
39 Sunshine C	175	1 830	314	21	2 340

APPENDIX 2d. Total area (hectares) summaries for deciduous inventory type groups

TSA	Type	Total Area
2	8	1 475
38	8	2 128
24	8	2 435
27	8	3 026
26	8	3 480
1	8	6 266
29	8	15 243
30	8	17 327
11	8	25 411
11	17	68
29	17	117
24	17	150
27	17	188
3	17	434
1	17	452
38	17	603
10	17	2 176
30	17	3 199
12	17	5 632
1	26	62
30	26	85
27	26	89
2	26	452
10	26	2 252
11	26	2 951
26	26	6 382
3	26	7 829
29	26	9 076
12	26	10 162
41	26	39 741
24	26	91 503
40	26	108 817
8	26	336 012
38	31	3
27	31	82
30	31	441
10	31	915
2	31	2 641
1	31	3 812
12	31	8 438
3	31	9 504
11	31	25 309
26	31	31 728
29	31	39 900
41	31	56 153
24	31	125 675
8	31	138 565
40	31	152 721
38	35	13
27	35	120
26	35	415
11	35	512
30	35	745
1	35	831
2	35	941
29	35	1 015
10	35	1 110
3	35	1 720
40	35	2 455
24	35	3 687
12	35	4 248
8	35	11 538
41	35	11 649
38	36	20
27	36	137
26	36	786
10	36	873
29	36	1 100
2	36	1 128
1	36	1 409
3	36	2 402
11	36	2 625
12	36	3 657
30	36	4 464
24	36	6 819
40	36	15 848
41	36	56 534
8	36	57 322
3	37	14
10	37	612
38	37	2 955
30	37	6 405
10	38	954
38	38	4 693
30	38	24 045
38	39	337
30	39	13 350
10	40	682
2	40	768
3	40	823
27	40	1 889
26	40	4 099
41	40	4 549
1	40	5 848
30	40	7 371
29	40	8 983
12	40	10 261
11	40	14 966
24	40	20 623
40	40	34 881
8	40	114 026
30	41	20
10	41	889
27	41	1 382
2	41	2 610
1	41	8 836
12	41	15 684
3	41	19 297
26	41	27 171
11	41	29 332
29	41	41 646
41	41	75 782
40	41	165 751
24	41	172 642
8	41	289 567
30	42	52
10	42	547
27	42	672
2	42	886
3	42	10 870
1	42	10 901
11	42	23 701
12	42	33 230
29	42	55 470
24	42	233 530
41	42	359 532
40	42	508 685
8	42	819 759

APPENDIX 3. Birds identified in Table 8 as having some use for hardwood stands

Accipitridae	Broad-winged Hawk Cooper's Hawk Bald Eagle Northern Goshawk Osprey Sharp-shinned Hawk
Aegithalidae	Bushtit
Anatidae	Barrow's Goldeneye Bufflehead Common Goldeneye Common Merganser Hooded Merganser Wood Duck
Ardeidae	Black-crowned Night-Heron Great Blue Heron Green-backed Heron
Columbidae	Band-tailed Pigeon Mourning Dove
Emberizidae	Black-throated Green Warbler Brewer's Sparrow Brown-headed Cowbird Lazuli Bunting MacGillivray's Warbler Orange-crowned Warbler Nashville Warbler Canada Warbler Connecticut Warbler Ovenbird Wilson's Warbler Yellow-breasted Chat
Falconidae	American Kestrel
Hirundinidae	Tree Swallow
Mimidae	Grey Catbird
Muscicapidae	Swainson's Thrush Western Bluebird

Paridae	Black-capped Chickadee Boreal Chickadee Chestnut-backed Chickadee Mountain Chickadee
Phasianidae	Blue Grouse Ring-necked Pheasant Ruffed Grouse Sharp-tailed Grouse
Picidae	Downy Woodpecker Hairy Woodpecker Lewis' Woodpecker Williamson's Sapsucker Northern Flicker Pileated Woodpecker Red-breasted Sapsucker Red-naped Sapsucker Three-toed Woodpecker Yellow-bellied Sapsucker
Sittidae	Red-breasted Nuthatch White-breasted Nuthatch
Trochilidae	Calliope Hummingbird Rufous Hummingbird
Troglodytidae	Bewick's Wren House Wren Winter Wren
Tyrannidae	Alder Flycatcher Willow Flycatcher
Tytonidae and Strigidae	Boreal Owl Common Barn-Owl Great Horned Owl Long-eared Owl Northern Hawk Owl Northern Saw-whet Owl Western Screech-Owl
Vireonidae	Veery Hutton's Vireo Philadelphia Vireo Red-eyed Vireo Solitary Vireo

Animal species using specific hardwood types

Black cottonwood *Populus trichocarpa*

Bald Eagle
Great Blue Heron
Lewis' Woodpecker
Barrow's Goldeneye
Bufflehead
Mourning Dove
Wood Duck
Cooper's Hawk
Great Horned Owl
Western Screech Owl
Northern Flicker
Red-naped Sapsucker
Yellow-bellied Sapsucker
Red-breasted Sapsucker
Downy Woodpecker
Red-eyed Vireo
House Wren
Ovenbird
(Pileated Woodpecker)
(Hairy Woodpecker)
(Common Goldeneye)
(Common Merganser)
(Hooded Merganser)
(Boreal Owl)
(Northern Saw-whet Owl)
(Tree Swallow)
(Osprey)
(Ruffed Grouse)

Roosevelt elk
Pacific water shrew
Southern red bat
Grizzly bear
Beaver
Bobcat
Mule deer
White-tailed deer
Hoary, silver-haired, and other myotis bats
Porcupine
(River otter)
(Ermine)
(Mink)
(Black bear)
(Moose)
(Pacific jumping mouse)
(Northern long-eared myotis)

Painted turtle
(Clouded salamander)
(Giant salamander)
(Western toad)
(Long-toed salamander)
(Canadian toad)
(Striped chorus frog)
(Wood frog)
(Tailed frog)

Alder ***Alnus rubra, tenufolia, crispa***

Black-crowned Night Heron
Great Blue Heron
Green-backed Heron
Band-tailed Pigeon
Mourning Dove
Wood Duck
Boreal Owl
Cooper's Hawk
Great Horned Owl
Western Screech Owl
Alder Flycatcher
Willow Flycatcher
Red-breasted Sapsucker
Downy Woodpecker
Red-eyed Vireo
Black-capped Chickadee

Pacific water shrew
Northern long-eared myotis
Grizzly bear
Townsend's chipmunk
Beaver
Moose
Mule deer
Raccoon
Deer mouse
Columbia black-tailed deer

Birch ***Betula papyrifera, glandulosa***

Black-crowned Night Heron
Black-throated Green Warbler
Brewer's Sparrow
Sharp-tailed Grouse
Boreal Owl
Cooper's Hawk
Great Horned Owl
Long-eared Owl

Northern Saw-whet Owl
Calliope Hummingbird
Red-naped Sapsucker
Red-breasted Sapsucker
Nashville Warbler
Canada Warbler
Connecticut Warbler

California big-horned sheep
Beaver
Rocky Mountain elk
Painted turtle

Trembling aspen ***Populus tremloides***

Black-throated Green Warbler
Brewer's Sparrow
Lewis' Woodpecker
Williamson's Sapsucker
Barrow's Goldeneye
Blue Grouse
Bufflehead
Common Goldeneye
Pileated Woodpecker
Ruffed Grouse
Wood Duck
American Kestrel
Boreal Owl
Broad-winged Hawk
Cooper's Hawk
Northern Goshawk
Great Horned Owl
Long-eared Owl
Sharp-shinned Hawk
Northern Saw-whet Owl
Northern Hawk Owl
Hairy Woodpecker
Three-toed Woodpecker
Calliope Hummingbird
Yellow-bellied Sapsucker
Red-naped Sapsucker
Red-breasted Sapsucker
Downy Woodpecker
Nashville Warbler
Orange-crowned Warbler
Canada Warbler
Connecticut Warbler
Ovenbird

White-tailed jackrabbit
Nuttall's cottontail
Beaver

Black bear
Long-tailed weasel
Mule deer
Rocky Mountain elk
Hoary, silver-haired, and other myotis bats

Western rattlesnake
Painted turtle

Mixedwood forests

Barn Owl (edges)
Northern Goshawk (edges)
Sharp-shinned Hawk
Western Screech Owl
Northern Saw-whet Owl
Northern Hawk Owl
Three-toed Woodpecker
Yellow-bellied Sapsucker
Downy Woodpecker
Veery, Hutton's, Warbling and Philadelphia Vireo
Orange-crowned Warbler
Nashville Warbler
Ovenbird
Tree Swallow
Black-capped Chickadee
Bushtit

Black bear
Moose
Muskrat
White-tailed deer

Willow ***Salix* spp.**

Black-crowned Night Heron
Cooper's Hawk
Great Horned Owl
Long-eared Owl
Alder and Willow Flycatchers
Black-capped Chickadees
House Wren

Beaver
Moose
Porcupine
Mountain beaver

Maple *Acer macrophyllum, glabra*

Red-breasted Sapsucker

Columbia black-tailed Deer

Balsam poplar *Populus balsamifera, trichocarpa*

Bald Eagle
Great Blue Heron
Bufflehead
Wood Duck
American Kestrel
Northern Goshawk
Long-eared Owl
Northern Saw-whet Owl
Yellow-bellied Sapsucker
Red-naped Sapsucker
Red-breasted Sapsucker
Downy Woodpecker
Ovenbird

Moose

Deciduous - Riparian forests

Fringed myotis
Keen's long-eared myotis
Townsend's big-eared bat
Pacific water shrew
Northern long-eared myotis
Townsend's chipmunk
Western small-footed myotis
Bobcat
Muskrat
White-tailed deer

APPENDIX 4. **Hardwood polygons where >50% of compartment is pure deciduous wood, their general location (from 1: 2 000 000 scale mapping), and their primitive and semi-primitive status: primitive = 01, semi-primitive nonmotorized = 02, semi-primitive motorized = 03, water feature = 08, other = 09.**

Polygon	TSA	General location	Biogeoclimatic zone classification	Primitive classes
1	Fraser	Cultus Lake	CWH	09
2	Fraser	South Fraser River, E of Kent	CWH	09
3	Fraser	South Fraser River, E of Matsqui	CWH	09
4	Fraser	Garibaldi Mountain, E drainage	CWH	09
5	Soo	Highway 99, N of Squamish	CWH-MH	09
6	Quesnel	Quesnel River	SBS	09
7	Quesnel	Monroe Heights, N of Quesnel	SBS	09
8	Robson Valley	~40 km ESE of McBride	SBS-ICH-ESSF	09, 02, 01
9	Robson Valley	S of McBride	SBS-ICH-ESSF	09, 02
10	Prince George	~30 km S of Prince George, at Red Rock	SBS	09
11	Prince George	~80 km E of Prince George, at Penny	SBS-ICH-ESSF	09
12	Prince George	Salmon River, at Salmon Valley	SBS	09, 02
13	Prince George	Fraser Lake, at Fraser Lake	SBS	09, 08
14	Lakes	Francois Lake, at Southbank	SBS	09
15	Bulkley	Bulkley River south, at Telkwa	SBS-ESSF	09

Polygon	TSA	General location	Biogeoclimatic zone classification	Primitive classes
16	Prince George	Stuart Lake to Pinchi Lake	SBS	09
17	Prince George	~30 km N of Bear Lake (~100 km N of Pr.George)	SBS	09, 02
18	Mackenzie	E of Tudyah Lake, on Highway 97	SBS-ESSF	09, 02, 03
19	Kispiox	S of Hazelton	ICH-ESSF	09, 02
20	Kispiox	Kitwanga	ICH	09, 02
21	Kispiox	Cedarvale	ICH	09, 02
22	Kalum	Nass River	CWH-MH-ICH	09
23	Kispiox	Kispiox River	ICH	09, 03
24	Mackenzie	S end of Williston Lake, west side	SBS	03, 02
25	Mackenzie	S end of Williston Lake, east side	SBS	09, 08, 02
26	Fort St. John	Dawson Creek , Chetwynd to Fort St. John	BWBS	09
27	Mackenzie	head waters of Ospika River at Williston Lake	ESSF-SBS	09, 08, 03, 02
28	Fort St. John	junction of Beatton and Doig Rivers	BWBS	09
29	Fort St. John	Goodlow	BWBS	09
30	Fort St. John	Beatton River	BWBS	09, 03
31	Mackenzie	Finlay River head, at Williston Lake	BWBS-ESSF-SWB	09, 03, 02
32	Mackenzie	Finlay River, ~10 km N of Williston Lake	BWBS-SWB	09, 03, 02, 01
34	Fort Nelson	Prophet River and Richards Creek	BWBS-SWB	03, 02

Polygon	TSA	General location	Biogeoclimatic zone classification	Primitive classes
35	Fort St. John	Chief River and Trutch Creek	BWBS	03
36	Fort Nelson	Prophet River E Klua Creek	BWBS	03
37	Fort Nelson	Muskwa River	BWBS-SWB	01
38	Fort Nelson	Gathto Creek	AT	01
39	Mackenzie	Finlay River, 10 km S of Braid Creek	AT	01
40	Fort Nelson	Tuchodi Creek	AT-SWB-BWBS	03, 02, 01
41	Fort Nelson	Kluachesi River, at Gethto Creek	BWBS	03, 02
42	Fort Nelson	Tenaka Creek	BWBS	03
43	Fort Nelson	Fontas River, at Conroy Creek	BWBS	09, 02
44	Fort St. John	Fontas River, at Etthitun River	BWBS	03
45	Fort Nelson	Hay River, ~50 km W of Rainbow Lake, Alta.	BWBS	03
46	Fort Nelson	Fontas River, ~70 km W of Rainbow Lake, Alta.	BWBS	03
47	Fort Nelson	Fontas River, SE of Clarke Lake	BWBS	09, 03
48	Fort Nelson	Kyklo Creek, ~80 km E of Fort Nelson	BWBS	09, 03
49	Fort Nelson	Prophet River at Jackfish Creek	BWBS	09, 03
50	Fort Nelson	Prophet River at Fort Nelson	BWBS	09
51	Fort Nelson	Chiska River at Muskwa River	BWBS-SWB	03

Polygon	TSA	General location	Biogeoclimatic zone classification	Primitive classes
52	Fort Nelson	Muskwa River, ~50 km W of Fort Nelson	BWBS	03
53	Fort Nelson	N of junction of Kitcho and Shekilie rivers	BWBS	03
54	Fort Nelson	S of Thinatea Lake, on Petitot River	BWBS	03
55	Fort Nelson	Sahtenah River (Etsho Plateau)	BWBS	01
56	Fort Nelson	N of Old Fort Nelson on Fort Nelson River	BWBS	09, 08, 03
57	Fort Nelson	~10 km N of Muskwa River	BWBS	09, 03
58	Fort Nelson	Kiwigana River (Etsho Plateau)	BWBS	03
59	Fort Nelson	~20 km S of Estsine Lake, on Petitot River	BWBS	03
60	Fort Nelson	Petitot River at northern B.C. boundary	BWBS	03
61	Fort Nelson	Petitot River at northern B.C. boundary, Emile Creek	BWBS	03
62	Fort Nelson	~30 km N of Nelson River	BWBS	09, 03
63	Fort Nelson	Fort Nelson River, Dunedin River, Liard River junction	BWBS	08, 03
64	Fort Nelson	Dunedin River ~45km S of Liard junction	BWBS	03
65	Fort Nelson	Toad River junction with Liard River	BWBS	08, 03, 01
66	Fort Nelson	~25 km W of Fort Nelson and Liard River	BWBS	03

Polygon	TSA	General location	Biogeoclimatic zone classification	Primitive classes
67	Fort Nelson	Liard River between Scatter and Beaver rivers	BWBS	03, 01
68	Fort Nelson	between Scatter and Crow rivers	BWBS	02
69	Fort Nelson	Highway 97 at Liard River, ~70 km E of Fireside	BWBS	09, 08, 01
70	Cassiar	Ketchika River	BWBS-SBS	03, 02, 01
71	Fort Nelson	Toad River	BWBS-SBS-AT	09, 03, 01
72	Cassiar	Klastline Creek	BWBS-SBS-AT	01
73	Cassiar	junction of Stikine and Chutine rivers	MH-ICH-ESSF	03, 02, 01
74	Cassiar	Telegraph Creek	BWBS-SWB	09, 02, 01
75	Cassiar	Sheslay River	SWB	02, 01
76	Cassiar	Taku River at Yeth Creek	MH-ICH-ESSF	02, 01
77	Cassiar	Taku River	ESSF-CWH-MH	02, 01
78	Cassiar	Alsek and Tatshenshini rivers	CWH-AT	01
79	Cassiar	Tatshenshini River	SWB-AT	01
80	Cassiar	Tatshenshini River, 30 km from Kelsall Lake	SWB-AT	01
81	Cassiar	Tatshenshini River, 45 km from Kelsall Lake	SWB-AT	01

APPENDIX 5. Recent hardwoods utilization activity in British Columbia

The following listings are taken from general sources and indicate activity within the last three years (1990-1992). The listings are not complete as some firms may not be reported and some produce intermittently. The listing is intended to show general activity and supports the discussion in Section 5.2

Timber harvesting	Location	Annual Harvest (m^3)
A.M. Cedar Ltd.	Nelson	6 000
BVR Contractors Ltd.	Chase	1 000
A.H. Green Log Hauling Ltd.	Lake Cowichan	15 000
Marling Logging Ltd.	Duncan	12 000
Murch Timber Ltd.	Mission	15 000
Norvik Timber	Delta	65 000
Pacific Ridge Logging Ltd.	Port McNeill	40 000
Perkins Bros. Logging Ltd.	Pemberton	6 500
Wiltshire Contracting Ltd.	Yarrow	1 000
Woodrow Contracting Ltd.	Silverton	8 000
Zaul Zap Industries (1983) Ltd.	Terrace	20 000
		189 500

Lumber	Location	Domestic hardwood use
B.W. Creative Wood Industries Ltd.	Maple Ridge	some hardwood
Carlwood Lumber Ltd.	Maple Ridge	9000 m^3 purchased
Primex Forest Products Ltd.	Delta	200 000 m^3 purchased
Wynndel Box & Lumber Co.	Wynndel	3200 m^3 purchased
Darfield Building Products	Darfield	10% birch and aspen
Midget Mills	McBride	some birch and aspen
Omineca Enterprises Ltd.	Fort Nelson	some birch, aspen, cottonwood
Pacific Green Gold	Richmond	birch, aspen, cottonwood
Reko Industries Ltd.	Quesnel	some aspen and birch
Slocan Forest Products Ltd. (Sluggett and Brown Div.)	Victoria	some maple, alder, birch
Stege Logging Ltd.	New Hazelton	some cottonwood
West Hill Lumber (1988)	Prince George	some birch
Kyah Forest Products Ltd.	Smithers	occasional hardwood
Pacific Pallet Ltd.	Aldergrove	alder
Peace Wood Products (Canfor)	Taylor	5% aspen

Plywood and Veneer	Location	Domestic hardwood use
Crestbrook Forest Industries	Cranbrook (Creston)	hardwood
Coastland Wood Industries	Nanaimo	some domestic hardwoods
Dawson Creek Waferboard (Louisiana-Pacific)	Dawson Creek	aspen
Victoria Plywood Co-op	Victoria	some poplar
West Coast Plywood Co.	Vancouver	some domestic hardwoods

Remanufacture	Location	Domestic hardwood use
Accra Wood Products	Burnaby	some hardwoods
Mol-ner Lumber Products	Fort Langley	some hardwoods

Crown hardwood timber allocations (1992)

Company	TSA	Volume (m^3)
Canadian Chopstick Manufacturing	Fort Nelson	77 000
Norvik Hardwoods Inc.	Fraser	65 000
Louisiana-Pacific Canada Ltd.	Dawson Creek	904 000
Makin Pulp & Paper Ltd.	Fort St. John	220 000
Scott Paper Ltd.	Van. Reg. TFL	49 600
Scott Paper Ltd.	Fraser	1 728
Scott Paper Ltd.	Kingcome	5 000
Scott Paper Ltd.	Soo	5 000
Fibreco Pulp Inc.	Fort St. John	500 000
Tackama Forest Products Ltd.	Fort Nelson	145 000

Source: Canadian Forest Industries Directory, 1992.
Madison's 1991 Canadian Lumber Directory.
B.C. Min. For., Linkage and Licensee Report, 92/03/12, Working document, Timber Management Branch, Victoria, B.C.

APPENDIX 6. Production statistics[1]

In 1987 and 1988, Statistics Canada reported the production of hardwood logs at 5 788 000 and 6 237 000 m^3, respectively.

Hardwood lumber production and export data are more readily available, as shown in the following table.

Birch and maple sawnwood production and export volumes and values 1980–1991

Year	Production (000s m^3)	Export (m^3)	Export ($000)
1980	1 471.5	12 1640	28 166
1981	980.1	103 607	25 681
1982	1 088.4	87 202	27 769
1983	1 042.7	83 632	21 776
1984	1 280.5	87 366	23 536
1985	n/a	85 944	23 887
1986	n/a	103 692	31 845
1987	946.0	125 602	37 712
1988	986.0	147 815	46 459
1989	1 245.0	130 876	46 658
1990	1 131.0	152 658	60 659
1991	1 003.0	n/a	n/a

Source: Statistics Canada, Cat. No. 35-003.

1 The figures reported in this appendix are for all of Canada, and can only be taken as indicative of the industry size and the magnitude of export markets.

Production and export statistics for sliced and rotary peeled hardwood veneer and for hardwood plywood are listed in the following tables.

Hardwood veneer (sliced and rotary peeled) production, export and export value, 1980–1990

Year	Production (m^3)	Export (m^3)	Export ($000)
1980	124 546	113 122	75 116
1981	137 885	115 312	79 416
1982	126 206	95 947	76 843
1983	173 471	125 728	99 599
1984	173 879	115 352	106 586
1985	n/a	91 095	82 814
1986	n/a	98 565	100 435
1987	n/a	109 638	120 602
1988	220 993 *	106 856	121 891
1989	222 237 *	105 874	115 743
1990	n/a	100 581	132 222

Source: Statistics Canada, Cat. No. 25-202.

Hardwood plywood production, export and export value, 1980–1990

Year	Production (m^3)	Export (m^3)	Export ($000)
1980	203 794	36 898	19 590
1981	197 904	35 521	20 487
1982	162 507	34 542	19 845
1983	200 374	37 232	19 772
1984	171 333	45 890	26 549
1985	n/a	52 595	28 675
1986	n/a	47 540	23 424
1987	n/a	56 510	33 068
1988	220 993 *	69 545	32 358
1989	222 237 *	70 366	41 592
1990	n/a	78 044	38 561

Source: Statistics Canada, Cat. No. 25-202.

* Combined plywood and veneer.

Statistics for the production and export of OSB/waferboard are much better in both availability and detail. The following table shows production of OSB/waferboard in North America, and Canadian exports for the years 1986–1991.

North American OSB/waferboard production, and Canadian export 1986-1991, MMSF, 3/8" basis

Year	Production United States	Production Canada	Total	Export from Canada
1986	3 545	2 121	5 666	695
1987	4 102	2 519	6 621	800
1988	4 606	2 443	7 049	858
1989	5 101	2 447	7 548	1 240
1990	5 640	2 227	7 867	1 249
1991	5 613	2 455	8 068	n/a

Source: American Plywood Association "Structural Panel Statistics", Membership Report. Statistics Canada Cat. No. 35-250 and Cat No. 35-2593 (discontinued).

No meaningful statistics are available for hardwood pulp, chopsticks, and pulp chips.

APPENDIX 7. Glossary of terms and abbreviations

BDT	Bone Dry Ton (2000 pounds)
BDU	Bone Dry Unit (2400 pounds)
CDN	Canadian
CIF	Cost (including) insurance and freight to a named destination
CSA	Canadian Standards Association
CSP	Canadian Softwood Plywood
FBM	Foot, Board Measure
FOB	Free or Freight, on board
JAS	Japanese Agricultural Standard
MFBM	Thousand Feet, Board Measure
MMFBM	Million Feet, Board Measure
MSF	Thousand Square Feet
MSM	Thousand Surface (feet) Measure
NHLA	National Hardwood Lumber Association
NHPMA	National Hardwood Plywood Manufacturers Association
OSB	Oriented Strand Board
SWE	Solid Wood Equivalent
TAPPI	Technical Association of the Pulp and Paper Institute
TDIB	Top Diameter Inside Bark
USPS	United States Product Standard

APPENDIX 8. Examples of specifications for hardwood production in British Columbia

a) Summaries of specifications applicable to provincial hardwood resources

b) West Coast Plywood Company Ltd.—Cottonwood Log Specifications

c) Louisiana-Pacific Panel Products, Ltd. —Log Quality Specifications

d) Francois Lake Woodworking Ltd.—Specification Birch Lumber

e) Canadian Chopstick Manufacturing Co. Ltd.—Chopstick Manufacturing Specifications

Summaries of specifications applicable to provincial hardwood resources logs

Company:	Norvik Hardwoods Inc.
Species:	Alder, some maple and birch
Use:	Sawlogs
Specifications:	BCFS Log grading rules, I & J

Company:	West Coast Plywood Company Ltd.
Species:	Cottonwood
Use:	Veneer
Specifications:	See Appendix 8(b) TDIB (min.) 12" Butt (max.) 50" Lengths: 17.5' min., 43.8' max.

Company:	Richmond Plywood Corporation Ltd.
Species:	Cottonwood
Use:	Plywood
Specifications:	TDIB 8-14" Rest similar to West Coast Plywood

Company:	Slocan Forest Products Ltd.
Species:	Cottonwood
Use:	Veneer/plywood
Specifications:	TDIB 8-14" Round, sound & no sweep

Company:	Coastland Wood Industries Inc.
Species:	Alder
Use:	Veneer
Specifications:	TDIB (min.) 8" Round, sound & free of rot

Company:	Delvin Fry
Species:	Aspen
Use:	Thin veneers (1/16") - Export
Specifications:	Butts: 12" & over Round, sound & free of rot

Company:	Louisiana-Pacific Canada Ltd.
Species:	Aspen, balsam poplar
Use:	Waferboard
Specifications:	See Appendix 8(c)

Company:	Scott Paper Ltd.
Species:	Cottonwood
Use:	Groundwood pulp
Specifications:	Logs: TDIB (min.) 6"
	Butt (max.) 48"
	Lengths - min. 3'
	min. 50% sound wood
	Blocks: l = 22"
	debarked
	split to maximum 14" diagonal

Company:	Canadian Chopstick Manufacturing Co. Ltd.
Species:	Aspen
Use:	Chopsticks
Specifications:	See Appendix 8(e)
	Sound, clear, knot-free
	Max. 25% stain

Sawnwood

Species:	Alder, Birch	
Specifications:	Domestic	- NLGA
	Export (USA)	- NHLA
	Export (Japan)	- JAS S1S 19

Veneer: Sliced

Species:	Birch
Specifications:	Export - NHPMA

Veneer: Rotary Peeled - Thin

Species:	Birch, Aspen
Specifications:	Export - NHPMA

Veneer: Rotary Peeled - 1/10" & over

Species:	Cottonwood, aspen	
Specifications:	Domestic	- CSA 0121 - Douglas Fir Plywood
		- CSA 0188 - Hardwood Plywood
	Export	- USPS 1-83
		- JAS S1S-8

Plywood

Species: Cottonwood
Specifications: CSA 0121 - Douglas-fir plywood

Species: Aspen
Specifications: CSA 0188 - Hardwood plywood

OSB/waferboard

Species: Aspen, balsam poplar
Specifications: CSA 0437 - OSB/waferboard
PS - 83 (USA)

Pulp Chips

Species: Alder/cottonwood
Export - Japan)*
Export - USA)*

---

* See Appendix 9

WEST COAST PLYWOOD COMPANY LTD.

COTTONWOOD LOG SPECIFICATIONS

LOG DIAMETER	-	Minimum top 12"
	-	Maximum butt 50"
SURFACE GRADE	-	Any number of visible knots under 1"
	-	Maximum of four visible knots 1-1/2" maximum diameter per 8' of log length, knots must be sound not
	-	Burls permitted if sound
	-	Straight logs, no sweep
TOPS AND BUTTS	-	Logs should be reasonably round with a minimum of butt flare or fluting
	-	No rot, ends should be firm, no ring shake or splits
	-	Only minor stump tear
LENGTHS	-	17.5' (minimum length)
	-	26.5'
	-	35.0'
	-	43.8'

WLR/sc
January 21, 1992

LOUISIANA-PACIFIC PANEL PRODUCTS, LTD.

LOG QUALITY SPECIFICATIONS

SPECIES: Accepted species are aspen Populus tremuloides the most common species also known as white poplar. Black cottonwood Populus trichocarpa is also known as balm, black poplar. Balsam Poplar Populus balsamifera is the least common species which occurs in the Peace River Area.

Any other species shall be treated as junk if included in wood deliveries.

LENGTH: Logs must be 100 inches or within ± 2 inches. In metric 2.54 m length ± 5 cm.

ROT: Logs must be 50% or greater firm wood by end. A rule of thumb for heart rot shall be that 2/3 of the inside diameter shall equal 1/3 of the outside log diameter. Therefore for 12 inches diameter log: then the maximum heart rot allowed is 8 inches, approximately 50%.

For any tree which has over 50% rot it must be checked (by boring into it with the power saw) every 2 feet (Fig. 1) until 50% or greater firm wood is found. This checking must be done before measuring the next log multiple.

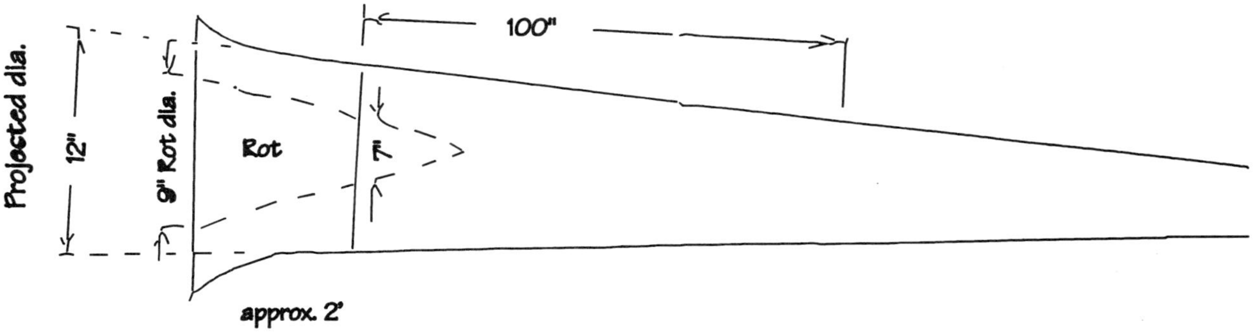

Fig. 1

Figure 1 shows 2 feet of the butt of this tree is waste and must be cut off before the next 100 inch multiple is bucked. Note also the butt flare is not included in the butt diameter. Butt diameter is the diameter of the log which normal log taper has been projected to the butt end. This is not to be confused when determining over size logs. (See OVER SIZE)

Evidence of rot inside a tree may appear as old scars or fungi growing on the tree outside. Fungi may appear from old branch stubs.

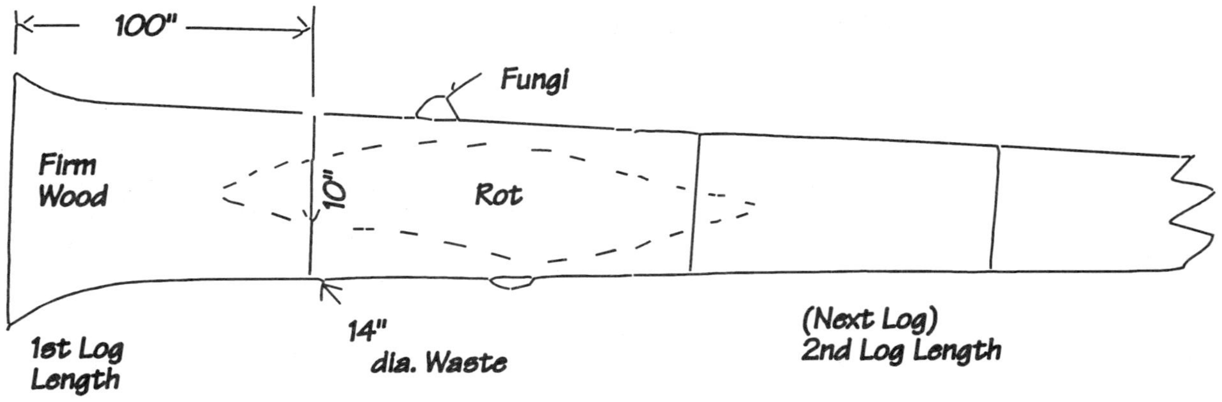

Fig. 2

Figure 2 shows the top end (14 inch diameter) of the 1st log length has rot (10 inch diameter) which exceeds 50% firm wood. It is from the top end of the 1st log length that the tree must be bored (checked) every 2 feet until 50% or greater firm wood is found. The next log length is then measured and bucked.

Rot can easily be determined with a pencil. Firm wood has resistance when a pencil is pressed into it. Therefore rotten wood has weaker fibre and less resistance. This can be achieved with a power saw. Rotten wood has less resistance. Therefore it will cut faster and more easily than firmwood.

Wood may be stained and yet is firm wood.

Rotten wood creates excess fines in our operation, greatly increasing the risk of fires.

BUTT OR TOP ROT: Butt or top rot is determined by end which is over 50% rot. Points charged shall be the portion of log length over 50% rot times the points charged should the piece have over 50% rot for the full length - e.g. a 30 cm diameter log with over 50% for ¼ the length would be charged 4 points (¼ x 16).

ROT FULL LENGTH: Is a log which has greater than 50% rot at either end - e.g. a 30 cm diameter log which is greater than 50% rot by end at each end shall be charged 16 points.

BUTT FLARES: Logs with excessive flares will impede our line flow and will jam during the debarking process. These logs are required to have the flare trimmed prior to delivery.

BAD CROOK: Logs must not have more than 6 inch deviation within the log length. Logs with more than one crook are not accepted. Debarking becomes a problem with bad crooks.

FORK: Forks are a problem with handling and at the debarker, they are not accepted.

EXCESS LIMBS: Limbs must be cut flush with the bole of the tree. Short stubs shall be considered as limbs.

Limbs are a problem on chain conveyors and at the debarker.

SNIPE: Snipes create truck loading, pond filling and slasher deck difficulty.

A snipe is the piece of wood left attached to the log end. This is usually caused
by the bucker not cutting the log entirely through. It may also be from falling.

Each of the logs which we receive shall be slashed into three pieces. As the logs are fed to the slasher deck they are butted against a steel plate. Should a snipe strike the plate first, then the other end of the log is wasted.

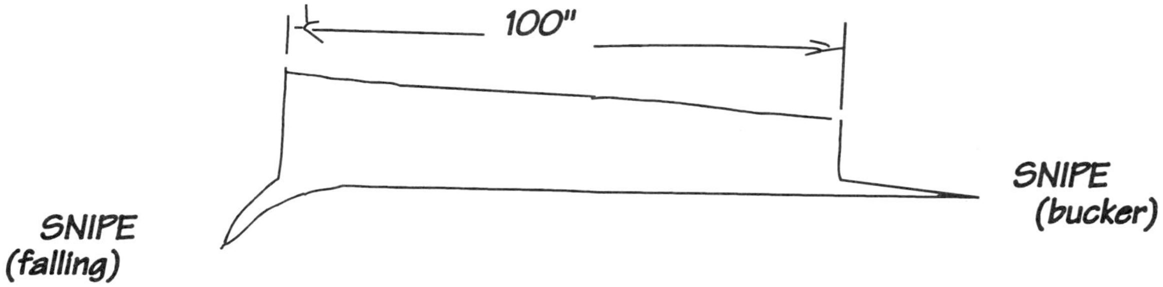

DRY WOOD: More fines are produced with dry wood. Dry wood tends to burn the waferized knives due to low natural moisture content.

Under summer conditions logs must arrive at the log yard within three weeks from the time the tree has fallen.

Logs which are deemed to be cut over a three week period shall be treated as dry wood. Dry wood is evident by excessive end checking, brown inner bark, weathered exposed wood, or dry (dead) trees.

JUNK: Junk includes any of the following:

1. Any species which is not accepted. (See Page 2)
2. Sticks, brush, rotten pieces, limbs.
3. Short chunks.
4. Large pieces of foreign material - i.e. ice, dirt, stones.
5. Firm wood which cannot be milled. (split pieces)

OVERSIZE: A log which at any point across the diagonal of the log that is greater than 20 inches at the widest point outside the bark is an oversize log.

Our debarker will not handle logs over 20 inches (51 cm) diameter. Logs must pass through a debarking ring in the debarking process. The ring has a maximum opening of 20 inches. If a log is too large (over 20 inches) they will jam within the debarker.

UNDER SIZE: Logs must be at least 5 inches (13 cm) inside the bark diameter for 3/4 of the log length Logs must not decrease under 4 inches (10 cm) diameter in the last ¼ log length. Small diameter logs must be straight and free of rot.

Small diameter logs tend to be broken during the debarking. Also, small logs become crossed in the conveyor enroute to the waferizer.

OVER LENGTH: Logs which are over 102 inches (2.59 m)

UNDER LENGTH: Logs which are under 98 inches (2.49 m). Short pieces cannot be debarked properly and cannot be held firm during the waferizing process.

FRANCOIS LAKE WOODWORKING LTD.

FRANWOOD

PO Box 100 Francois Lake BC V0J 1R0 Canada Phone (604)695-6616 FAX (604)695-6550

<u>SPECIFICATION BIRCH LUMBER</u> Febr. 14, 1991.

<u>General Grade:</u> free of rot, bluestain, split and wormholes
basically free of wane - some pencil wane accepted
Only clean bright lumber will be accepted.
Trees must be harvested during the winter season

No. I Grade: WHITE WOOD ONLY (No dark center stain allowed)
Thickness of cants: 3-3/16"
Widths of Cants: 3-1/2"; 4-3/4"; 6"; 7-1/4"; 8-1/2"; 9-3/4" and 11"

- No undersize -

No. II Grade: Two-tone-color allowed
The heart center (dark stain) must not exceed 1/3 of the width of the cant. Thickness of cants: 3-3/16" and/or 7"
Widths of cants: 3-1/2 ; 4-3/4"; 6"; 7-1/4"; 8-1/2"; 9-3/4 " and 11"

- No undersize -

Side lumber: graded as above (No. I and II Grade)
Thickness: 1-1/16"
Widths: 3-3/16" and /or 7"

<u>Lengths</u>: of all Cants and Sidelumber: 6 - 12 ft. (random)

Example for cutting logs:

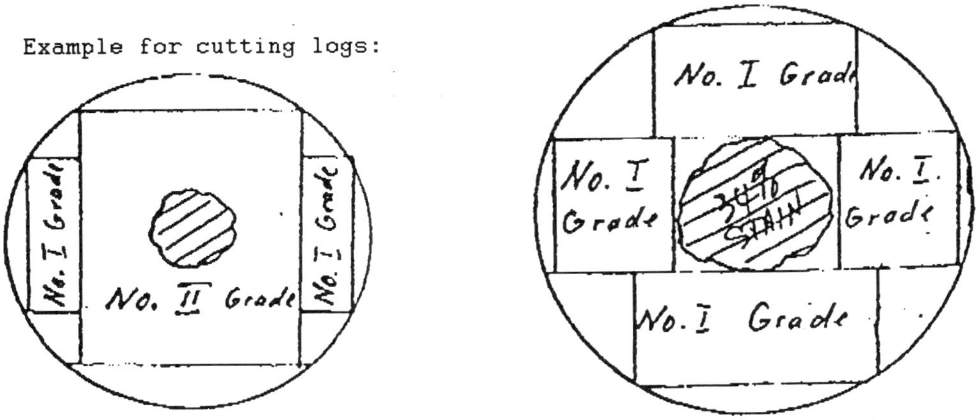

CANADIAN CHOPSTICK MANUFACTURING COMPANY _____(the "Company") and

____(the "Contractor")

dated for reference the __th day of Ju__. 1992

1. Clause 3.2 - Species of Timber:

Aspen and Conifer

2. Clause 3.2 - Logging Standards:

Aspen will be manufactured for Chopsticks and other markets as prescribed in Addendum No. 4 of this contract. If chopstick logging only is directed by the woodlands manager the following specifications will be adhered to:

Chopstick Mfg. Specifications

Every Aspen tree will be merchandised to maximize the chopstick recovery at a preferred length of 5.7 meters and a length of 2.85 meters. Merchandising will recognize C.C.M.C. Sort 1 as the preferred sort with other sorts prioritized by descending order. (See C.C.M.C. Sort Specifications). Merchandising will also consider C.C.M.C. woods mismanufacture specifications, logyard quality assessment system, as well as the manufacturing specifications below.

1. Processing & Long Butts: firm wood dependent, no more than 0.35 meters will be bucked off to determine grade. If the stain is greater than 15 percent of the gross scale, but less than 20 percent of the gross scale, a 0.35 meter piece will be bucked off. If stain appears to be increasing, then a 1.0 meter piece will be bucked off. If; however, the stain is decreasing, a 0.35 meter piece then a 5.7 meter piece will be manufactured. At the butt, if the stain is greater than 20 percent of the gross scale the log will be processed in 1 meter lengths until the log contains less than 20 percent stain. At 20 percent stain the log will be processed in 0.35 meter lengths until stain is less than 15 percent of the gross scale. A 5.7 meter log will then be processed. The above manufacturing sequence will be used on all logs unless defects are present. Clear butts, with moose browse will be manufactured to 5.7 meters or 2.85 meters to maximize tree recovery.

The following are some examples of log processing as per C.C.M.C. specifications.

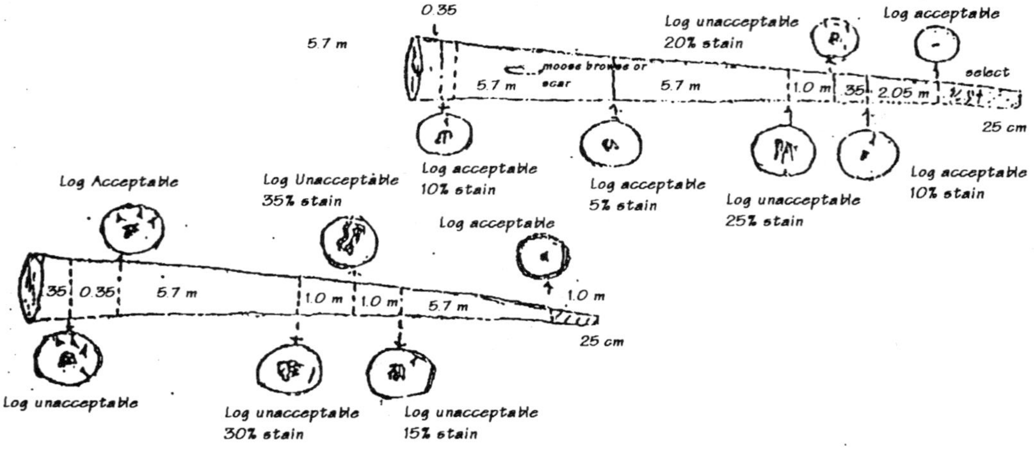

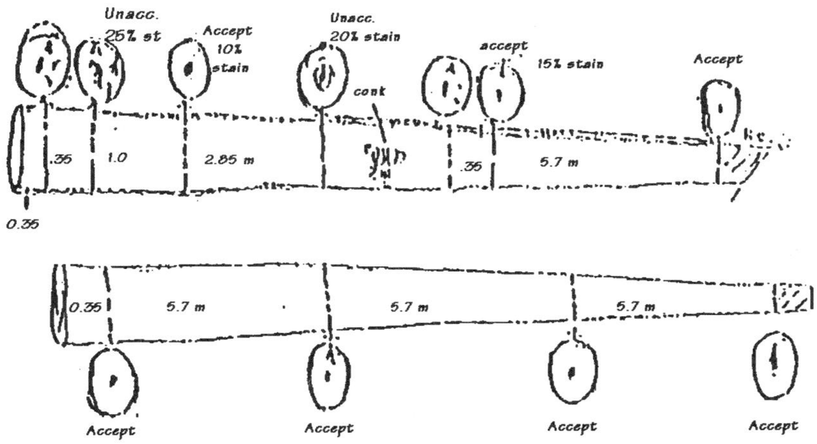

Rot Definition: if bits of fragments of wood can be picked out easily with a sharp object the wood is rotten and not firm wood. Aspen characteristically has white rot. The rot is generally whiter than the firm wood and may have a black zonal line around its circumference. Chopstick grade may not have greater than 2 percent of the gross scale as rot.

Stain Definition: Stain is discoloration of the wood fibre thought to be caused by the oxidation of minerals and varying wood fungai. Frequent stains encountered are blue stain, black stain, red stain, green stain, yellow stain and Water stain, of which only water stain is permissible. The other stains must be less than 15 percent of the gross scale. A minimum of 5 percent of the stain must be concentrated to the centre. The balance of the stain must be concentrated in one third of the log.

Acceptable and unacceptable logs are described in C.C.M.C. Scaling and Quality assessment system as well as illustrated below.

Rot

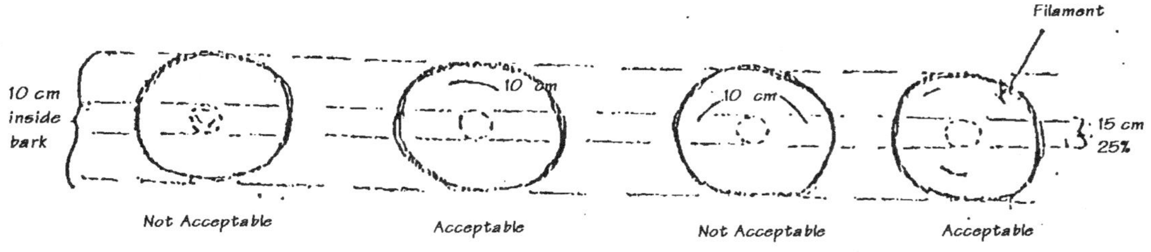

* Exception to 1.0 above is ring rot. Ring rot not otherwise located in the inside 25 percent of diameter may be accepted so long as not greater than 3 filaments exceed 10 cm. in length and 0.5 cm thick.

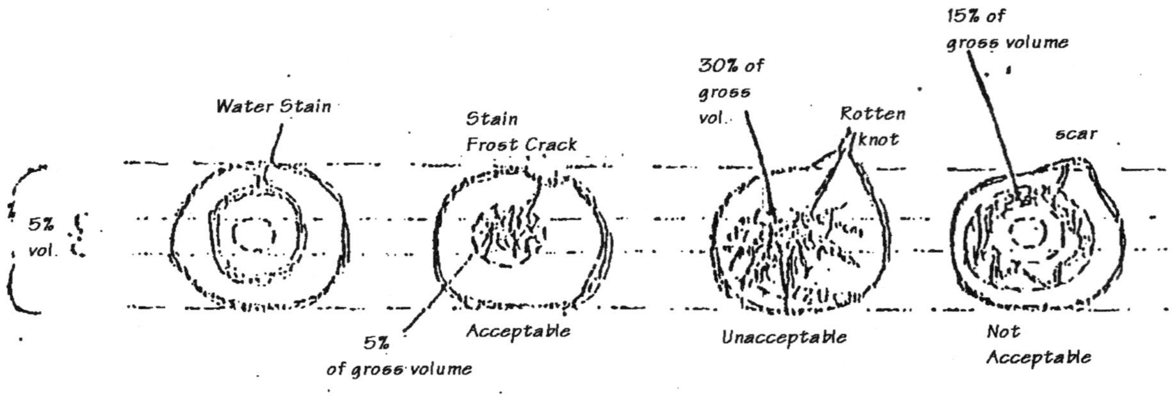

* As a rule of thumb water stain has a circular pattern following the growth rings of a tree. UN permitted stains generally radiate (star shape) from the pith to source of infection such as a knot or frost crack.

2.0 Buck Out all forks, rotten scars, cat faces, burls, and dog leg crooks. Look for old scars, conks, cat faces, spikes, rotten branch stubs or knots that indicate rot or stain inside and test with saw if necessary.

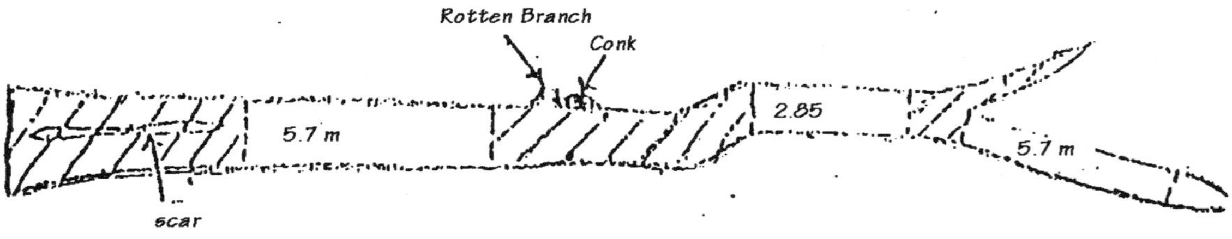

3.0 Excessive sweep must be bucked out. Excessive sweep is defined as a log that curves greater than 30 cm from a straight line that extends from the centre of the butt to the centre of the top.

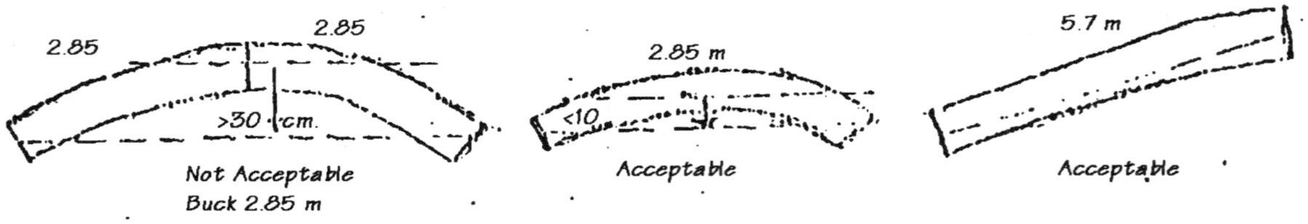

4.0 Top all logs no smaller than 25 cm. diameter inside bark.

5.0 The bucker must <u>mark all logs</u> plainly that do not meet chopstick grade so they may be sorted adequately.

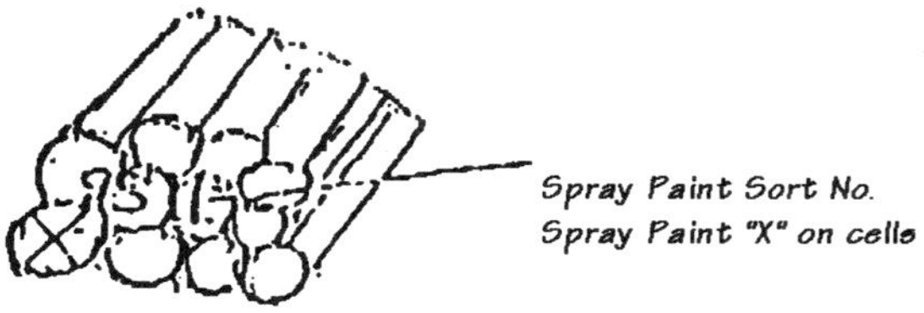

6.0 <u>Remove all limbs</u> from logs, flush to stem before loading. This includes swellings associated with knots, which are elevated in excess of 15 cm. from the stem.

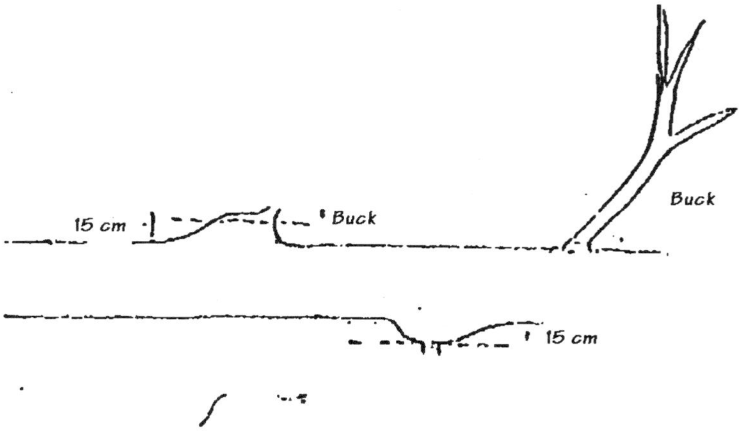

7.0 <u>Square all butts</u> where excessive falling snipes occur. Any falling snipe greater than 6 cm. must be bucked square.

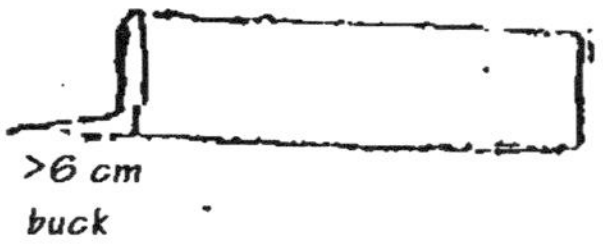

8.0 Cut all cull logs with powersaw at least every 2.0 m to prove extent of rot or stain.

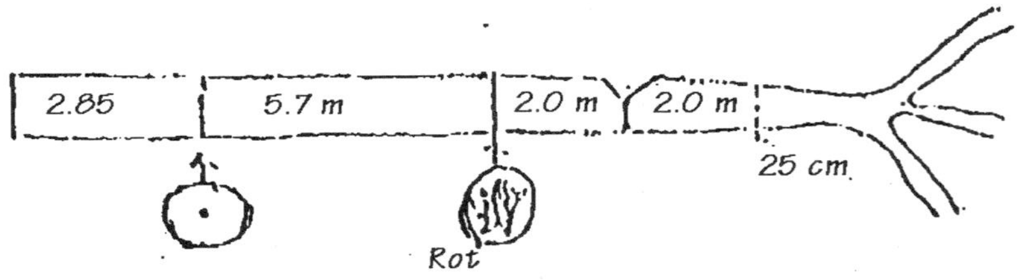

9.0 Trim all shattered logs back to sound wood. Evidence of the shatter must remain following trimming.

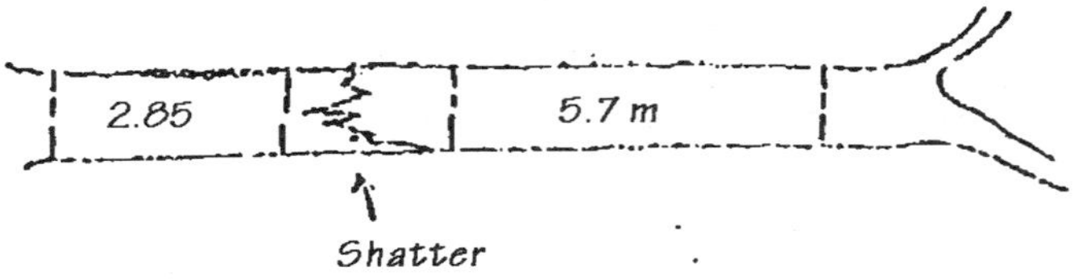

10.0 Piece length acceptable is 2.85m or 5.2m (preferred). Shorter pieces must be culled. Longer pieces must be bucked to tolerance. Tolerances are, 5 cm. on short logs and 10 cm. on long logs. See C.C.M.C. Sort Specifications No. 1.

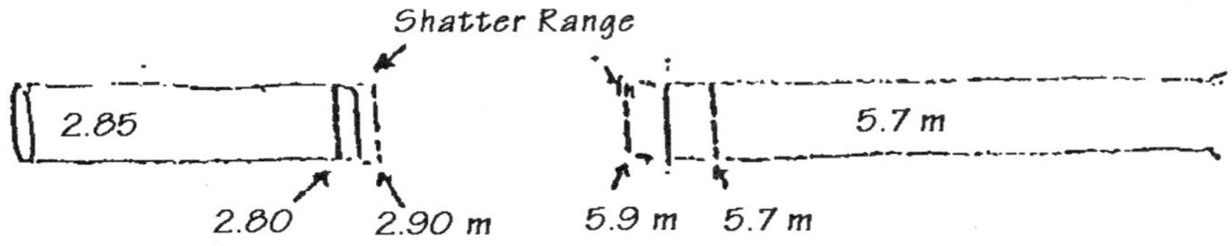

11.0 Top Diameter acceptable is 25 cm. or 13 rads. inside bark. Tolerance is one rad. See C.C.M.C. Sort Specifications No. 1.

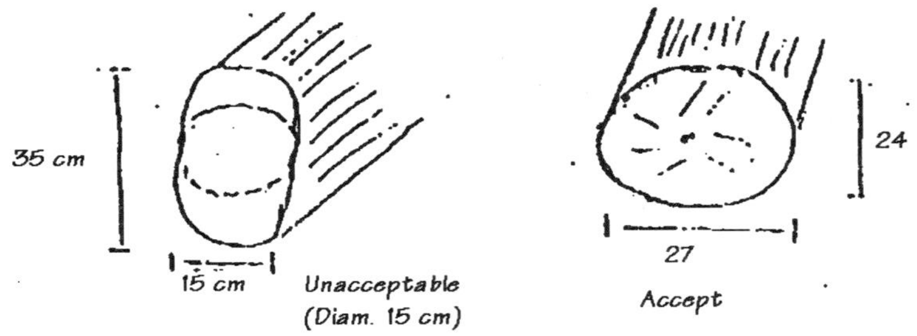

12.0 Cull all logs, with Spiral check or straight open check.

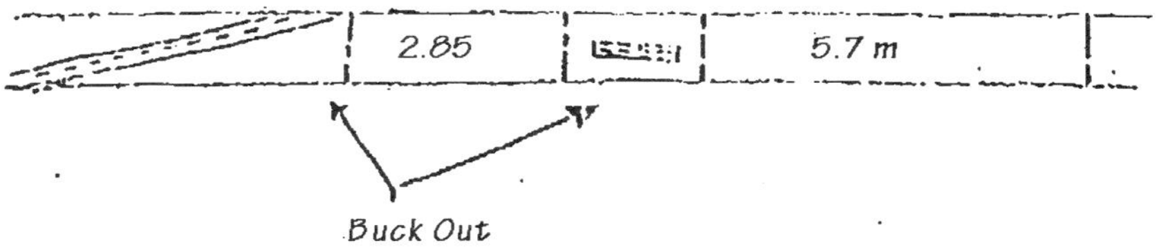

13.0 Buck out oblong parts of trees.

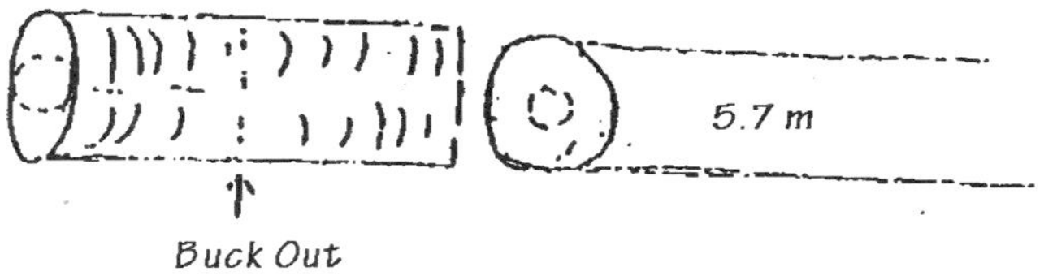

14.0 Cull all dead and dry logs.

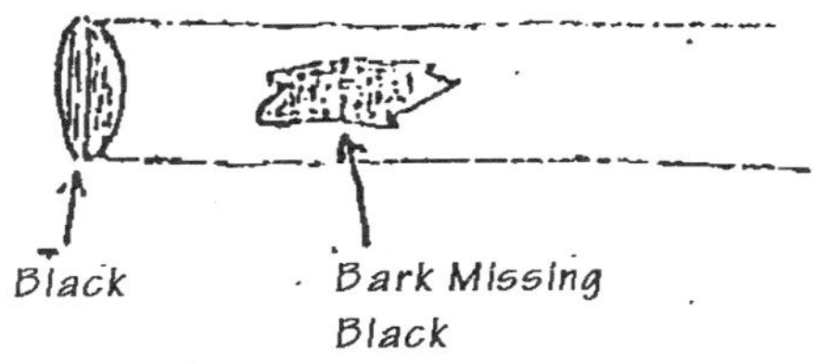

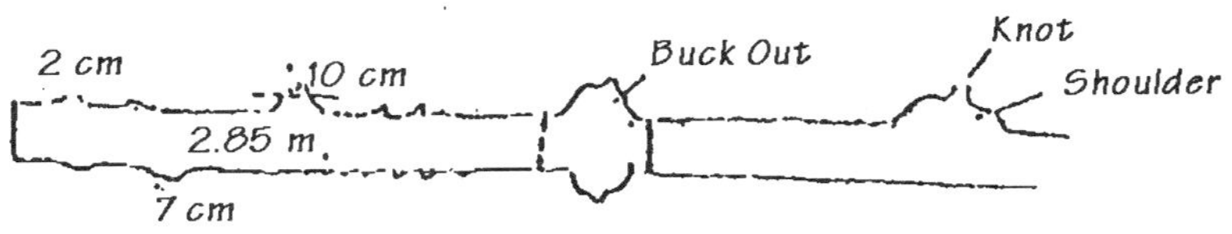

16.0 Blue Stain or sun checked logs will be loaded onto truck in such a manner that it all faces one direction. This will increase sorting efficiency at the logyard.

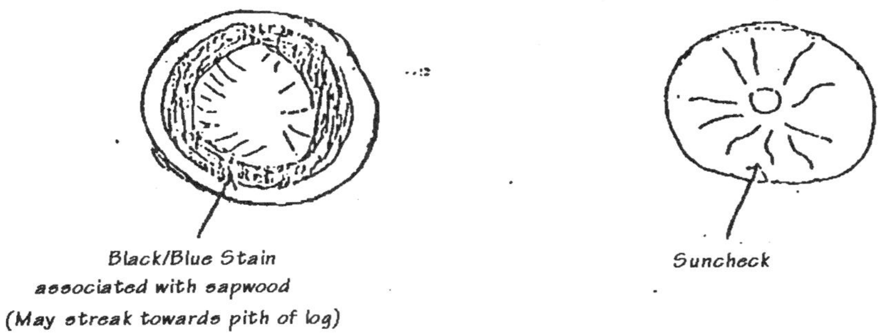

APPENDIX 9. Specifications for chip exports to Japan and the United States

A. Specifications for chips exported to Japan

Chips will be measured in accordance with TAPPI technical standard No. T16-ts-61 using the screen size for nominal 3/4" wood chips:

Over 1 1/2"	maximum 5%
Between 1 1/2" and 3/16" (inclusive)	minimum 90%
Under 3/16"	minimum 5%

Species: Whitewood from the interior of the province consisting of spruce, lodgepole pine, and balsam with traces only of other species being permitted. The chips must contain a minimum of 50% spruce.

Contaminants: The chips shall be substantially free of contaminants and other foreign materials and may not contain more than:

Bark	maximum 1%
Rot	maximum 1%

B. A practical composite of the chip specifications used in British Columbia

WFPL* Classification		Specification
Percent oversize	+45 mm	– 3.0
Percent over thick	+ 1 mm	
Percent acceptable	+ 7 mm	+ 89.0
Percent pins	+ 3 mm	– 7.0
Percent fines	– 3 mm	– 0.5
Percent bark		– 1.0
Percent knots		– 2.0
Percent rot		– 0.25

Note: These specifications will not necessarily add to 100%. They represent minimum and maximums acceptable.

Compiled by R.J. Hyslop & Associates.

* Western Forest Products Laboratory (Now FORINTEK Canada Corp., Western Laboratory).